BRITISH POLICY IN THE NORTH-EAST FRONTIER AGENCY

By the Same Author

- Development of Administration in Assam: With Special Reference to Land Revenue Justice and Police (1874-1920)
- Historical and Constitutional Documents of North-Eastern India (1824-1973)
- History of Arunachal Pradesh
- Social and Cultural History of Ancient India (Revised and Enlarged Edition)
- Social History of Assam

About the Author

Prof. M.L. Bose has been teaching in the Dibrugarh University (Assam) for about thirty years and has contributed more than thirty papers in Regional and National Seminars and Journals of Repute. An Aurobindite Prof. Bose has guided many research scholars to produce Ph.D. thesis. His earliers published works are *Historical and Constitutional Documents of North-East India; British Policy in the North-East Frontier Agency; Development of Administration in Assam; Social History of Assam; Social and Cultural History of Ancient India*; and *History of Arunachal Pradesh* were well received in the academic world.

BRITISH POLICY IN THE NORTH-EAST FRONTIER AGENCY

M.L. BOSE

CONCEPT PUBLISHING COMPANY PVT. LTD.
NEW DELHI-110059

ISBN-13: 978-81-8069-419-6

First Pubiished 2017

Published and Printed by

Concept
Since 1974

Concept Publishing Company Pvt. Ltd.
A/15-16, Commercial Block, Mohan Garden
New Delhi-110059 (India)
T: 25351460, 25351794, *F*: 091-11-25357109
E: publishing@conceptpub.com, W: www.conceptpub.com
Editorial Office: H-13, Bali Nagar, New Delhi-110 015, India.

Cataloging in Publication Data--Courtesy: D.K. Agencies (P) Ltd. <docinfo@dkagencies.com>

Bose, Manilal, author.
British policy in the North-East Frontier Agency / M.L. Bose.
pages cm
Includes bibliographical references and index.
ISBN 9788180694196

1. Aruna?chal Pradesh (India)--History. 2. Great Britain--Colonies--Administration. I. Title.

DS485.N68B67 2017 DDC 954.163 23

Preface

THE WELL-KNOWN term NEFA—short form of "North-East Frontier Agency"—came into existence in 1954. The territories which came to be known as the Union Territory of Arunachal Pradesh from December 1972 were known as Frontier Tracts till 1954. The Indian Constitution of 1950 defined these territories in Part B of the Sixth Schedule as : (1) North-East Frontier Tract, including the Balipara Frontier Tract, Tirap Frontier Tract, Abor Hills District, and Mishmi Hills District; and (2) Naga Tribal Area. In 1954, T.N. Kaul, Joint Secretary in the Ministry of External Affairs, organised a new Frontier Service, to be called Frontier Administrative Service. The members of this service were to be recruited from amongst the ex-army personnel and others to serve under the Governor of Assam, who was entrusted with the responsibility of looking after the administration of these frontiers as the deputy of the President of India. He was to act under the advice of the Ministry of External Affairs. The Governor of Assam was assisted by an Adviser of the rank of a senior Secretary to the State Government and as such, carried on the business of the administration of the frontiers like a Chief Secretary. In 1954, this set-up of the Frontier Administration headed by the Adviser was given the name of the North-East Frontier Agency and the territory henceforth came to be known as NEFA in short.

Till December 1972, NEFA was constitutionally a part of Assam State. But because of its backwardness it was kept under the formal control of the President of India, like other tribal areas of the Union. In 1951, the plains portion of the territories of Balipara Frontier Tract, Tirap Frontier Tract, Mishmi Hills District and Abor Hills District were transferred to the administrative jurisdiction of the Government of Assam. The rest of the administrative units were given a uniform nomenclature in 1954 and the administrative centres began to be pushed up into the hills in central positions. Thus, there were now, from West to East, Kameng Frontier Division, instead of the Balipara Frontier Tract; Subansiri Frontier Division, created out of Balipara Frontier Tract; Siang Frontier Division instead of the Abor Hills District; Lohit Frontier Division instead of the Mishmi Hills District; and Tirap Frontier Division instead of the Tirap Frontier Tract. These Divisions were termed Districts and subdivided into Sub-divisions and Circles in 1965 for administrative purposes.

After the Chinese occupation of Tibet in 1950 and the subsequent flight of the Dalai Lama, the North-East Frontier began to assume a new political significance and its problems began to draw the attention of the Government of India. But the problems of the frontier were brought to the notice of the public in general after the major Chinese thrust in 1962 and the hitherto unknown North-East Frontier Agency now became the NEFA. Articles, books, pamphlets and stories on this region began to be published in newspapers, journals and magazines all over the world.

The present study was, however, not stimulated by the Chinese invasion of 1962. While the author was engaged in search of materials for the study of the development of the administration of Assam, he realised the complexity of the problems of the North-East Frontier. With a view to bringing forth the viewpoints of the NEFA Administration, the Defence personnel, scholars and academicians, a seminar on the North-East Frontier was organised and directed by the author at Dibrugarh University in 1971. Some of the problems focused during the discussions at the seminar highlighted the necessity of a study of the frontier from a different angle, and as the sponsor of the seminar the author took up the task. The present work is the result of his study in depth over the last three years.

The North-East Frontier was a closed land, and it continues to be so in the sense that travel across the Inner Line is not allowed; even now a person has to obtain a pass to cross that Line from the competent authority. Usually such a pass is issued temporarily to traders who carry on business in the territory. Such passes were issued even during the British regime; but generally speaking, except for Europeans the land remained virtually hidden behind an iron curtain, and all sorts of mysterious and absurd stories were associated with the life and culture of the tribes living there. In the nineteenth century, as also in the early twentieth, a thorough study of the culture of the Indian people was undertaken by nationalist scholars and the past was glorified. But the Frontiers still remained in the womb of darkness. The political parties and their activities were not allowed there. Consequently, the nationalistic and patriotic upsurge which swept the country and bound the people of India in a common bond of union for the sake of liberation from foreign rule, did not create in the Frontiers any change in outlook. The North-East Frontier remained out of the stream of India's national development.

That does not mean that no account of this secluded land was available. Right from the beginning of British rule in India, it had caught the attention of the British and reports on them were prepared even before the annexation of Assam to the Company's territories. The Company had entrusted Francis Hamilton (later known as Buchanon Hamilton) and Pemberton to prepare reports on the provinces on the Frontiers of Bengal. After the annexation of Assam, the officers serving in Assam were required to prepare reports on the frontier tribes and the officers of the Company, both civil and military, sent their exploratory reports to the government. Although vitiated in many cases by bias and lack of understanding, these reports suppy valuable information on tribal life and organisations.

The Christian missionaries did not lag behind. Just after the annexation of Assam they began to explore the possibilities of proselytisation in the new region. They ventured to cross the Frontiers and found their way even into Tibet. But gradually their interest in the Frontier began to chill and they found themselves busy in the hills on the south bank of the Brahmaputra. The initial interest in the Mishmi Hills (1835) and the belated interest in the Abor Hills (1885) did not leave behind any considerable impression except in the Abor Hills where some people still follow the religion of Christ.

The general policy of the Administration was to keep the Frontier in stagnation and till the end of British rule in India the British Indian Government did not allow tribal life to be disturbed by any new idea or development of any kind. Not even the survey of and enquiries into the topography of the territories were completed. After the Chinese movements of 1910 on the Frontiers, collection of information on the topography of the tracts became imperative for the finalisation of the hitherto unsettled boundary between the two countries. Some exploratory teams were sent to the territories for survey and exploration of the interior of the Hills. But such hasty and unconcerted exploration did not produce satisfactory results. Knowledge about these areas, though increased, was by no means complete.

In fact, the British never attempted to prepare a coordinated account of the different tribes of the Frontier region. From 1881 onwards, monographs on the Frontier tribes began to be included in the Census of India Reports and by 1947 all but the tribes of the western hills and those who lived on the fringes of the border were covered in these reports. But the reports were incomplete and undependable, particularly in respect of statistical data, as none of the officers went inside the hills to collect them. Meanwhile books and accounts of these tribes written by those who visited the hills began to come out; but they also were equally incorrect and incomplete as the authors lacked understanding and were biased. The only trustworthy and reliable accounts are available in the works of E.T. Dalton and George Grierson.

In one sense, we have no dearth of materials on the Frontier tribes; rather we have a bewildering mass of reports and accounts of various kinds. But all are elusive, some are biased, others suffer from lack of understanding, and a few are partial and incomplete. Much of these were in the form of notes, articles, essays, reports and monographs; but no comprehensive work including all aspects of the life of the Frontier people, their land, economy and culture, together with the Government measures and policy with regard to the region, has yet been written.

In the post-independence period, a number of works on the Frontier came forth, particularly in the wake of the Chinese invasion of 1962. But they are concerned mostly with the border problems and the military debacle, as they appeared at a time when the political and military issues dominated the official and public thinking. Works such as P.C. Chakravarty's *India-China Relations* (1965); *Evolution of India's Northern*

Borders (1969); John Rowland's *A History of Sino-Indian Relations* (1967); Alastair Lamb's *The China-India Border: The Origins of the Disputed Boundaries* (1964); *The McMahon Line: A Study in the Relations Between India, China and Tibet 1904 to 1914* (1966); S.P. Verma's *The Struggle for the Himalayas* (1971); N. Maxwell's *India's China War* (1970); Brigadier J.P. Dalvi's *The Himalayan Blunder* (1969); B.M. Kaul's *The Untold Story* (1967), Kusum Nargolkar's *In the Wake of Chinese Thrust* (1965); and G.S. Bhargava's *The Battle for NEFA: The Undeclared War* (1964) may be classed in this group. The only book which has examined the different problems of the North-East Frontier people in some depth from various angles is Sitaram Johri's *Where India, China and Burma Meet* (1962). But this work is mainly an examination of the policy matters in relation to the administrative developments in the perspective of the land, people and culture of the Frontiers, and though it contains many references it does not provide a connected account of the growth of British administration in the North-East Frontier *vis-a-vis* the North-East Frontier Policy of the British. Moreover, since it has reflected on the recent trend of developments, it has assumed the nature of a pedagogic directory, instead of an objective analysis of the facts based on the data of a particular regime.

Some books exclusively on the North-East Frontier and particular tribes and their institutions and culture have been issued in recent years from the NEFA Administration. The Administration has published *A Philosophy for NEFA* (1959), *The Myths of the North-East Frontier of India* (1958), *The Art of the North-East Frontier* (1959), *Democracy in NEFA* (1965) all by Verrier Elwin; *Constitutional and Administrative Growth of the North-East Frontier Agency* (1971), by Col. P.N. Luthra; *The Adi Religion* (1971), *Hill Miris of Subansiri* (1970), by J.N. Chowdhury; *Mopin* (1966), by Kumar Ishan; *NEFA—The Land and People*, reprinted from the *India Quarterly*, Vol. XIX, No. 4, of 1963; *Games of NEFA* (1959), by Marion D. Pugh; *Glimpses of the History of Arunachal* (1973) by L.N. Chakravarty. Besides some small books on individual tribes like *The Sherdukpens* (1961), by R.P.R. Sharma, *The Idu Mishmis* (1961), by T.K.M. Barua, *The Tangsas* (1959), by P.C. Datta, *The Daflas* (1959), by R. Sinha have also been published by the same authority. Of the works published by the Agency Administration, Elwin's *Philosophy for NEFA* and Luthra's *Constitutional and Administrative Growth of the North-East Frontier Agency* deserve greater attention; the rest are treatises on either a particular tribe or on a particular aspect of tribal culture. The first contains directives to the Agency officials and till the publication of the *Important Directives on the Administration of NEFA* in 1967 served the purpose of guiding the latter. The second is practically a compendium of the notices published from time to time to specify the Inner Line in particular and the administrative and constitutional provisions for the Frontier Administration after 1914, prefaced by a very brief history of the growth of the administration of the Frontier from 1914 to 1967.

Besides the Agency publications, we have Elwin's *Hill People of the North-East India* (1959), *Kingdom of the Young* (1968), *Leaves from the Jungle* (1958), *India's North-East Frontier in the Nineteenth Century* (1955), *The Tribal World of Verrier Elwin* (1964). Very recently, a book named *Arunachal Panorama* (1973) has been published by J.N. Chowdhury. Two more books which appeared after 1973 are P. Mehra's *The McMahon Line and After* and K. Gupta's *The Hidden History of the Sino-Indian Frontier* have significantly increased the knowledge of Frontier history. These throw much light on several aspects of Frontier history; but concerned as they are with some aspects of tribal life, they cannot satisfy the need of a connected history of the Frontier people in the perspective of British policy.

This book attempts to draw, in five chapters, a connected history of the North-East Frontier Agency, complementing two well-known works, *History of the Relations of the Government with the Hill Tribes of the North-East Frontier of Bengal* (1884) by Sir Alexander Mackenzie, and *History of the Frontier Areas Bordering on Assam from 1883-1941* (1942) by Sir Robert Reid. In its span it covers, generally speaking, the entire period from the annexation of Assam in 1826 to the end of British rule in 1947 in order to provide an understanding of the development of the North-East Frontier during the British period from a historical angle.

For the preparation of the book, the relevant proceedings of the revenue, judicial, police and political departments of the Government of Bengal between the years 1826-1874, and the Secret Consultations of that Government, in the West Bengal State Archives, Calcutta, as well as the Home, Public, Judicial, Police, and Foreign Political proceedings of the Government of India, in the National Archives of India, New Delhi, for the same period were examined. (The history of this period has been laboriously written by Sir Alexander Mackenzie, who served under the Government of Bengal and the Government of India and had full access to all the official papers of those Governments. The book is well written, though with a purpose.) Besides, the following have also been thoroughly studied: all the proceedings of the Chief Commissioner of Assam between 1874-1905 in the Foreign Department of the Government of India; all the relevant proceedings of the Government of Eastern Bengal and Assam in the Political Department between 1906-1912; and all the proceedings of the Government of Assam for 1913-1920, 1921 and 1937 have also been consulted. Subsequent developments have been studied from the proceedings of the Tribal Affairs Department of the Assam Governor's Secretariat. The study was considerably facilitated by the author's discovery of the records preserved in the Lakhimpur Deputy Commissioner's Record Room at Dibrugarh; all the original papers relating to the Frontier, particularly of the period between 1874 and 1914, and all the reports on the administration of the North-East Frontier till the end of the British period are available there. Finally, all the relevant proceedings of the Government of India in the Foreign Political and Secret Department had to be consulted for connecting the missing links in the development of the Frontiers. The study at the National Archives of India was, however, greatly handicapped by restrictions on the use of records relating to certain periods and certain aspects of the subject. But the difficulty has been partially removed by the publication of some White Papers by the Ministry of External Affairs. To the study of the unpublished documents was added a thorough survey of reports and articles on the Frontiers published from time to time in different journals as also books which have been published in recent times, particularly those mentioned in the preceding parasgraphs.

Thus, the present study may claim originality in respect of collection of new facts from hitherto unexplored source materials as also in respect of new interpretation of some already known facts. It is an original work also in the sense that it has treated the history of the Frontier from a fresh point of view. It is a comprehensive study of: (*i*) relation of the Government with the Frontier Tribes up to the end of the British period; (*ii*) emergence of the Inner Line, Outer Line and the McMahon Line; (*iii*) the evolution of the Constitution and administration of the North-East Frontier, in the perspective of the land and the people. Secondly an attempt has been made to study British policy against the background of political realities. Adverse criticism of that policy is usually based on the charge that it was because of the British neglect that the present problems have cropped up. This is true in a general sense, but then it is only one aspect of the issue. We cannot, as students of history, overlook the fact that British interest was concentrated on the plains—and not on the hills—for practical reasons. No threat of foreign aggression across the eastern frontiers seemed possible after the British had come to Assam; what caught their attention were the raids of the tribes from above the hills. The British were anxious to ensure safety of the plains below the Frontier Hills and for this purpose they strengthened the security measures on the foothills. Then after 1910, when the Chinese appeared across the frontier and foreign aggression became possible, the frontier was delimited and development and security measures began to be provided. It was already too late; the frontier people, deprived of governmental attention for about eight decades, remained far behind their brothers in the plains in respect of social and economic development. Administrative and security measures were thought of and provided for by the British Government during the last three decades of its rule. But this was only a beginning, and they left a complicated legacy for free India.

The book is based on my thesis submitted for the Ph. D. degree of Jadavpur University which was awarded in 1976.

For the help I received in preparation of the book, I am indebted to many, particularly A.C. Banerjee, Ex-

Centenary Professor of International Relations, Calcutta University and retired Professor of Guru Nanak University for supervising my research. I am also grateful to P.C. Sharma, Keeper of Records, Assam Secretariat, the authorities of the National Archives and West Bengal State Archives and Dibrugarh District for permitting me to collect research material from their respective archives and libraries. I am also grateful to B. Datta Ray and his family in Shillong who extended warm hospitality to me during my stay there in connection with the preparation of the book.

Department of History
Dibrugarh University

M. L. Bose

Contents

1

North-East Frontier Agency : Land, People and Culture

THE LAND

THE NORTH-EAST Frontier Agency (NEFA), now Arunachal Pradesh, comprises mountainous territory on the southern slopes of the Eastern Himalayas with the spurs coming down from north to south from the crest of the main range to the valley of the Brahmaputra in the State of Assam, except in the district of Tirap where the territory consists of the north-eastern slopes and spurs of the Patkai range, the crest of which divides India and Burma. Thus, the province is separated on the north by the province of Khams or Khamsyul of Tibet along the 700 mile long crest of the eastern Himalayas, known since 1914 as the McMahon Line[1], to the Talok (Diphuk) Pass to the north-west of Burma, from the tri-junction of Bhutan, Tibet and India to the tri-junction of India, Tibet and Burma; on the west by Bhutan; on the east through the crest of the Patkai range which separates India and Burma; and on the south by Assam and Nagaland. The province is the home of twenty-five major tribes with a number of sub-tribes totalling a population of 4,67,511 according to the 1971 census. The total area is said to cover 80,481 square kilometres divided into five districts from west to east : Kameng, Subansiri, Siang, Lohit and Tirap.[2]

Geopolitically speaking, the province was regarded as unimportant[3] till 1910 when the contingent of Chao Er-feng, after occupying Tibet, appeared at Rima and demanded the submission of the Mishmis to their orders, bounded as it was on three sides by states which were neither powerful nor potentially dangerous for the British Empire. The Himalayas always provided India with natural defence and the Eastern Himalayas were regarded as a barrier against the invaders from the north-east. To the east, Burma, after the first Anglo-Burmese war (1824-26) was regarded as an aggrieved and powerful state and to stop an immediate attack on the British territory by Burma, a hedge of semi-independent petty states was created between Burma and the British possessions in Assam. In the north-east —the Khampti and Singpho tracts—were the Ahom principality of Upper Assam and Manipur. As the easiest approach from Burma to British India lay through the Kubo Valley, a contingent called the Manipur Levy equipped, paid and commanded by a British officer was maintained there. To strengthen and gratify Manipur, some tracts of Cachar were made over to the Raja of Manipur.[4] But after the second Anglo-Burmese war (1852), when Lower Burma was annexed to the British Empire, the dangers of Burmese aggression receded to naught; finally the Chinese over-lordship over Burma was brought to an end by an agreement between China and Great Britain in 1876.[5]

To the west of the province, along a frontier of 159 km (98 miles) lies Bhutan which was a petty vassal of Tibet. The location of Bhutan, between the Tibetan plateau and the plains of Bengal and Assam, gives it a highly strategic importance. But Tibetan control over Bhutan had become extinct and Bhutan had become independent for all purposes; the Bhutanese ruler became practically sovereign. The British had come to the rescue of the ruler of Cooch Behar in 1772 when the latter had been carried off by the Bhutias. The East India Company's army marched into Bhutan and defeating the Bhutia army not only brought back the Cooch Behar prince but also got a treaty signed by the Bhutia authorities to the effect that they would never entertain hostility against the British nor would they give asylum to any enemy of the British.[6] Gradually Bhutan Duars were annexed to the British Empire. In 1857, the Bhutia sympathy for the Sepoys in the Mutiny, antagonised the English. After the suppression of the Mutiny, the English deputed Ashley Eden, then Secretary to the Government of Bengal, on a Mission to Bhutan to obtain a fresh treaty on favourable terms. The Bhutias instead got Eden to sign a treaty which pledged the restitution of the Duars to Bhutan. On the return of Eden, the English declared war on Bhutan. The Bhutias were defeated; a fresh treaty was concluded. This ceded Kalimpong to the British and the Bhutias agreed to refer disputes between them and Sikkim and Cooch Behar to the English arbitration. The English agreed to raise the subsidy to Bhutan to Rs. 50,000 per annum. Since then peace was not disturbed till 1910 when the army of Chao Er-feng invaded Tibet. The British, suspicious of the Chinese motive, got a new treaty signed by Bhutan. The Bhutias agreed to be advised by the English in the conduct of foreign affairs and the Bhutia subsidy was raised to Rs. 1,00,000 per annum.[7] The threat on the Arunachal area from the Bhutan side thus disappeared altogether.

To the north of the Eastern Himalayan range lies the eastern division of Tibet known as Khams or Khamsyul extending from the frontiers of China in the east to the Tibetan province of U in the west.[8] The region was regarded as ethnographic Tibet rather than political Tibet as the Tibetan Government exercised jurisdiction in the province only in certain places and at irregular intervals. For the most part, the local lay or monastic chiefs ruled the districts of varying size at their discretion.[9] Again China, Tibet's suzerain, herself showed symptoms of decay and disintegration and till 1910 her control or direction of affairs in Lhasa was nominal rather than real. Neither Tibet nor China showed signs of virility or aggressive propensity. No danger thus loomed across the northern frontiers. Therefore, the British, instead of guarding the frontiers and arranging for their proper defence, remained unconcerned about the province[10] and left the affairs there to the helpless people themselves.

Geographically, the Eastern Himalayan range of Arunachal from the eastern border of Bhutan through the gorge of the Tsangpo (Dihang) up to the syntaxial bend in the Mishmi hills lies entirely within Tibet and Assam.[11] The Mishmi hills and that part of the Patkai range which falls within the Tirap district of Arunachal are within Burma and Assam. Compared with the Sub-Himalayas, the information about the more interior parts of the Himalayan mountains is restricted and vague. The main trafficable trade route from south to north runs along the Kameng Valley through Bomdi La, Se La and Tawang in the present Kameng district; along this route, the Dalai Lama fled into India in 1959 and then three years later the Chinese troops made their major thrust into Assam. Further east, no important trade routes cross the range and that factor accounts partially for lack of full information about this region of the Himalayas.

According to Augusto Gansser, the Eastern Himalayas can be divided into four structural units : (i) The Sub-Himalayas consist of Siwalik sediments of the Tertiary period, lying mostly in the southern part of the region ; (ii) the Lower Himalayas lying between the main boundary fault and the main central thrust comprise varied sedimentary and metamorphic rocks ranging in age from Palaeozoic to Mesozoic ; (iii) north of the central thrust lies the basal crystalline thrust sheet of the Higher Himalayas ; (iv) a great thickness of fossiligeorous Telhys sediments cover the crystalline thrust sheet of the Higher Himalayas.[12] The geological structure and process of erosion have influenced the surface appearance of landforms, which are intricately related to man's use of the land. But in this part of the country, the natural environment has remained inhospitable and adverse features have seriously impeded human development over large areas.

Very little informotion is available about the soils. The rocks are generally of the Himalayan type—shabs, schists and conglomerates; the derived soils are sandy and progressively clayey in the lower reaches of the valley. Soil acidity caused by heavy rainfall is high. The recently cleared forest lands exhibit a thick layer of leaf mould, rich in organic matter, but as a result of early rains the top soil is easily washed off. Soils in the foothills are alluvial in nature, being either loam or sandy loam mixed with pebbles, brought down by rain from higher altitudes. Soils in the valleys are clayey alluvium and rich in organic content.[13]

At least three major climatic zones can be recognised on the basis of temperature although temperature, pressure, precipitation and winds vary with altitude. The foothill area is hot and humid and has a sub-tropical climate; the lesser Himalayas enjoy cooler or microthermal climate; and finally in the higher region, a Himadri type (Alpine) climate is found. The flora and fauna of the province vary with the climate and soil. The forest types range from tropical evergreen in the foothills, through temperate evergreen in the middle ranges, to the coniferous in the higher elevations and the high Himalayas in the extreme north.[14]

Be that as it may, the hills of this province up to the Mishmi hills may be sub-divided into sections based on the major tribes that inhabit the respective mountains. From the west at the eastern border of Bhutan to the east, they are the Mompa, Sherdukpen and Aka hills in the Kameng district, the Dafla (Nishi) hills in the Subansiri district, the Miri hills and Abor (Adi) hills in the Siang district, the Mishmi (Idu, Taraon and Miju) hills in the Lohit district; the Daphabhum and Patkai ranges are known by their names even to the tribes that inhabit them. The Daphabhum range is populated by the Singphos and the Singphos, Wancho, Nocte and Tangsas populate the eastern Patkai range of the Tirap district.[15]

THE AKA, SHERDUKPEN (THONGJI) AND MOMPA HILLS

The Kameng district (14,000 sq km or 5,469 sq miles) is the habitat not only of the Mompa, Sherdukpen (Thongji) and Aka tribes but some other tribes live there as well. The Mompas live in the Tawang sub-division as well as in the Dirang and Kalaktang circles of the Bomdi La sub-division, that is to say, in the hills of west north-east region. The Sherdukpens (Thongji) live largely in the Rupa circle and some parts of the Kalaktang circle, that is to say, in the hills east of the Mompa, but covering the hills of the south-western part of the Kameng district. The Aka hills are bounded on the north by the Miju hills, on the west by the Sherdukpens, on the east by the Bengni hills and on the south they stand above the Darrang district of Assam. In between the Dafla hills to the east and the Mompa, Sherdukpen and Akas to the west, and bounded by the northern border of the Darrang district of Assam on the south and the territory of the Bangros and Sulungs on the north, lie the extensive Bengni hills. From the Bengni hills on the south to the McMahon Line on the north and between the Mompas of Kameng and the Tagins of Subansiri stand the Sulung and Bangro hills. Besides some

Mijis live in the hills near central Mompa tracts and a few Buguns are found in between the Sherdukpens and Akas of Kameng district.[16] Thus, the territory of the district is bounded by Bhutan on the west, the Tibetan province of Khams on the north along the McMahon Line, the Dafla hills on the east and the Darrang district of Assam on the south.

On the west, from the Mompa region of Tawang, flows the Nyamjang chu (Dargong) drawing the waters of the Mela ridge. It flows from north to south and a number of tributaries having their origin in the Mela ridge debouch their waters into it flowing eastward. The waters of the Namka chu, which assumes the name of Tawang chu and receives the waters of the Thangla ridge, are discharged into the Nyamjang chu.[17] After flowing through the Mompa hills, the Nyamjang enters into Bhutan and flowing through that country discharges its waters into the Brahmaputra through the Manas river. East of Tawang through Se La flows the Dirang which draining the western Mompa hills feeds the Kameng river. From the south-west, the Rupa river through the Sherdukpen hills sends its waters to the Kameng which with the waters of the Dirang flows into plains under the name Bhorali and discharges its waters into the Brahmaputra.[18] So the rivers of the eastern Kameng hills flow in the south-westerly direction and the rivers in the eastern region flow in the south-easterly direction.

The altitude of the hills in the Kameng district is comparatively lower except in the north than the other hills of this region of the Himalayas. The hills in the lower region on the plains are steep and inaccessible. The pass leading to Tawang along the Kameng valley and then through Bomdi La and Se La lead through higher altitude; at Se La the elevation is 4,680 m. But the Tawang region is relatively lower and the altitude of the Tawang itself is, 3,000 m above the sea level.[19] The climate of the district is humid up to 1,200 m, temperate up to 2100 m, and cold with heavy snowfall beyond that. Rich with evergreen deciduous forests, the hills in the upper region are dressed in pine, oak and fir. Carpeted with wild strawberries and a display of rhododendrons and a score of other multicoloured flowers, the district is the most picturesque of all the Arunachal hills.[20]

DAFLA HILLS

The Subansiri district (15,319 sq km or 5984 sq miles) covers mainly the Dafla hills.[21] Only a few Apa Tanis are found engulfed in and about Ziro, the headquarters of the district, and a few Hill Miris are found on the north-eastern extremity of the Dafla hills, adjacent to the Abor hills of the Siang district. The Miri hills are bounded on the south-east by the Dirjemo river which separates them from the Abors inhabiting the low hills north of Dibrugarh; on the north-east by a low range of hills forming the southern boundary of the Dihang valley; on the south by the Sub-division of North Lakhimpur; on the south-west by the hills to the east of the Ranga river which separate them from the Daflas. The Subansiri river divides the hills east and west. To the north up to the McMahon Line and between the Bangros and Sulungs of north Kameng in the west and Membas and Gallong Abors in the east are found over extensive territory the Tagins who are regarded as Tagin Daflas.[22]

Robinson places the Dafla hills between 90°50″ to about 94° north longitude and forming the northern boundary of the valley of Assam from the Kuriapara Duar to where the Subansiri debouches into the plains. G.W. Dun, in his preliminary notes on the Daflas, holds that the Daflas are a tribe of the "outer hills" of the southern slopes of a spur of the Himalayas which divides the Bhorali from the Subansiri drainage. "This spur is well defined as far as a peak called Lollupo, but at the point it is split into numerous minor valleys and spurs among which the Daphalas have established their villages. On the west, a very distinct ridge coming down from Lollupo separates the Daphalas from the Akas, who inhabit the basin of the Bhorali. On the east, another district ridge starting from Lollupo peak divides the Daphalas from the Miri of the Khru river (an afluent of the Subansiri) and of the Subansiri."[23] Thus, the Dafla hills are bounded on the north by the McMahon Line, on the west by the Bhorali river, on the east by the Sundri river and on the south by the Naoduar of Darrang and Cheduar of Lakhimpur districts of Assam.

The hills of the region are rugged and the lower region is covered by dense forest. The hills rise towards the north to

6000 m (20,000 feet) on the Tibetan border and remain snow-covered all the year round.[24] The valley in the hills lies east and west. The distinguishing feature of the territory of this district is a remarkable level valley, 4 km × 125 km (or 2½ × 7½ miles) at Ziro which is 1,500 m high.[25] Between Bhutan and the Subansiri river the Kandgu massif (7,089 m) forms the only major culmination. It forms a marked southward-directed spur and it seems possible that this culmination coincides with a southward-extended 'bulge' of the main thrust zone. From the Subansiri river to the east-north-east, the main range is surprisingly straight and no river flowing to the south crosses it. The Tsangpo, flowing from south of Lhasa in an easterly direction has approached the range to as near as 15 km and now follows its north-eastern track.[26]

Two principal streams drain the interior of the triangle enclosed by two spurs of the Dafla hills, *viz.* the Humderi or Ranga on the east and the Dikrang. The Dikrang has a small tributary from the east called Barpani, and further west are the still smaller stream of the Buroi with its tributaries the Poma and the Papum, and still further west the Borgang, a stream of the other slopes. The general direction of the rivers in this triangle is easterly.[27] But, by far the largest river of the district after which it has been named is Subansiri. It has a long course through the Himalayas and flows through a series of gorges and rapids. This river cuts the main Himalayan range in Arunachal Pradesh east of Bhutan and sends its headwaters into Tibetan territory pushing the actual watershed almost to the Tsangpo river. It is known as Tsari chu in Tibet and in the upper course of Arunachal as Mara where in the Tagin territory the Galen, a tributary, discharges its waters.[28] The principal tributary of Subansiri in Arunachal are the Kamla and Sidan draining the west and east respectively. The range from which the Sidan flows is a comparatively low one on the south-west of Dihang. The Kamla flows from the high mountains of the north-west.[29]

ABOR HILLS

Between the Dafla hills on the west and the Dihang river which borders on Mishmi hills on the east and in between

Lakhimpur district of Assam and the McMahon Line on the north lie the extensive Abor (Adi) hills of Siang district (20,981 sq km or 8,196 sq miles).[30] These hills constitute the slopes of the main Himalayan ranges which at the very eastern extremity rises to the highest elevation of the whole eastern Himalayas in the still practically unknown Namche Barwa (7,755 m).[31] The northern region is full of high, steep and inaccessible mountains and wild valleys. The southern part is comparatively flat. But the mountain in the south running north-east to south-west stand as a solid wall and shut the Brahmaputra valley from the north.[32] The passes along the northern boundary on the main range are surprisingly low; the tree studded Tum-La is only 3,600 m high and the more eastern Shoka La apparently still lower: We have here one of the lowest passes crossing the whole Himalayan range, similar to or even lower than the Zoji La in Kashmir (3,529 m) and only 600 m higher than the Tsangpo river which meanders in a rather steep gravel-filled valley, flanked by impressive terraces.[33]

The Tsangpo known in Assam as Dihang (now known as Siang-Brahmaputra) turns its north-easterly course into a southern and south-western direction at Namche Barwa. As the counterpart to the famous Indus gorge at the western end of the Himalayas north of Nanga Parbat, the Tsangpo cuts exactly through the highest culmination of the eastern end of the Himalayas. Down to Pe or Timpa, just west-south-west of Namche Barwa, the Tsangpo flows placidly in a gravel-filled, though rather steep-walled valley. From here downstream, the river which was previously over 1 km wide suddenly narrows to a mere 90 m and tumbles through a deep gorge with enormous boulders in most impressive cataracts.[34] The Tsangpo-Brahmaputra is one of the longest rivers of the world traversing a distance of 2,900 km through Tibet, India and Bangladesh.[35]

The Siang-Brahmaputra (Tsangpo-Dihang) flows through the centre of the Abor territory. Those living on the left or east bank of the Siang river up to the Dihang are called Bar Abors or Great Abors. Those living on the right or west bank of the Siang are known as Pasi-Meyond and formetly only Meyond Abors.[36] With the variation in altitude, the topographical and climatic conditions vary from south to north. The whole ranges are covered by dense forests and between October and January gorge wind occurs.[37]

MISHMI HILLS

South-east of the Siang (Tsangpo-Dihang) valley, the Mishmi hills form the still very obscure eastern syntaxial bend of the Himalayas.[38] It consists of a continuous chain of hills which in the higher region of the northern boundary remain perpetually covered with snow. The firs, and the highest in the horizon is the turret-form which is commonly known as the Sadiya peak; its base extends to Dihang on the left, and to the right it covers a considerable extent, allowing a more distant class of mountains to peep above its sloping sides. The next is the huge three-peaked mountain; the Mishmis call it as Thigritheya. It is succeeded by a wall after which Thathutheya, a round-backed ridge, rises high above the ranges near Parasuram Kund. Then there is a fall filled in by low mountains. Immediately to the east, at about a distance of 65 km the ranges are high and snow is seen above them throughout the cold season. The last peak in that direction is known as Beacon or Daphabhum as it is called by the Singphos. The lofty mountain retrogrades to a considerable distance beyond Daphabhum and forms a deep basin, the southern and eastern sides of which are alone visible; through the centre of this basin, the Dihang winds, having its source in the most distant point.[39]

Thus, the Mishmi hills are flanked on the west by the Dibang river, on the north by the McMahon Line and on the north-east by Burma, while in the south-west it is bounded by the valley of the Brahmaputra and the Patkai range. The hills and mountain ranges up the Lohit river from the Parasuram Kund as far as the Tibetan frontier on the east and round to west as far the Digaru up to the Tibetan frontier on the north are inhabited by the Digaru Mishmis.[40] The territory to the south-east is occupied by the Mijus, and to the west of the Digaru up to the Dibang on the west and Tibetan border on the north live the Idu or Chulikata Mishmis, to the south-east of whom, up to the foothills, live the Bibijias.[41] Some Khamptis live on the plains just below the Mishmi hills and a few Singphos inhabit the Daphabhum range part of which lie in the Lohit district. These areas have been brought under the Lohit district (23,191 sq km or 9,059 sq miles).[42]

The altitude of the hills of the Lohit district ranges between 600 m and 5,100 m. The craggy hills and blue green valleys are very narrow and steep. High river terraces, some 200-300 m above the stream level, border the valley.[43] The hills in the Dibang valley are generally more pointed and the hill slopes are steep and precipitous.[44] The plain areas in the foothills are covered by tropical jungle and are intersected by numerous ravines and water courses. Because of the inaccessible nature of the terrain, population in the Mishmi hills is sparse, particularly in the eastern region which embraces a number of high mountain ranges. The majority of the population is concentrated in the western part, chiefly in the southern portion of the Lohit valley.[45]

The principal rivers drain the Mishmi hills; both originate across the border within Tibet and flow down from south-eastern slopes of the Namche Barwa. The Lohit, known in Tibet as Zayul chu, flows into the Mishmi hills from the Tibetan post Rima, and through Menilkrai it approaches the Parasuram Kund across the high mountain and debouches into the wild valley below at a short distance from it.[46] A number of tributaries both across the Indian border and from the Digaru and Miju Mishmi hills feed it to make it a mighty river. From the western side, the Dibang, similarly drawing waters of tributaries of Tibet and upper hills of Bibijia and Chulikata or Idu territories, flows into the plains and unites with the Lohit below Sadiya.[47]

The climate of the Mishmi hills is generally moderate throughout the year. The foothill areas are warm during the summer, but the temperature in the high region goes down even in summer. As a result, innumerable varieties of trees grow in the district and some of them make good timber.[48]

DAPHABHUM AND THE EASTERN PATKAI RANGES

South of the Mishmi hills, where the Daphabhum and Phunganbhum meet, the Patkai range begins. It separates Assam from Burma and stands in a south-westerly direction projecting spurs on the Assam side in the northerly direction.

The portion of the range in Arunachal is almost uniformly high, 1,500 m above the sea level. Only the Pangsau Pass connecting the upper valley of the Brahmaputra with Burma stands at 1,238 m above the sea level. The elevation of the range varies from 2,040 m at Maium Peak in Upper Burma to 924 m in the Sympana Saddle.[49]

Towards the north-east fringe along the Daphabhum and Phunganbhum and the Patkai live some Singphos who have been in close connection with the Kakheyans of Burma.[50] Adjacent to them in the northern spurs and slopes of the range live the Tangsas who were known as Sarkari Nagas; next to them along the main range and the middle spurs are found the Wanchos who were known as Rangpangs and further south-west along the Tuensang district of Nagaland live the Noctes known as Namsangias.[51] The Noctes, Tangsas and Wanchos were regarded as Nagas and they still have close connections with their Burmese counterparts across the Patkai. A few Lisu or Yobins, Chakmas, Huzongs, Deonias, Kacharis and Miaos also live on the hills of the Miao sub-division on the north-eastern extremity of the Tirap district. This district (6,988 sq km or 2,730 sq miles) borders with Burma on the east, Nagaland on the south-east and Assam and the Mishmi hills on the north-east.[52]

Towards the north-east originates the Namphuk river which drains the north-eastern spurs and valleys and discharges its waters into the Buri Dihing river. The Tirap river, after which the district has been named, drains the huge valley along the eastern flank of the Patkai and after a long course falls in on the left bank of the Buri Dihing.[53] But the Buri Dihing is by far the largest of the rivers of the district that drains the entire basin of the northern slopes of the Patkai and receiving the waters of all the streams that flow from the north-eastern slopes of that range discharges its water into the Brahmaputra south of Dibrugarh.

The altitude of the hills of the district varies from 400 m in the Daphabhum range to 150 m in the foothills of the Patkai range.[54] The general relief over the entire north-western part of the Tirap district is low and the district is highly dissected by a number of wide river valleys like those of the Tirap and the Nou-Dihing. It is in these river valleys, particularly along the Brahmaputra plains, that the major part of the population is concentrated. The eastern part of the district is comparatively sparsely populated.[55] The climatic conditions also vary to a great extent. The climate of the foothills and plains valley is hot and humid whereas that of the higher hills is moderate and pleasant. As a result, the district is rich in sub-tropical evergreen forests and varieties of fauna.[56]

INFLUENCE OF GEOGRAPHY

The physical features of the territory of Arunachal have restricted the mingling of the people of different tribes and retarded the growth of national consciousness among the people; geography of the area favours retention of local identity, and lack of transport and communication facilities have kept the tribes separate from each other. Much of the land in the northern region of the Greater Himalayas has remained virtually empty; the middle zone is moderately populated; but the foothills and valleys are relatively closely populated and are characterised by the scattering of population clusters. The uneven distribution of population among several small valleys without adequate communication with each other hinders cohesiveness among the people. To the people the tribal loyalties come first and national allegiance—if there is any such sentiment at all—comes second. The enrivonment is largely responsible for the multiplicity of language and customs of the tribes which do not have easy communication with the neighbouring areas.[57]

Geography has influenced the cultural development of the province to a great extent. The northern region had little contact with the lower region, particularly the valley of the Brahmaputra, and has been greatly influenced by the Indo-Tibetan culture. For the past many centuries, the Tibetan traders crossed the borders and traded in the region; many of them settled down in the valleys of the Greater Himalayas. This accounts for the large Buddhist settlements in the Siang district and the Buddhist impact is visible in the way of life in the higher regions. The southern belt of the foothills has had similar contact with the plains of Assam. The results are manifest in the religion, language, clothing, food habits and mode of agriculture. But the middle zone has remained comparatively backward and both Tibetan and Assamese influence are visible in their way of life there. The tribes living in this region had very little contact with the outside world and even today they are living in extremely primitive conditions.[58]

But nature has endowed the land with beauty and hydro-electric potential which, if developed properly, can more than offset the physical difficulties. The province is full of scenic beauty and can attract tourists from all parts of the world. If transport facilities are improved and the restriction on the movement of visitors is removed, a flourishing tourist trade will develop. The hydro-electric potetial, if developed to its logical capacity, will transform the face of the land. If human efforts come to the aid of nature, Arunachal can develop into a second Switzerland.[59]

PEOPLE

ORIGIN AND MIGRATION OF TRIBES

History furnishes a very imperfect insight into the origin and descent of the tribes of the North-East Frontier. Robinson in his *A Descriptive Account of Assam* observes: "It seems almost vain to attempt to lift up the dark veil which conceals the origin of the tribes, to trace back their history, or to gain any information of the various revolutions by which they have been influenced; these subjects belong to times and circumstances which are beyond the limit of certain knowledge. It would be most cautious and perhaps the most philosophical course, to abstain from any conjecture relative to their origin or from any attempt to penetrate into the nature of causes of which even the most distant results are but partially known to us. Therefore, we must depend on the reflected light which is obtained by the comparison of language, by the analysis of civil and religious institutions and mythological fables, or by tracing clearly marked affinities in the manners and customs of different tribes."[60]

Indeed, it is very difficult to arrive at any definite conclusion regarding the original home, the routes of immigration and the dates of settlement of the myriad tribes of the North-East Frontier. Even the names by which they were popularly known were attributed to them by the neighbours in the valley of the Brahmaputra and were quite unknown to the tribal people themselves who had no contact with the plains.[61] The tribes of the present Kameng district were collectively known by a generic name Bhutia, except the Hrussos who were known as Akas for their custom of tattooing their bodies.[62] The Nishis were known as Daflas but the reasons why they were so called are still to be ascertained. The inhabitants of the present Siang district were called Abors, perhaps for their unruly nature, but they call themselves "Adi" which means "hillmen".[63] The tribes of the Lohit district were called Mishmis, but they have objected to be known as such and are now known by their group names, *e.g.* Idu, Miju and Taraon. Of the North-East Frontier tribes, only the Khamptis and the Singphos do not express any objection to being called by their agelong popular names. The tribes of the Tirap district were called Nagas; they are now recognised by their group names like Wancho, Nocte and Tangsa.[64]

But the identification of the tribes by their proper names has not in any way established the link with their past history. It has been pointed out that the assumption of the present nomenclature is perhaps more due to the rise of a sense of dignity and pride among the tribes who no longer like to be branded by their plains fellows in any manner they want.[65] It is not due to a tendency to identify themselves with a glorious race or kingdom elsewhere in the past or present as is the case with the Ahoms who now establish their connections with the empire of Pong which existed to the north of Burma and the Shan tribes who live in Thailand or Siam.[66]

The tribes of the North-East Frontier trace their origin in the north-east. George A. Grierson holds: "North-western China between the upper waters of Yang-tse-Kiang and Ho-ang-Ho was the traditional cradle of the Indo-Chinese races, and from that starting point successive waves of immigrants entered Assam. The first were the Maan-Ahoms who have left Khasis and are now to be seen in Annam and Cambodia. Second came the Tibeto-Burmans, the ancestors of the Bodo tribes with whom the Abors, Miris and the Daflas are clearly connected."[67]

C.H. Hesselmayer says: "The Himalayan mountains as they form the northern boundary of Assam are inhabited by two distinct races of men. Originally probably one and the same race, they seem to have undergone a change sufficiently marked to authorise their being considered at the present moment as two distinct races. The mountaineers who occupy the eastern half of these frontier hills seem to be original occupants, or first arrivals, and to have retained their original habits and customs. Those who live to the west appear to belong to a later period of immigration, subsequent to their descent from Central Asia."[68]

It is very difficult to ascertain the date of immigration of the tribes. But the statement of Hesselmayer also seems to be untenable. Beginning from the west, we know that the father of the Mompa tribe, Rupati of Kameng, had migrated to its present home in the hills from the plains of the Brahmaputra valley in the tenth century and is said to have married the daughter of a prince of Kamrup.[69] The progenitor of the Sherdukpen tribe is the grandson of an eighth century king Srongtson Gempo; he again is an immigrant from Tibet and is said to have come from the ancestral home in the eighth century.[70] According to a tradition recorded by Capt. Kennedy, the Akas trace their origin from the east. They trace their descent from Arima who migrated from the plains below the hills in remorse for having killed his father in ignorance.[71] The date of their immigration is not known, but it must have been after the decline of the dynasty of Bana, whose relics are found in Bhalukpong and Tezpur sometime after the twelfth century."[72]

The origin of the Daflas is not known. They trace their descent from a legendary ancestor whose three sons are believed to have been the forefathers of the three clans known as Dapum, Dodum and Dol respectively.[73] The first mention of the Daflas is found in the *Ahom Buranjis.* Their atrocities caused the Ahom kings to hold a portion of their territory and erect a line of fortifications along their hills.[74] But no account is available regarding their migration and origin elsewhere. It seems possible that they came from across the McMahon Line from the Khamsyul division of Tibet. To the north of the Daflas live the Tagins who are definitely immigrants of Khams. Some Tagins are to be seen across that Line in Tibet. The Daflas in the north are called Tagin Daflas and the Tabins, though a separate group, are off-shoots of one and the same stock.[75] The two other tribes, Apa Tanis and Sulungs, have been overwhelmed by the Daflas. They seem to have been living in the region before the coming down of the Daflas from across the McMahon Line. The Apa Tanis have remained independent, but the Sulungs have been reduced to the status of serfs in relation to the numerous and powerful Daflas. The Apa Tanis trace their migration from a valley of two rivers Supupad-Pudpumi. They have cultural affinities with the Abors and the Nagas.[76]

The tradition of origin among the Abors, as recorded by R.C.R. Gumming in 1931 for the Census Report, is as follows: "In none of these tribes there are any traditions of origin which go back very far. All claim origin from one race or tribe settled at Killing in the Bomo-Janbo country. From Killing, part of the tribe journeyed south across the Siyom river and occupied the hilly country between that river and the Subansiri and the Brahmaputra. These are now known as Galong. Others crossed the Dihang (San Fo) or settled on its bank or neighbourhood."[77] In the Census Report of 1961 they have been stated to be immigrants from the Khams province of Tibet.[78] The Abors probably had close relations with the Ahoms of the Brahmaputra valley, for during the Moamaria rebellion of 1792-93 twenty to thirty thousand Abors are said to have assisted the Ahom monarch.[79]

About the Mishmi immigration, J.P. Mills wrote that they were immigrants from Burma who entered Assam 500 years ago.[80] The Mishmis were followed by the Khamptis and the Singphos. The Khamptis began to migrate to Assam from Khampti-long in the east of present Lohit district, and to the north of Burma, somewhere in the 18th century.[81] The Singphos followed them from north Burma much later. During the decay of the Ahom kingdom the Singphos crossed the Patkai *circa* 1793, entered into Assam, and capturing Assamese slaves settled down on this side of the Patkai range.[82] The Wanchos and Tangsas of the Tirap district perhaps were preceded by the Ahoms who entered the valley of the Brahmaputra along the Buri Dehing valley crossing the Patkai range in the vicinity of present Vijaynagore, c. 1226.[83]

Thus, it seems that the present tribes of the North-East Frontier in Arunachal had entered into their present homes at different times and from different directions. The Sherdukpens, Daflas and Adis had come from across the McMahon Line from Tibet and settled over territories displacing the tribes who were already living there. The Mishmis, Khamptis and Singphos had migrated to Assam from the Irrawady-Salwen valley, commonly known among the tribes as Khampti-long or Bor Khampti country, over hundreds of years before the coming of the British into Assam in 1824-26. They neither came from the upper waters of the Yang-tse-Kiang and Ho-ang-Ho, nor were they of common origin as stated by Grierson and Hesselmayer.

TRIBAL LANGUAGES

The languages spoken by the tribes of the North-East Frontier reveal diversity of origin rather than confirm the unity of origin. The Tibeto-Burman family is the most important of the group of Indo-Chinese languages spoken by the tribes of the region, but it is by no means the only group that is found among the people here. The Mompas, the Sherdukpens (extra-Bhutan-Bhutias), the Khambas and the Membas (immigrants from Khams) speak languages of the Tibeto-Himalayan group of the Tibeto-Burman family;[84] the Akas, the Daflas, the Tagins, the Bangros, the Sulungs, the Mijis, the Bangnies, the Adis and the Mishmis speak languages of the North Assam group of the Tibeto-Burman family;[85] the Khamptis speak a language of the Tai group of the Chinese-Siamese family;[86] the Singphos speak a language of the Kachin group of the Tibeto-Burman family;[87] and the Noctes, the Tangsas and the Wanchos (Nagas) speak languages of the Naga group of the Tibeto-Burman family.[88] Thus, there are at least two families and four groups of languages prevalent in the area. Of these again the Mompas and the Khamptis speak languages which possess some literature, the one in Tai and the other in Tibetan language; the rest of the languages are practically dialects and they have neither scripts nor any literature. The Tai language has nothing in common with the rest of the languages; it is closely related to the Chinese language and is a distinct family as compared with the Tibeto-Burman forms of speech. The languages of the North Assam group, however, provide a link between the Tibetan spoken in the north beyond and the Bodo group of languages spoken below in the valley of the Brahmaputra. Similarly, the Kachin group and Naga groups are links between the Tibeto-Himalayan and Tai languages of South-East Asia.[89]

But the physical features of the tribes of the North-East Frontier offer striking similarities. The Mompas, Sherdukpens and Akas have yellowish brown Mongolian faces. Their women are pale-yellow and have a reddish tinge on their cheeks. Their nose is flat and eyes black and straight.[90] The Daflas are a very well-built and muscular people with a decidedly Mongolian cast of face. There is no beard on men's faces and their hairs are straight.[91] The Adis are of short stature but stockily built. Their complexion is yellow, eyes straight and black. The face is generally flat, the forehead broad. The nose is upturned with wide nostrils but many boast almost acquiline noses.[92] The Mishmis are a small but hardy race with a Tartar cast of features. Their eyes are blackish brown but straight. The nose is flat but not very broad; many possess acquiline noses. The Idus are sallow in complexion whereas the Taraon and the Mijus are reddish. But all possess handsome features.[93] The features of the Singphos are of the Mongolian type: "very oblique eyes and eybrows, mouths wide, cheek-bones high and very heavy square jawbones. Their complexion, never ruddy, varies from a tawny yellow or olive to a dark brown."[94] The physique of the Tangsas, Noctes and Wanchos is stockily built as is the case with other Mongolian tribes, and their complexion comprises every shade of brown. But a remarkable feature in them is the deficiency of hair on the face.[95]

TRIBAL SOCIETY AND GOVERNMENT

The myriad tribes of the North-East Frontier my be conveniently classified into three cultural groups, as V. Elwin has done. The first group includes the tribes who follow the Buddhist religion or have been influenced by Buddhism. The Mompas and Sherdukpens of Kameng, the Khambas and Membas of Subansiri and Siang and the Khamptis of Lohit follow Buddhism; the Buguns and Akas of Kameng, the Dhammai of Susbansiri and the Singphos of Lohit and Tirap have been influenced considerably by Buddhism. Common artistic pursuits, including making of wooden masks, are a distinctive feature of this group. The second group consists of the Daflas, the Adis, the Mishmis and sundry tribes inhabiting the hills stretching from Se La in Kameng through the greater parts of upper Subansiri, Siang and Lohit districts. These tribes have varying traditions but are culturally united by their attachment to weaving, absence of wood-carving and a degree of excellence in fine works of cane and bamboo. The last group is confined to the present Tirap district of the North-East Frontier and are composed of the Noctes, Tangsas and Wanchos of Tirap.[96] All these tribes have still wide contacts with their brethern across the Patkai in Burma and have been influenced to a great extent by them. They inter-marry with the Burmese tribes and do their hair and dress in imitation of them. They also are experts in wood-carving and personal decorations.

TRIBAL SOCIETY

Notwithstanding these cultural divisions, the tribes of the North-East Frontier have some common social features. The social organisation among them without any exception is patrilineal and the oldest male member is regarded as the guardian of the family; marriage is usually negotiated and the groom has to pay a bride-price to the guardian of his wife; members of the tribe marry within it but members of a clan outside it; polygamy is permitted but monogamy is the usual practice; polyandry is restricted to only some Adi tribes and is practically dying out; women in general enjoy a good deal of respect in society; slavery existed among all tribes throughout the British period. There is no casteism or racialism in any tribal community though social grades exist.[97]

Each tribe of the North-East Frontier lived an exclusive life of its own which the difficulties in communication and terrain had fostered to some extent. Each tribe, however, is divided into endogamous clans. The Daflas are divided into exogamous groups; clan divisions hardly exist among them.[98] The Adis are subdivided into exogamous clans which are further subdivided into smaller clans or families among which endogamy is strictly forbidden.[99] The Mishmis are endogamous and are divided into sects rather than clans.[100] The Khamptis, Singphos, Wanchos, Noctes and Tangsas are also divided into exogamous clans.[101]

Each clan breaks up into numerous families each of which consists of husband, wife and their children. A grown up son, when married, sets up a separate house unless he is the eldest and becomes a member of the village community which allocates a plot of land for his subsistence.[102] Families of the same clan may live in separate villages over which there is one chief or Gam or Gaobura, as he is known now a days. The villages in the Apa Tani plateau and Wancho and Tangsa are the largest and houses are built close to each other. The Apa Tani villages accommodate even 100 families.[103] The smallest villages are seen in the Mishmi Hills where a village is practically the home of a single family.[104] Social habits and customs are peculiar to a particular tribe, but there are some basic similarities though there may be difference of details from group to group. Every tribe has club houses or dormitories where youths are trained in civic duties, tribal disputes are resolved in meetings of the village elders, youths sleep in the night. Tribal guests are accommodated in these Morangs.[105] The accommodation of the youths in the Morangs served some other useful purposes as well. If the village is in danger and the youths are required to be mobilised to face the emergency, then the youths from the Morang could be given instructions quickly. In the Tirap and Siang districts, these Morangs serve as meeting places for youths to select their marriage partners. Among the Tirap and Siang tribes, their were separate Morangs for girls.[106]

The position of women in North-East tribal society is respectable is not very high. The system of polygamy, particularly among the Dafla and Mishmi tribes, no doubt has lowered their position, and sometimes wives are foresaken without being divorced. In spite of laxity in sex relationship, prostitution is practically unknown in the North-East Frontier.[107] Ordinarily, women lead a busy life, helping the menfolk in all walks of life. They wake up early in the morning and prepare meals for the family. Taking their morning meal, they proceed to the fields carrying their noonday meal and drinks. They work in the fields and return home in the evening. Again, they cook the meal for the night. Women took part in folk-dance where it existed and the entertainment of the guests was their privilege.[108]

Life of the people

The tribal people have a knack of celebrating festivals with a mounting crescendo of activity. Generally these festivals are connected with deaths, marriages and sowing and harvesting of crops. The Mompas of Kameng celebrate the Losar festival which is a kind of new year's festival on the occasion of Buddha Purnima.[109] The Adis celebrate Arau and Mopin festivals for a good harvest.[110] The Khamptis and Singphos celebrate Buddhist festivals. But the tribes of Tirap usually celebrate the settlement of disputes with feast and drinks.[111] Individual dances are practically unknown among North-East Frontier tribes; but community dances are also unknown among the Daflas, Apa Tanis and Mishmis. The Mompas and Sherdukpens of Kameng are most skilful dancers. People in colourful make-up and gorgeous costumes perform dances representing the world theatre in various religious functions to teach moral lessons to the people.[112] The Adis and Hill Miris of Siang and the Wanchos and Noctes of Tirap perform community dances or folk dances during community feasts. During these occasions, people drink liquor in large quantities so as to become intoxicated.[113]

The staple food of the people in the North-East Frontier consists of rice, millet and wheat which are supplemented by vegetables and forest produce. Fish and meat are consumed by all tribes, whether followers of Buddhism or of a tribal religion. Even Buddhist monks eat fish and meat but they do not catch and kill any fish or animal.[114]

Tribal houses are made of bamboo, timber, leaves and grass. Stones and mud are used extensively in Kameng where houses are comparatively small. In other parts, the houses are long and are raised on posts of cleft timber. The Adi houses are raised about 5 feet from the ground and posts are not used.[115] Four or five pieces of wood at an angle resting on the surface take the place of a post. Houses are constructed indiscriminately either on the top or side of hills, but the levels of the floors are maintained. The floors are of split bamboo not woven and walls are made of rough planks. For the roofs, palm thatch and wild plantain leaves are used. Roofs of the houses come down so low that externally the wall is not seen. But division of a house into compartments depends on social customs of the tribes and there is no distinction between individuals. The Wanchos and Noctes have two rooms in each house, one for the men and the other for women;[116] the Mishmis have as many rooms as the number of wives of the master of the house;[117] the Apa Tanis and Hill Miris have only one long room.[118] The houses of the tribes are 18 to 20 feet wide and 100 feet long; the interior is divided into chambers for private use and reception, and at the front there is an open balcony, a prolongation of the floors beyond the eaves providing for an airy place for the family to sit or work or lounge in (this is not so in the case of the Khamptis, whose chiefs possess two houses contiguous to each other).[119] Every house at the rear is provided with a veranda with a hole in the floor where the domestic stock is accommodated and these serve as scavengers. There are no sweepers and scavengers among the Frontier tribes.

Slavery

As mentioned above, slavery as an institution existed in the North-East Frontier all through the British period; slaves were objects of merchandise liable to be bought and sold. The unyielding and unproductive terrain of the Himalayas was perhaps conducive to slavery ; it was strengthened by tribal beliefs and the superstition that a person would get after his death as many slaves as he commanded in this world. People fell into slavery for many reasons. War captives might be sold as slaves in accordance with the custom existing in India from primitive times. The children of slaves became slaves automatically. Sometimes people committing offences against the community were condemned to slavery. The tribal people, however, treated their slaves quite well and their hardships were not as severe as depicted in *Uncle Tom's Cabin*. The position of the slaves in the tribal community is well described in a letter of the Chief Secretary of the Chief Commissioner of Assam : "Word (slave) connotes nothing more than a very mild form of servitude. The so-called slaves in the unadministered areas usually live in the house of the family for which they work, though occasionally they have separate houses of their own. Their clothing, food, house accommodation and general domestic equipment do not differ in any way from that of the ordinary hillman. They not infrequently possess private property which they obtain by trading during the months of the year when they are not required to work in the fields or in the case of women, by weaving clothes and rugs. A slave, in the event of the death of all the males inherits his master's property including his house. A master during his life time often sets up a slave in a separate house, finds him a wife, and gives him livestock and fields for his support, allowing him to live an independent life. It is true that slaves receive no actual cash wages, but money is exceedingly scarce in the hills and is used very little by the hillmen in their ordinary transactions. The slaves live in the same style as other hillmen and take as well as they do and it might, therefore, not unreasonably be urged that the wages which they receive in kind are as good as any servant can expect in such a quarter of the world. Moreover, there seem to be good grounds for holding that in the immense majority of cases, these so-called slaves remain with their masters of their own accord. No physical restrictions are placed upon their liberty and there is nothing to prevent them, if they wish to do so, from coming down and settling in the plains. In spite of this, the number of slaves who actually leave their master is very small."[120]

Political organisation

The tribes of the North-East Frontier know no kingdom or king; but each tribe or clan or village has its own head styled as Gam or Gaonbura, that is the village head, who is sometimes known as Sat Raja, as is the case with the Mompas and Sherdukpens, or Raja as the case with the Aka chiefs.[121] But the management of the internal affairs of the village or clan and its relations with the neighbours is vested in the village council which consists of the elders of the village. In such a village council, all members have equal powers and each such council is independent of all external influences.[122]

The most conspicuous of these village councils is the Adi Kebang. Its members, known as Kebang Abus, are chosen for their experience, ability and capacity to present and decide cases according to the traditional customs and conventions of the tribe. The Kebang controls the entire village activities and punishes those who deviate from the right path. The allocation of plots out of the *jhum* land of the tribe to each family, including plots for residential houses, and settlement of the village disputes—are all discussed and decided in the meetings of the Kebang. In settling disputes the view points of both the parties are taken into account after a careful hearing. Inter-village disputes are composed in the meetings of the inter-village council known as Bangos. All villages are divided into several groups for this purpose. The Bangos are composed of all the Gams of the member villages and such other members as have distinguished themselves in Kebang meetings and a secretary. Money collected in Bangos as fines are spent for the welfare of the village under the Bango. The inter-Bango disputes are settled in the meeting of the institution known as Bogum Bokang which is temporarily created for a particular case with members of all the Bangos and some distinguished persons who do not have any interest in the dispute and are impartial.[123]

Though the composition and functioning of the village councils differ from tribe to tribe, it is the main administrative, judicial and political institution throughout the North-East Frontier. Among some tribes, like the Wanchos, and the Noctes of Tirap, the Khamptis and the Singphos of Lohit, the Akas (Hrussos) of Kameng, the chief of the tribe or clan is hereditary and possesses more power and influence over their tribesmen. The Dafla chiefs are less influential as they are divided into innumerable petty divisions.[124] But the Tagin chiefs seem to be little more influential than their fellow Daflas.[125] Among these tribes, inter-village disputes and political decisions are within the jurisdictions of the chiefs.

But the Mompa and the Sherdukpen set-up is a little different. There were chiefs known as the Sat Rajas who were subordinate to the Governor of Tawang. In between the Governor of Tawang and the Sat Rajas of the different regions, there were some Gellings who were appointed by the Governor of Tawang for three years.[126] Under the Sat Rajas operated the village councils (Tsorgens) in different areas. The villagers elected the village council for a term to manage the affairs of the village according to the tradition of the tribe. But inter-village disputes and political decisions lay in charge of the Sat Rajas and their superior, that is, the Tawang Deo.[127]

ECONOMY

AGRICULTURE

The economic life of a country is largely conditioned by its physical and topographical features. Man tries to adapt himself in his natural surroundings with his technological equipment and social resources. The tribes of the North-East Frontier testify to the truth of this natural law. The mountains of this region are of younger age and break up into soil easily. The rainfall is heavy except in the north-east of the Kameng district with an average of more than 100 inches per annum. This has made the economy of the hills jhum-agricultural, which is supplemented by hunting and fishing. Generally, by the end of the winter an area is selected for cultivation and the jungle is cleared and fire is set to burn the dry bushes and trees that are felled. Before the onset of the rainy season, the soil is prepared with primitive implements, *e.g.* dao, axe, iron-hoe, pointed bamboo, and seeds of various crops are sown in the same plot. Seeds are often placed in separate holes with pointed bamboo but broadcasting of seeds is not uncommon. Different crops are reaped at different seasons from the same field. A clearing is used for two or three years and when its fertility is lost, it is abandoned and a new site is selected.[128].

Wet-rice cultivation and terrace cultivation are also prevalent among some tribes. The Mompas, the Khambas, the Membas practise terrace cultivation, wet-rice cultivation is popular among the Apa Tanis of Subansiri and the Wanchos, Noctes and Tangsas of Tirap and the Khamptis and Singphos of the Lohit district. The Mompas, Khambas and Membas plough their fields with yak or mithun and the tribes practising wet-rice cultivation employ cattle for ploughing their fields like the people of the plains.[129]

All tribes grow paddy, maize, millet, and vegetable of different varieties. The most popular and widely grown vegetable is *aram* which is grown in abundance all over the hills and is a common item of food of many people. The Adis and Mishmis grow tobacco; cotton and some barley are raised in some places.[130] The Wanchos and Noctes grow tapioca and cotton.[131] The domestic animals are pig, cow and mithun; the

Mompas, the Khambas and Membas keep horses and are very fond of them. But the mithun is, by far the most important and valuable domestic animal and usually the yardstick of wealth of the rich.[132] Fowl are found almost in every household along with pigs.

Land is said to be more important to an indian farmer than his wife and there is no exception in case of the North-East Frontier tribes. Land is the bedrock of the tribal economy in the hills and it is the mainstay of their subsistence. On land, the tribes grow their food and rear their herds, and from the forests around their villages they gather their housing materials like timber, bamboo and grass and collect firewood and fuel and go for hunting. Since the tribal people live on hill sides and cultivated the hill sides which are subject to erosion and land slides, the importance of land is more keenly felt.

There are three kinds of ownerships of land: personal land, clan-land and village-land. The land which is held in individual ownership and is inherited through the father is personal land; the land which is utilised by different villages of a particular clan for burial or grazing purposes is clan-land; the land on the fringes of villages where there are forests providing the villagers with firewood, roots and herbs as also hunting or fishing is the village-land property. The Apa Tanis and the Mompas who practise permanent or terrace cultivation have strong attachment to personal lands. The individual's status in society is determined by his possession of land. But the burial ground and the pasture are in all cases the property of the clan or the tribe. The forests on the periphery of each village is the property of the village.[133] The tribes who practise jhumming hold the agricultural land in common and the village council allocates to each individual family a plot of land for its use in each clearing.[134] The family enjoys it as private property till it moves away for a fresh site.

TRADE

Almost all the tribes grow all that are necessary for them and yet barter or trade is quite familiar. The Mishmis and the Khamptis are inveterate traders;[135] the Akas and the Mompas carry on extensive trade and act as middlemen for their neighbours;[136] the Adis trade with their brethren living behind them. What the tribes do not produce and require to procure from outside is salt. A small quantity of clothes, utensils and agricultural implements and some ornamental beads were the other items that they purchased at the fairs or from traders or businessmen are gold, yak-tails, wool and woollen blankets, ponny, sheep, dogs musk, ginger, Mishmiteeta, wax, honey, chillies, spices, madder, walnuts, rock-salt and oranges. Rubber and elephant tusk were at one time objects of a prosperous and lucrative trade.[137] But the introduction of synthetic rubber and indiscriminate tapping of rubber trees brought the rubber traffic to an end, and the government's policy of wild life preservation has stopped elephant catching.

INDUSTRY

Industry in the modern sense practically did not exist among the tribal people of the North-East Frontier. But cottage industry to produce the household requirements existed almost among all tribes. Marketable surplus of cottage industry products consisted of wooden-musks and utensils, carpet and tribal dresses, painting and religious scrolls called "thang-kas." In addition, there were a little handmade paper from the Mompa tribe,[138] cotton blanket of artistic design called "Jom" from the Adis,[139] coats and houses from the Mishmis,[140] and at one time artistic jewellery inlaid with stones from the Khampti tribes.[141] The Daflas produce fine hats from cane and bamboo but they did not have a market.[142]

FAIRS

Inside the hills there are practically no daily or weekly bazars or marts where the tribal people may sell their products and purchase their requirements excepting some trading shops set up in the later period by tradesmen who, with official licence, went for business inside the Inner Line. In the foothills, outside the Inner Line, there were some weekly marts where people from inside the hills went from time to time for marketing purposes. But the best time and occasion for purchase among the tribal community were the fairs that were regularly held among the foothills either inside the Inner Line, as was the case with the Sadiya fair, or outside the Inner Line as at Udalguri or Daimara in the Darrang district of Assam.[143] It was at these fairs that the government also paid the *Posa* or stipend payable to the tribes who with the money thus obtained purchased their requirements from the fairs. Here at these fairs again the tribal people sold their surplus products and purchased their annual requirements and cattle.[144]

Fair is a conspicuous institution in an agricultural economy. Usually after the end of the agricultural season, *i.e.*, after harvesting, people take stock of last season's balance and plan for next year. They sell what they can afford to forego and purchase what they think necessary for the coming year. Alexander Mackenzie writes that the whole amount paid to the Bhutias, after they were put off the Duars, was spent by them for purchases at the Udalguri fair. The Government Report on fairs gives the export and import figures of 1885 at Udalguri as Rs. 90,380 and Rs. 1,20,792 respectively.[145] As early as 1837, the Government of India instructed the Bengal Government to arrange a fair and make it a rendezvous for the tribal chiefs. Rabijit Choudhury writes : "It (fair) was advertised among the ryots and the different chiefs of the Singphos, Khampti and Abor and Mishmi tribes through interpreters. A sports ground was prepared and accommodation was arranged for the visitors. . . .The total expenditure in getting up the fair and in feeding the tribal visitors was Rs. 1000 only, double the amount originally assessed."[146]

Cross-country trade which continued from time immemorial between India and her neighbours could not be revived during the British period. Only trade between Tibet and India *via* Tawang continued to be carried on a limited scale. Trade between the Chinese province of Yunan and Assam *via* Upper Burma and Szechuan and Assam *via* the Mishmi hills fell gradually to extinction due to government antipathy. "The India Office did not favour a route through Burma to Western China."[147] But during the years of British rule, there were several attempts to restore the trade between India and China *via* the Mishmi hills and even survey and exploratory teams were successfully sent through the hills. Cooper's journey through the Mishmi hills to Western China roused much interest and people looked with attention for its results. A rail line with Western China *via* Mishmi hills also was mooted. In 1908, Sir Thomas Holdrich advocated a railroad from Sadiya to Szechuan and Noel Williamson, the Assistant Political Officer of Sadiya, also supported the idea.[148] After 1910, strategic considerations negatived the proposal of rail link with China through Sadiya. Yet the Mishmis of Lohit, the Adis of Siang and the Tagins of Subansiri along the McMahon Line continued to have trade with the Tibetan merchants till almost the end of British rule in India.[149]

Trade between Tibet and India *via* Tawang continued throughout the British period and at the annual fairs held at Udalguri and Baimara the Tibetan merchants continued to trade with the merchants of India. Being unsuccessful in establishing trade contacts through the western passes through Ladakh and Leh, the East India Company's Government tried to open Tibet to British trade through the Eastern Himalayas. In 1840's, the Commissioner of Assam advocated opening up of regular trade with Tibet through Tawang.[150] He held that the tribes who inhabited those tracts and had commercial intercourse with both the plains of the Brahmaputra valley and Tibet would welcome such development and co-operate with the government with the prospect of more profit. He requested to send members of the Boundary Commission then in Tibet back to India *via* Tawang or alternatively to give him permission to send an envoy to Lhasa by the same route from Assam.[151] Unfortunately, the British Government did not take any step to implement the idea though the issue was discussed time and again. The specification of the Inner Line on the Darrang frontier again put a barrier on Indian traders to trade freely with Tibet and the hills leading to Lhasa.

RELIGION AND CULTURE

MIXTURE OF RELIGIONS

To satisfy his mental and spiritual hunger, man has through the ages built up a spiritual world from which he derives guidance for every-day life. The people of the North-East Frontier are no exception; they also have developed a supernatural world to brighten the stark realities of life. They believe in a world of good and evil spirits hovering in the air about them and on the earth below, and long to appease enmity or enlist the aid of these secret powers by sacrifice.

Unfortunately, the European officers on whose reports we have to depend mainly for our information on the North-East Frontier during the British regime have not left any favourable account of the religious practices of the tribal people. "In no field are our old records more imperfect than in that of religion", observes Elwin.[152] The general attitude of the European writers towards the tribal religion is that the tribes did not have any religion at all, or that it was a mixture of all the various idolatries and superstitions.[153]

But a careful study of the religious practices of the tribal people show that in building the spiritual world the people of the frontiers have been influenced by the religious practices of their neighbours and have adapted some of their practices or beliefs to their requirements. The Mompas, the Khambas and Membas profess the Mahayana form of Buddhism.[154] Some Khamptis follow Hinayana Buddhism which they brought with them from Khampti Long, while others worship the Hindu goddess Devi or Durga.[155] The Singphos who have accommodated the religious practices of their neighbours follow Buddhism and Brahmanism and have decorated their temples with images of different gods and goddesses.[156] Some Noctes of Tirap profess the Mahapurushia form of Vaishnavism propagated by Srimanta Sankardeva in Assam, while the Wanchos and Tangsas of Tirap follow their tribal religion.[157]

The people who have been influenced by the religion of their neighbours have also built temples or sanctuaries like their neighbours. In the Buddhist region of Kameng, every village has a Gompa or temple and every house has its own chapel and altar with a statue of the Buddha. The Buddhist monastery of Tawang, which accommodates a magnificient statue of the Buddha, is the largest of its kind in India.[158] During the Buddha Purnima, the Mompas celebrate the Losar festival in a spectacular manner with the accompaniment of musical instruments, like clarionet—made of silver, brass and wood—, reed-pipes, horns, shells, cymbals, drums and gongs. There are many shrines and temples in the Khamba and Memba villages of Subansiri.[159]

But still a considerable number of people of the North-East Frontier follow what may be called tribal religion or the so-called animism which is a sort of primitive religion to be found anywhere in the tribal societies. The characteristics of primitive religion, as Will Durant has observed, "are an animistic fear and worship of spirits lurking anywhere, a poetic reverence for the impressive forms and reproductive powers of earth, and an awed adoration of a heaven whose energising sunlight and fertilising rains are parts of the sky."[160] This definition of animism is corroborated by Prof. E.O. James who writes: "The doctrine of animism represents a complex attempt to interpret the material and spiritual aspects of the phenomenal world by resolving the universe into a fundamental dualism of Body and Soul."[161]

The Abors of Siang, the Akas and Khowas of Kameng, the Daflas of Subansiri, the Mishmis of Lohit and the Wanchos and Tangsas of Tirap believe in a number of heavenly spirits and offer sacrifices to propitiate them. The Akas regard the sun and the moon as the male and female god and goddess respectively who have the powers of peace and prosperity, and they offer sacrifices to enlist their support.[162] The Daflas regard moon as male and sun as female deity and trace their descent from their union.[163] The Abors of Siang and the Mishmis of Lohit regard Donyi-Polo or the Sun-Moon god as the supreme reality and offer sacrifices for his favours.[164] The Wanchos believe in Rang, the benevolent god of the skies, who cares for men and beasts, and Baurang, the malevolent god of earth and destroyer of living creatures, and offer sacrifices to appease them.[165]

The remarkable feature of the tribal religion as practised in the North-East Frontier is the absence of shrine or temple, as also of image worship. Nor is any organised clergy or priesthood dependent on religious performances as distinct from the rest of the community to be found among the tribes except some religious functionaries like the Epak Miris and the Nyibo[166] of Abor society and the Tumsawa of the Singphos[167] and the Opa or Nampa Aja, Rampa and the Rammi of the Wancho society.[168] Women usually do not take part in religious functions; worship among them means prayer and offering sacrifices. Sacrifice is followed by community feast and wine is consumed on the occasion of offering sacrifices.[169]

Emile Lasbax, in an article on *Rhythm of Sacrifice and Prayer*, has observed, "Primitive sacrifice is always an offering under one aspect or another; it is a sacrifice of the firstlings. The sentiment which inspires it is that the materials should never be used without some reserve; for it becomes an absolute master who has himself produced them to sacrifice them without some reserve. It should not be forgotten that their true creator is God, and therefore it is equitable to offer Him the first fruit, which it has permitted to us to gather, in gratitude for this first gift. The sacrifice of man thus appears to be the exact counterpart of the creative work of God.'"[170]

But the tribes of the North-East Frontier are practical people. Their attitude to religion might originally have been influenced by the sense of awe and reverence, but it is now based on the system of barter and purchase. So the sacrifices performed by them are mostly performed for worldly gains. The agricultural ceremonies and sacrifices are performed with a view to ensuring good growth of healthy crops and preventing disease and failure of crops.[171] Other rites are performed either to keep away the evil spirits or to bring in prosperity.[172] Thus, their sacrifices have nothing to do with the firstlings as suggested by Lasbax.

The world of the spirits is not confined to the forces above the earth alone; it extends to the world of the dead as well. Most of the tribes believe in a separate world of the dead. The Akas believe that the spirits of the dead go under the earth and proceed westward until they come to the place where the sun and the moon set; then they ascend to heaven. But the souls of those who die unnatural death and of the children too . . . ascend direct to heaven without undergoing the pilgrimage under the earth.[173] The Daflas have similar notions about the dead, but they hold that there are villages under the earth for those who die a natural death and villages in heaven for those who die unnatural death and for the children's spirits.[174] The Miris and the Mishmis also ascribe an abode underneath for the spirits of the dead.[175]

Since the tribes believe in the existence of the spirits of the dead, they put in the graves of the dead some food, clothes, weapons and other items of daily use to aid the journey of the spirits. The Abors place in one hand of the dead a small knife as an aid for getting food on the way to the spiritual home. A gourd of rice beer is tied under the grave and various garments of the deceased; any heads of mithum, etc. killed by him and used to feast the community are suspended on the posts nearby or under the shelter.[176] The Akas and Daflas hang a basket of rice, meat, beer, etc., near the grave of the departed.[177] The Mishmis put the corpse on a wooden couch, fully clothed and armed and with food, money, utensils etc. under the grave.[178]

In fact, the religious philosophy of the Arunachal tribes, be it Buddhist or Hindu or Animist, is based on a strong sense of history, a pride in the descent of the race from a great ancestor, and a belief in the value of sacrifice for the common good.[179] This is again founded on five cardinal tenets. First, the tribes believe in a supreme god who is just, benevolent and good. Their religion emphasises the spiritual realities behind the daily life. The tribes have faith in kind tutelary spirits and emphasise the spiritual cause of tragedy. Religion in North-East Frontier, as elsewhere, is closely associated with social ethics that unites the tribe in its discipline and promotes virtues like generosity, hospitality, truth, kindness and devotion to work. Finally, their religion gives them the power to reconcile themselves to the frequent emergencies of life.[180]

The study of the Arunachal tribes, thus, reveals strange contrasts. Some of these tribes, like the Mompas and Sherdukpens of Kameng and the Khamptis of Lohit, together with the Khambas and Membas of Subansiri, possess a remarkable culture and an advanced form of religion in contrast to the rest who follow more or less their ancestral religion which is again typical of primitive society everywhere in the ancient world. In some areas, the tribes practise what may be called permanent cultivation on irrigated terraces and valleys, whereas in others, tribes follow jhuming or shifting cultivation. In some tribes, workmanship in cane and bamboo shows remarkable dexterity while in others it is practically unknown, but then they are far more dexterous in wood carving and painting. It is quite difficult to state categorically whether these people are

Hindu or anything else, for the term Hindu is so catholic and elaborate as to embrace not only the followers of Gautama Buddha and Mahavira, the great teacher of Jainism, but also the worshippers of snake and spirits, supposed to be the presiding deities of natural forces or calamities and diseases.

ORIGINS OF RELIGION AND CULTURE

But the recent excavations at the foothills of NEFA have brought to fore yet another problem. The ruins of Bhismarkanagar about thirty miles from Sadiya,[181] the Tamreswari temple nearby and the ruins of a palace at Malinithan, a place near Likhabali in the Siang district, prove conclusively that these are of Hindu origin and construction.[182] Besides, there are some relics of Hindu culture at Bhalukpong in the present Kameng district to the north-west of Tezpur; a Buddhist gompa or cave exists at Dirang in the Subansiri district, a stupa has been found at Vijaynagar in the Tirap district, and there is the Bhairav Kund on the western tip of Kameng district.[183] Parasuram Kund, a famous place of Hindu pilgrimage in the Lohit district, still attracts numerous Hindu pilgrims from all over India. How do we relate these sites to the present tribes?

A recollection of the traditions associated with these places may suggest some solution. In the sacred Vaishnava work, *Srimad Bhagavata*, there is a story that the king of Vidarbha, Bhismaka, had a beautiful daughter Rukmini by name. The king had arranged her marriage with a prince named Sisupala, the ruler of a kingdom in the neighbourhood; but Sri Krishna, the lord of Dwaraka, carried her away by a stratagem and married her.[184] The present Bhismaknagar on the river Kundil near Sadiya was known in ancient times as Vidarbha. The ruins are said to represent the palace of the king Bhismaka alluded to in the Bhagavata.[185] Excavations in 1967 brought to light a phallic stone representing lord Siva. The Chutias of Assam claim to be descendants of the same king. The copper temple near Bhismaknagar is also attributed to the Chutia kings of Vidarbha. The temple is the shrine of Kechai Gohaini which still now is revered by the Chutias and Cacharies of Assam. Two copper plates in Sanskrit have been restored from this place.[186]

The next important site excavated is Malinithan. It is not at a great distance from Bhismaknagar. Local traditions say that Krishna while going back to his home, Dwaraka, rested here with Rukmini, the daughter of Bhismaka, whom he had married, as the guest of Lord Siva and his consort Parvati. During their sojourn, Parvati had offered garlands of beautiful flowers from her garden. Lord Krishna, who was overwhelmed with the charm and beauty of these flowers, addressed Parvati as Malini or mistress of the garden. Since then the place was known as Malinithan or the abode of mistress of the garden. The *Kalikapurana* says that when the body of Sati, wife of Siva, was cut to pieces by Vishnu with his holy discus, her head fell somewhere on the Akasi Ganga. Some hold that the same river flowed once by the present site of Malinithan. The North-East Frontier Agency authorised L.N. Chakravarty, Deputy Director of Research (History), who had traced out the Sivalinga or the phallic stone at Bhismaknagar in 1968, to undertake the excavation of Malinithan. He has already exhumed over one hundred images of various gods and goddesses of Hindu pantheon, Yaksas in dancing postures, figurines, sculptured panels, animal motifs such as those of bull, lion, elephant, etc., and some iron dowels or clamps used to hold building materials instead of mortar; some geometric and floral designs have also been discovered by him. An eight-foot high plinth of a temple, most beautifully and florally decorated, has also been unearthed. Images of Indra, seated on elephant, Kartikeya on a peacock and Ganesh have also been found, besides Sarswati and Nandi, the vehicle of Lord Siva. The excavations have proved conclusively that the ruins are of a Hindu civilisation that flourished perhaps before the tenth century.[187]

Moving westward up the hills one comes across the cave temple of Dirang associated with the Buddhist religion in Subansiri. But further west at the foot of hills below in the Kameng district at Bhalukpong there are the ruins of yet another palace with temple sites in and around it. This place is associated with the name of another Puranic king Bana. In the *Vishnu Purana*, we have a reference to king Bali whose son Bana was a contemporary of legendary Naraka of Kamakhaya. The king Bana, who had a palace at Bhalukpong, had a very beautiful daughter Usha by name. Krishna's son Aniruddha was charmed by her beauty and she consented to marry him; the two lovers secretly escaped from the palace. Bana, enraged at this, chased the fugitives, but they were rescued by Krishna who had meanwhile arrived on the spot and defeated Bana's contingent.[188] Besides, the Bhairav Kund of this district is associated with the king Bana who was a devotee of Lord Siva.

Parasuram Kund, where the holy river Lohit, known as the Brahmaputra, descends on the plains, is regarded by the Hindus as a place of pilgrimage, and on Magh Bihu in the middle of January pious people and pilgrims from all over India came to take a dip in its holy waters. There is a story that Parasuram had killed his mother with an axe at the command of his father and had thus committed a great sin. His father told him to take a dip in the Brahmakund at the place now known as Parasuramkund which would absolve him of his ghastly sin. He did accordingly and was purified by this act.[189]

Now the association of Hindu legends with these places, references to these places in the Puranas and Tantras, and excavations carried out so far prove beyond doubt that people of these places were influenced by Hindu religion and civilisation right from very ancient times. But when and how Hindu civilisation penetrated into Assam can only be conjectured, for no connected history of Assam in its religious and cultural aspects till the advent of Ahoms in 1226 A.D. is available. Then we have only accounts of Ahom warfare with the Asssam valley chiefs with occasional references to some customs and costumes with artifices. The condition of Assam at the time of the Ahom incursion is not known in its all aspects. The remains of civilisation that have been unearthed are said to be remnants of the culture of the Chutias, Kalitas and Bhuyans, who have almost merged their identity with the rest of the people of the valley. The problems of identity of the people with this civilisation can be solved in the light of "Sanskritisation" theory of Srinivas.[190] Then the claim of the Mishmis that they descended from Bhismaka, the legendary king of Kundil, and the tradition of the Akas who regard themselves as descendants of king Bana can be resolved.

An analysis of the culture and the people involved may help an understanding of the problem. The Chutias who are identified with the Kacharis of the south bank of the Brahmaputra are a people of the Mongolian stock without any doubt. Again, it is a proved fact that they had come to stay in the valley right from the beginning of the Christian era. The present state of their (Chutias) culture and living may lead to the conclusion that the culture which flourished at Bhismaknagar, Malinithan and Sonitpur (Tezpur) could not have been developed by them alone; there must have been some outside Aryan influence over them. But at the same time it is also clear that they continued to be the predominant people before the flood of C.A.D. 1750, and were gradually dispersed thence by the Ahoms and other people.

The Kalitas and Bhuyans were almost the same people and perhaps were pioneers of the Aryan elements in the Assamese population. If we accept the view of Gait that the Aryans penetrated into the Kirat country and established petty kingdoms we may assume that these Aryans established themselves among the Kirat people and in course of time became princes, as their counterparts did in the Malay peninsula and archipelago.[191] S.K. Chatterjee also holds the same view.[192] Thus, a new type of culture began to generate in the upper valleys of the Brahmaputra and it subsequently flourished at places like Bhismaknagar and Malinithan.

A critical appreciation of the stories relating to the origin of the ruling dynasties of the localities brings one to the conclusion that these kingdoms and cultures were the results of the labours of the indigenous Kirat people who had immigrated from Mongolia in China to the valleys of the Brahmaputra and the Aryan people who fused themselves with these people. Stories of union of the native princes with Hindu gods in the guise of some kings or princes and queens with Brahmanas or some Aryan chiefs are frequently brought forth in tracing the origin of different powerful chiefs. Thus Gourinarayan, the celebrated Chutia king, is said to be an offspring of the union of Kuber in the guise of Bispal with his queen Rupabati.[193] Another powerful prince of Arimatta was born of Ramchandra's wife Chandraprova when she eloped with the Brahmaputra.[194]

J.P. Wade narrates an account of origin of the Jaintia Raja in the following words: "Zointeh Rai had no children but solicited Takoor Ranee by pious exercise to bless him with a son. Devee in a dream visited him and informed him that destiny had determined that he should not have offspring, but that she would supersede his destiny as a recompense for his devotions at her altar and grant his request. She accordingly promised to be herself the child, and to be born of the princess, his wife .... In due course of time, a most beautiful child saw the light in his family. The king sought in vain a husband worthy of her and ultimately married the daughter to his confidential adviser Sundobur's son Sundahburra, a Brahmin."[195]

In tracing the origin of Kacharis also the same author observes, "Deongdana had paid her assiduous devotion to Sioo to obtain the favour of a male child. The god appeared to her in a dream and directed her to receive a stranger who should visit her the ensuing day into her embraces, promising her a son who should become prince of that country". The two former races of princes are also said to have descended from the conquerer Bhim (an Aryan chief of the *Mahabharata*).[196] A similar origin is atrributed to the Koch king Biswa Singh. His father Hurria Mundal had two wives, Leela and Heera. The latter was carrying some repast for her husband who was at work in the field. On the way, Mahadeo, assuming the form of Hurria, surprised her under a tree and devoured the repast and caressed her on the spot. In due course, a son was born of this union and he became the founder of the kingdom of the Koches.[197]

When we study these stories in the larger perspective of Hindu expansion from the 3rd century A.D. to the 12th century A.D. in the countries adjacent to India, particularly in Burma, Malay, Siam, Cambodia and the Malayan Archipelago, it is quite clear that some adventurers from within India made their way into the valley of the Brahmaputra and, like their counterparts, in the South-East Asian countries, succeeded in establishing themselves as either rulers or advisers of the rulers in the region and thus laid the foundation of a new civilisation there. Maybe they were Kalitas and their successors (Bhuyans) who later on were expelled or absorbed by the Shan Ahoms and Khamptis after their incursion into the valley across the Patkai range.

But the problem of placing the present tribes of the North-East Frontier into line still remains. It appears that they came down from Tibetan territories when the Chutia kingdom began to decline and when these tribes originally one and the same came down on the Assam plains. But it may be conjectured that unless there was a major disturbance or upheaval in their original home they might not have migrated to their present homes. It is quite probable that when the Mongol leader Chengis Khan's descendant Godam, who was governor of the Kansu region of China, invaded Tibet in 1239 A.D. looting and killing everything before him, some tribes of the Khams region of Tibet descended on the southern slopes of the Himalayan ranges.[198] The Chutias faced the Ahoms from the south and the Tibetan hordes from the north. When the Ahoms gradually suppressed the Chutias of the north bank, these tribes further came down on the plains and established their sway over the helpless plains people. Further, the flood of the Dehing which submerged the plains of the Upper Assam valley for more than a fortnight in 1750 A.D. facilitated the tribal expansion and weakened the position of the people of the plains.[199] A section of the tribes, now known as Miri, came down to settle on the plains after the recession of the flood waters. Capt. Kennedy, who accompanied the Aka promenade of 1913-14, records an interesting tradition which says that the Akas along with other hill tribes went in search of land; the Akas lost time in resting and drinking beer when others took possession of better lands.[200]

The Linguistic Survey of India has shown that the tribes living in the present frontier tracts speak a language of Tibeto-Burman family of North Assam group with the exception of the Khamptis, who speak a language of Chinese-Siamese family of Tai group. The Khamptis from the Bar Khampti land began to migrate to Assam from the 8th century and gradually pushing the Chutias occupied territories on the Lohit and Dehing; the Singphos came much later in the wake of the Burmese in 1822-23, or just before them, from Burma. Again, the Khamptis profess the Buddhist religion which they brought from their original home, the Bar Khampti country. The tribes of the central tracts follow tribal religion. Therefore, it seems quite clear that the tribes living west of the Khamptis of the Lohit district belong to a separate race and the tribes of the Abor hills or Subansiri district and the Khamptis and Singphos of Lohit had nothing to contribute to the Hindu civilisation that flourished in Bhismaknagar and Malinithan. The tribes of the western district Kameng had not settled on the plains of Assam when these centres of Hindu religion and civilisation developed; they tended to come down when it had begun to decline.

A survey of the land, that is, the physical features and topography, of the North-East Frontier reveals that the natural frontier of North-Eastern India is the crest of the Eastern Himalayas and Patkai mountains which separate the Brahmaputra waterparting from the San Po and the Irrawady-Salwin watersheds. The study of the population shows that the population of the North-East Frontier is Mongoloid and is the predominant ethnic element in the population of North-East India. A review of the culture of the North-East Frontier leads one to conclude that it is an admixture of Indian, Tibetan and Burmese elements, and through the North-East, India has absorbed Tibeto-Burman cultural elements to enrich her variegated cultural profile.

It may be concluded, perhaps, without the risk of over simplification, that the Aryan civilisation which penetrated into the valley of the Brahmaputra before the beginning of the Christian era, continued to flourish through centuries of Ahom and British though there can be no denying the fact that the economy and culture of the hills on both sides of the valley influenced that growth. As a result of this mutual give-and-take, the economy and culture of both the hills and plains developed and prospered. As the San Po, originating from the Lake Manas, becomes the mighty Brahmaputra in the Assam plains, drawing the waters of innumerable tributaries coming down the hills, so also the economy and culture of the plains of Assam have flourished with the contributions of the hills. Again, as a powerful lamp radiates light and expels darkness around, the Hindu civilisation that flourished in the valley of the Brahmaputra enlightened the tribes living on the hills.

REFERENCES

1. The total length of the McMahon Line is 1,312 km (820 miles) of which 192 km. (120 miles) border with Burma and Tibet and 1,120 km (700 miles) border with Tibet. See Foreign Political (Secret) Proceedings (India), October 1914, Nos. 134-396.
2. Administrative Jurisdictions, p. 6.
3. Foreign Secret Proceedings (India), January 1911, No. 239.
4. A.C. Banerjee, *The Eastern Frontier of British India*, p. 365.
5. H. Vinacke, *A History of the Far East in Modern Times*, p. 62.
6. A. Amanatulla, *A History of Cooch-Behar* (in Bengali), pp. 39-43
7. Ram Rahul, *The Himalaya Borderland*, p. 64.
8. G.A. Grierson, *Linguistic Survey of India*, p. 136.
9. H.E. Richardson, *Tibet and its History*, p. 1.
10. Foreign Secret Proceedings (India), January 1911, No. 239
11. A. Gansser, *Geology of the Himalayas*, pp. 227-230.
12. *Ibid*, pp. 227-229.
13. R.L. Sing (ed), *India—A Regional Geography*, pp. 82-84.
14. *Ibid*
15. North-East Frontier Agency, henceforth referred to as NEFA, *The Land and the People*, p. 4.
16. *Ibid.*
17. T.S. Murty, "Historical and de facto position of the Buddhist pockets", An article published in the *Institute for Defence Studies and Analysis Journal*, vol. 3, No. 4, April 1971.
18. J.P. Dalvi, *The Himalayan Blunder*, pp. 108-109 (map).
19. F.M. Baily, "Explorations on the Tsangpo or Upper Brahmaputra," *The Geographical Journal*, vol. XLIV, p. 357, Nevill's and Dalvi's topographical features do not tally with Bailey's (Dalvi, p. 113).
20. *NEFA*, *op. cit.*, p. 4.
21. *Administrative Jurisdictions*, p. 6.
22. C. Von Furer-Haimendorf, *Ethnographic Notes on the Tribes of the Subansiri Region*, p. 3.
23. V. Elwin, *India's North-East Frontier in the Nineteenth Century*, p. 185, henceforth referred to as *North-East Frontier*.
24. *NEFA*, *op. cit.*, p. 8.
25. Ram Rahul, *op. cit.*, p. 7.
26. A. Gansser, *op. cit.*, p. 229.
27. V. Elwin, *North-East Frontier*, p. 185.
28. T.S. Murty, *op. cit.*
29. V. Elwin, *North-East Frontier.*
30. *Administrative Jurisdictions*, p. 6.
31. A. Gansser, *op. cit.*, p. 229.
32. NEFA, *op, cit.*, p. 11.
33. A. Gansser, *op. cit.*, p. 230.
34. *Ibid.*
35. S.D. Misra, *Rivers of India*, p. 28.

36. Ram Rahul, *op. cit.*, p. 9.
37. NEFA, *op. cit.*, p. 11.
38. A. Gansser, *op. cit.*, p. 229.
39. V. Elwin, *North-East Frontier*, pp. 9-10.
40. J.P. Mills, *Notes on the Mishmis*, p. 2.
41. *Ibid.*
42. *Administrative Jurisdictions*, p. 6.
43. A. Gansser, *op. cit.*, p. 230.
44. NEFA, *op. cit.*, p. 17.
45. R.L. Sing (ed), *op. cit.*, p. 486.
46. T.S. Murty, *op. cit.*
47. S.D. Misra, *op. cit.*, p. 29.
48. NEFA, *op. cit.*, p. 17.
49. V. Elwin, *North-East Frontier.*
50. A. Mackenzie, *History of the Relations of the Government with the Hill Tribes of the North-East Frontier of Bengal*, p. 61., henceforth referred to as History.
51. Lakhimpur Deputy Commissioner's Collection No. XII, F. 71, 1904-08.
52. V. Elwin, *North-East Frontier*, pp. 25-26.
53. *Ibid*, p. 104.
54. NEFA, *op. cit.*, p. 22.
55. R.L. Sing (ed.), *op. cit.*, p. 500.
56. NEFA, *op. cit.*, p. 22.
57. R.L. Sing (ed), *op. cit.*, p. 480.
58. *Ibid.*
59. *Ibid*, p. 492.
60. W. Robinson, *A Descriptive Account of Assam*, p. 335.
61. Census Report, 1901, vol. IV, Part I, Chap. XI, p. 120.
62. V. Elwin, *North East Frontier*, p. 438.
63. Assam Census Report, 1881, para 153, Census Report, 1931, vol. V, Part III, p. XIII.
64. Lakhimpur Deputy Commissioner's Collection, No. XII, F. 7, 1904-08.
65. S. Roy, *Aspects of Padam Minyong Culture*, pp. 1-5.
66. P., Buragohain, "Tai Jati" an article published from Assam in a journal named *Tai Sanskriti* in 1956, No. 2, aserts that the Ahoms are from Mongolia and are same with the Mongols of Mongolia.
67. Census of India Report, 1901, Part I, vol. IV, p. 120.
68. V. Elwin, *North-East Frontier*, pp. 435-436.
69. T.S. Murty, *op. cit.*
70. *Ibid.*
71. V. Elwin, *North-East Frontier*, p. 438.
72. E.A. Gait, *A History of Assam*, p. 16.
73. Census of India, 1961, p. 240.
74. W. Robinson, *op. cit.*, p. 353.
75. Census of India, 1961, pp. 246-50.

76. *Ibid.*
77. Census of India Report, 1931, Part III, p. xiv.
78. *Ibid*, 1961, p. 250.
79. W. Robinson, *op. cit.*, p. 353.
80. Census of India, 1961, p. 252.
81. L. Gogoi, *The Tai Khamptis*, p. ix.
82. Selection from Bengal papers, No. 23, p. 6.
83. H. Barua, *Asom Buranji*, pp. 11-12.
84. G. Grierson, *op. cit.*, p. 126, 136.
85. *Ibid*, p. 568.
86. *Ibid*, p. 141.
87. *Ibid*, p. 499.
88. *Ibid.*
89. *Ibid*, pp. 2-11.
90. Census of India Report, 1921, Part I, Appendix B, p. x.
91. *Ibid.*
92. *Ibid*, 1931, Part III, p. xiv.
93. *Ibid*, 1921, Part II, p. xii.
94. E.T. Dalton, *Descriptive Ethnology of Bengal*, p. 11.
95. Census Report, 1961, p 231.
96. V. Elwin, The Art of the North East Frontier of India, henceforth referred to as the Administrative, pp. 16-17.
97. NEFA, *op. cit.*, p. 1.
98. Census of India Report, 1921, Part I, p. xi.
99. *Ibid*, 1931, Part III, p. xiii.
100. *Ibid*, 1921, Part II, p. xii.
101. *Ibid.*
102. S. Johri, *Where India, China and Burma Meet*, p. 121,
103. Census of India Report, 1921, Part I, Appendix B, p. xi.
104. *Ibid.*
105. S. Roy, *op. cit.*, p. 194.
106. S. Johri, *op. cit.*, pp. 170-171.
107. *Ibid*, p. 155.
108. *Ibid*, p. 170.
109. V. Elwin, *The Art*, pp. 71-73.
110. J.N. Chowdhury, *A Comparative Study of the Adi Religion*, p. 45.
111. S. Johri, *op. cit.*, p. 169.
112. V. Elwin, *The Art*, pp. 71-72.
113. S. Johri, *op. cit.*, p. 171.
114. A. Das, 'Fish in Arunachal,' *Pines*, vol. I, Part III, p. 24.
115. Census of India Report, 1931, Part III, p. xiv.
116. S. Johri, *op. cit.*, p. 182.
117. V. Elwin, *The Tribal World of Elwin* henceforth referred to as *The Tribal World.*, p. 274.
118. S. Johri, *op. cit.*, p. 182.
119. V. Elwin, *North-East Frontier*, p. 366.
120. Lakhimpur Deputy Commissioner's Collection, xvii, F. 17, 1917.

121. *Ibid*, Collection No. XII, F. 7, 1884.
122. NEFA, pp. 18-19.
123. S. Roy, *op. cit.*, p. 223.
124. V. Elwin, *Democracy in NEFA* henceforth referred to as Democracy pp. 87-89, 177-78, 171-72.
125. V. Elwin, *The Tribal World*, p. 265.
126. Foreign Proceedings (Assam), March 1885, No. 40.
127. V. Elwin, *Democracy*, *op. cit.*, pp. 57-59.
128. V. Elwin, *The Art*, *op. cit.*, p. 20.
129. *Ibid.*
130. Census of India Report, 1921, p. xii.
131. NEFA, *op. cit.*, pp. 23-24.
132. V. Elwin, *The Art*, *op. cit.*, p. 20.
133. Col. C. Furer-Haimendorf, *op. cit.*, pp. 56-57.
134. S. Roy, *op. cit.*, pp. 121-122.
135. V. Elwin, *North-East Frontier*, p. 350.
136. Census of India, 1961, p. 233.
137. Report on the Trade between Assam and the adjoining foreign countries, 1890.
138. V. Elwin, *The Art*, *op. cit.*, p. 20.
139. *Ibid*, p. 10.
140. *Ibid*, p. 11.
141. E.T. Dalton, *op. cit.*, p. 9.
142. Census of India Report, 1961, p. 240.
143. Report on the Trade between Assam and adjoining foreign countries, 1890.
144. A. Mackenzie, *History*, p. 15.
145. Report on the Trade between Assam and the adjoining foreign countries, 1890.
146. R. Choudhury, 'A Note on the Sadiya Fair', *PINES*, vol. I, Part III, p. 77.
147. S.M.K. Shubani, "A Study in the Trans-Himalayan Trade through North East of India," *Journal of the Assam Research Society*, vol. XVII, 1963, p. 46.
148. Lakhimpur Deputy Commissioner's Collection, No. XVI, F. 3, 1904-08.
149. Annual Report, Sadiya Frontier Tract, 1937-1938.
150. S.M.K. Shubani, *op. cit.*, pp. 39-43.
151. *Ibid.*
152. V. Elwin, *North-East Frontier*, pp. xviii-xix.
153. *Ibid.*
154. V. Elwin, *The Art*, p. 16.
155. Assam Census Report, 1881, para 142.
156. V. Elwin, *North-East Frontier*, pp. 197-98.
157. Census of India Report, 1961, p. 232.
158. *NEFA*, *op. cit.*, pp. 4-5.
159. *Ibid*, pp. 14-15.

160. W. Durant, *The Story of Civilisation*, p. 783.
161. O.E. James, *The Beginning of Religion*, p. 15.
162. Census of India Report, 1921, Part I, p. x.
163. *Ibid*, Part, II, p.xi.
164. *Ibid*.
165. NEFA, *op. cit.*, p. 23.
166. S. Roy, *op. cit*, p. 244.
167. *Ibid*.
168. V. Elwin, *North-East Frontier*, p. 415.
169. S. Johri, *op. cit.*, p. 171.
170. Ramakrishna Mission, *Cultural Heritage of India*, vol. I, p. 176.
171. S. Roy, *op. cit*, p. 248.
172. *Ibid*.
173. Census of India Report, 1921, Part I, Appendix B, p.x.
174. *Ibid*, p. xi.
175. *Ibid*, p. xiii.
176. *Ibid.*, 1931, Part III, p. xiv.
177. *Ibid*, p. xi.
178. *Ibid*, p. xii.
179. V. Elwin, *A Philosophy for NEFA*, henceforth referred to as A Philosophy.
180. *Ibid*.
181. R.M. Nath, *Background of Assamese Culture*, pp. 63-64.
182. L.N. Chakravarty, *Malinithan*, A pretty nice illustrated booklet published by Arunachal Pradesh Administration, Shillong, 1974.
183. R.M. Nath, *Glorious Assam*, p. 24.
184. *Bhagabata*, Book 10, chapter, 52-59; *Vishnu Purana*, Chapter 33, Verses 7-50.
185. R.M. Nath, *Background of Assamese Culture*, pp. 63-64.
186. *Ibid*.
187. L.N. Chakravarty, *op. cit.*
188. *Kalika Purana*, Chapter 83, Verses 16-48.
189. *Ibid*.
190. M.N. Srinivas, *Caste in Modern India and other Essays*, pp. 56-57. Srinivas holds that when a social group aspires for higher social status it tries to find a place in the Sanskrit hierarchy.
191. E. Gait, *op. cit.*, p. 15.
192. S.K. Chatterjee, *The place of Assam in the History and Civilisation of India*, pp. 31-33.
193. Sarbananda Rajkumar, *Chutia, Bhuyan aru Matak Rajya*, p. 44.
194. J.P. Wade, *An Account of Assam*, (ed. B. Sarma), p. 37.
195. *Ibid*, pp. 38, 59.
196. *Ibid*, p. 184.
197. *Ibid*, p. 45.
198. H.E. Richardson, *op. cit.*, p. 33.
199. V. Elwin, *North-East Frontier*, p. 4.
200. *Ibid*, p. 438.

2

British Relations with the Tribes of the North-East Frontier

DURING THE decaying days of the Ahom regime, the different tribes of the North-East Frontier began to come down and establish themselves on the plains below their hills. The Ahom king Pratap Singha, to conciliate the tribes and secure the frontiers of his kingdom, granted them some lands in the Duars through which they came down. These grants were made usually to provide the hill people with articles which were not grown or available in the hills. The grants took the form of land, with people to cultivate the land, and sometimes some marshes were given in grant to enable the hillmen get fishes from them.[1] The *paiks*, as the subjects of the Ahom kings were called, who provided articles to the hillmen or served them, got remission of revenue from the Ahom authorities.[2] After the annexation of Assam to the British dominions, the British found the valley surrounded on the north, east and south by numerous hill tribes who advanced claims to rights, more or less definite, over lands lying in the plains; some claimed tributary payments from the villages below their hills or the services of the *paiks* in those villages.[3] To begin with, such claims had been, to some extent and in some places, formally recognised by the British authorities. The British relations with these tribes show a gradual extinction or commutation of such claims, as we shall see in the succeeding pages of this chapter.

EXTRA-BHUTAN BHUTIAS (MOMPAS AND SHERDUKPENS)

In the north-western part of the North-Eastern Frontier lay the hills inhabited by the so-called extra-Bhutan Bhutias. These tribes are now known as the Mompas and Sherdukpens (Thongjis) of the present Kameng district of Arunachal Pradesh. They were under the rule of the chiefs who were called the Sat Rajas.[4] But the term was used by the Bhutias to denote the petty local chiefs of the frontier hills. The word 'Sat' (meaning seven) had perhaps no literal meaning or relation to the actual number of chiefs. In the Darrang Books (Registers of Stipendiary chiefs) seven Rajas of Kuriapara were invariably recorded as pension or *posa* holders though the treaty edited by Aitchison shows that it was signed by only three Sat Rajas who perhaps were present at the time of the 1844 negotiations. But in case of the Charduar Bhutias, seven Rajas seem to have been always recognised.[5]

The Sat Rajas, who held Kuriapara, were subordinate to the governor of Tawang whom Aitchison calls 'Tong Debee Raja' and with whom the treaty of 1844 was concluded. The three Sat Rajas mentioned by Aitchison seem to be merely his subordinates.[6] Between the Sat Rajas and the governor of Tawang, there were two Gellengs who held office for three years.[7] The Bhutias of this area during the cold season used to make their headquarters at Amrotal, a place about half a day's journey from the border of the Darrang district, whence they came down to the Udalguri fair. Their houses were supposed to be five easy marches from Amrotal. The two Gellengs stayed at Amrotal and came to Udalguri if the Chief Commissioner or Deputy Commissioner specially sent for them, but usually they sent representatives who were merely traders.[8]

Before the British occupation of Assam, these tribes used to hold the Kuriapara Duars (situated between Bornadi in the west and Deoshan in the east) for four months a year, from the 15th October; during the remaining months these territories were held by the Ahom authorities.[9] Pratap Singha is said to have granted them this right to enable them to procure the commodities which were not available in their hills. The

Bhutias paid due tribute for their concession.[10] The Bhutias also came in large numbers from their hills to the fair at Udalguri and exchanged their goods with the merchants of the plains. After the annexation of Assam to the Company's territories, they continued to hold Kuriapara. The Collector of Darrang, Capt. Vetch, proposed in 1838 that the Bhutias should not be allowed to collect *posa* as they did during the Ahom days, and they should, instead, be paid in cash. It was troublesome and beyond the dignity of the British Government to allow the Bhutias to collect dues which they might have wrested from the effeminate Ahom authorities.[11] He estimated the revenue of the area to be somewhere between 10-12 lakhs of rupees, and if the lands were settled with the ryots, they would leave a good surplus after paying the *posa* to the Bhutias. The agreement, he suggested, should provide for recognition of the British authority up to the foot of the hills and the right of the British army to march through their hills, should that be necessary. The Bhutias should not allow criminals to settle or seek asylum in their hills and should not violate the British territory.[12] His proposal was approved of by the then Commissioner Jenkins and it was also agreed to by the Supreme Government of the Company.[13]

But the Bhutias refused the overtures for relinquishment of their rights in consideration of cash payment by the British.[14] Then on the score of a Bhutia raid in 1843-44, a blockade was instituted against the Bhutias of the Kuriapara Duars and negotiations were instituted with their chiefs for relinquishing their rights in the Duars.[15] Three agents of the governor of Tawang came down to negotiate along with the local chiefs with a view to concluding an engagement for settlement. It was finally agreed that the Bhutias would receive Rs. 5,000 in lieu of their *posa* in the Duars and would recognise the limit of the British jurisdiction up to the foot hills. They would not allow criminals to seek asylum in their hills and hand them over if asked for by the British authorities.[16]

The relations between the British and these Sat Rajas remained peaceful till 1852 when a misunderstanding arose. One of the Gellengs who was vested with supervisory powers over other chiefs declared himself independent of his authority and intercepted the money paid by the British Government to the Sat Rajas.[17] For some time, he held his own position but eventually he fled from the hills and took refuge in British territory. The army sent by these so-called Bhutias for the capture of the Gelleng demanded his extradition in peremptory terms from the British and threatened perpetual war in the event of refusal.[18] The British Government mustered 400 troops and a couple of six-pounders to face the imminent invasion of the Darrang frontier. But the effect of British concentration dampened the morale of the Bhutia army and they now assumed a compromising tone. Instead of the head of the Gelleng, they now asked from the Governor General's Agent a certificate to the effect that the rebel was no longer alive. This, they thought, would save their honour.[19] The certificate was denied and eventually they were made to sign the treaty again concluded in 1844, in which they gave an undertaking that the followers of the rebel in the hills would be pardoned.[20]

Since the confrontation of 1852-53, peace between the Tawang Bhutias and the British was never broken. The British Government did not interfere in the affairs within the hills nor did the Bhutias ever raid the plains. The retreating Bhutia army, in violation of the 1853 undertaking that they would not take action against the partisans of the Gelleng, did not honour their word; they brutally murdered supporters of the rebel. The British did not go for satisfaction of the breach of the undertaking as the event had occurred within the hills, outside the British jurisdiction.[21] In 1861, the Gelleng went back to the hills and was reconciled to his master, the governor of Tawang.[22] But once again, in consequence of a quarrel, he fled to the plains; the Bhutias did not purpsue him.[23] He continued to live in a house in Kuriapara. But in April 1864 a party of the Bhutias fell upon him by night and murdered him. The British Government did not take any action against the murder though it had occurred within the British jurisdiction; there was no breach between the Bhutias and the Government.[24]

To the east of the Rowta river and the west of the Bhorali (known as Belsiri in 1875) lay the Charduar territory from which the Rupa and Shergaon Bhutias (now known as Sherdukpens or Thongjis collected dues along with the Akas (Hrussos) and Daflas (Nishis).[25] The Bhutias of Rupa and

Shergaon were termed Bhutias Roop Roe Gya and Surgyah respectively in Aitchison's *treaties* (CVI). The hills of these Bhutias were two days' march from the plains of Charduar.[26] These Bhutias were supposed to be independent of the Tawang governor till 1875, and were under the authority of the local chiefs styled Sat Rajas like the hills north of Kuriapara as we have already seen. One of these Sat Rajas (who were seven in number) was Darji Raja of Rupa who was considered to be superior to others.[27]

L. Devi, in her book *Ahom Tribal Relations*, mentions that king Partap Singha had probably granted the right to *posa* to the Bhutias to keep uniformity with the other neighbouring tribes of the Akas and Daflas to whom he had granted similar privilege.[28] There is no authoritative record of the grant, however, in any document or in the Ahom Buranjis. Sir Alexander Mackenzie, in his *Memorandum* observes that the 'Assam Rajas' granted them this right to collect necessaries from the Duars in lieu of tribute paid to the 'Ahom Rajas.'[29] The British after annexation of Assam allowed the collection by the Bhutias to continue for some times. The Government of India held the view that the system should not be stopped because that might lead to troubles and since it did not affect its interest immediately the continuance of the practice "however injurious" was allowed.[30] Capt. White, however, was authorised to carry on negotiations for termination of the system.[31] He recommended money payment in lieu of 'blackmail' to be collected by the Bhutias.[32] Capt. Mathai, the Collector and Magistrate of Darrang, also regarded the system as detrimental to peace and prosperity of the Duars and he was authorised to conduct negotiation to substitute cash payment stopping direct collection by the Bhutias. The result was an engagement concluded between the Sat Rajas of Rupa and Shergaon and Capt. Mathai in 1836 wherein the former agreed to relinquish their rights to direct collection in consideration of an annual payment of Rs. 2526-7-0 as compensation. It may be observed that in the negotiations between the tribes and the British, no representative of the Tawang was present and that perhaps led the British to believe that these Bhutias were independent of the Tawang's authority.[33]

The British relations with the tribes of Rupa and Shergaon were strained in 1839 in consequence of the murder of Madhu Saikia a British subject, in a Charduar village. The Bhutias were charged with the murder and payment of *posa* was stopped.[34] The Darji Raja along with his other colleagues protested that for the alleged crime of two or three persons the whole community should not be charged, and promised good behaviour in future.[35] The British authorities were statisfied with this representation and on the recommendation of Capt. J.T. Gordon, the Collector of Darrang, payment of *posa* was resumed. But the amount of *posa* was reduced.[36] Thereafter the relations with them were never strained during the rule of the British in India.

Next to the Rupa and Shergaon tribes lived the so-called Thebenga Bhutias, who were later on called Tabang Bhutias or the tribe of Telenigah. They used to come down from their hills which were situated at a distance of 16 days' journey from Charduar. Along with the Rupa tribe, they collected dues from Charduar.[37] It was found later that the tribes of Rupa and Shergaon as also the Thebengas were subject to the Tawang governor but were under local chiefs called Sat Rajas. A resolution of the Chief Commissioner admits that those chiefs were subordinates of the Tawang governor. Their right to direct collection was replaced by the substitution of cash payment of Rs. 145-13-6.[38] The British never came to breach of peace with the Thebengas. In 1915, Nevill wrote to the Chief Commissioner to stop payment of *posa* to them as he considered that it had no effect in keeping them quiet and they hardly realised that they had any condition to fulfil.

In 1872-73 Lt. Col. Graham was authorised to demarcate boundary between Bhutan and the Extra-Bhutan Bhutia hills and the British districts of Kamrup and Darrang. He was instructed to exclude the Bhutia hills and to make the boundary line straight.[40] It appears from the records kept by Graham that the line he fixed up as boundary was accepted by the Sat Rajas of Tawang and Rupa and Shergaon, though the Sat Rajas of Shergaon and Rupa protested regarding the initial demacration along the foothills.[41] But at the time of the promulgation of the Inner Line Regulation in the Darrang district in 1876, the hill chiefs protested against the restriction put on ryots on their entry into the hills from British territory.[42] On representation from the chiefs, the restrictions on entry into their hills from the adjoining Duars were kept in suspension and all traders from beyond intending to go to the hills were granted permission to cross the Darrang Inner Line.[43]

After the division of the North-East Frontier into three charges subsequent to the Abor expedition of 1911 and the promulgation of the Assam Frontier Tract Regulation of 1880, as amended in 1884 and 1898, G.A. Nevill was appointed in 1914 as Political Officer of the Western Section of the North-East Frontier in which were included the hills inhabited by these Extra-Bhutan Bhutias or the Mompa and Sherdukpen tribes. The policy of the government was now to exercise "loose political control" over the chiefs of the hills. Nevill went on tour in 1914 to the hills starting from Jamiri above Kuriapara and through the Aka hills and reached Tawang.[44] Everywhere he was welcomed by the jubilant crowds which had mustered on the way. But though measures of control were contemplated, the outbreak of the First Great War prevented the government from going ahead with the new policy.

After the war, the freedom movement in India and introduction of reforms in administration kept the hands of the government tied for some time. Again, in the thirties, the government mooted measures for bringing these hills under direct control and Capt. Lightfoot, who had succeeded Nevill as Political Officer, went on tour to Tawang in 1937-38 and proposed measures to bring the hills under control.[45] But the outbreak of the Second World War again prevented the government from taking any effective step to administer these hills.[46] After the war, the British Government withdrew from India and independent India began to set up administrative centres within these hills to the great relief of the local people.

THE AKAS

The Akas, who lived in the hills north of Charduar along with the Rupa, Shergaon and Thebenga Bhutias and the Daflas, collected dues from Charduar.[47] The Akas were independent and had no formal connection with the Daflas or the Bhutias. Both the clans of the Akas—the Hazarikhowas and the

Kapachors—lived under the nominal control of the chiefs called Rajas who conducted relations with the outside world and presided over the meetings of the village council. The Akas had received from the Ahom king Pratap Singha the right to collect paddy and other articles which were not available in their hills.[48] The idea behind the grant was to reconcile the fierce hill tribes to Ahom rule and secure for the neighbouring villages immunity from their attack.

After the British occupation of Assam, following the Anglo-Burmese War of 1824-26, the Governor General's Agent, David Scott,[49] allowed the Akas to collect their dues from the Duars. It is found in the records that the Hazarikhowa Akas were entitled to receive from each house of their allotted 'Khels' one portion of a female dress, one bundle of cotton thread and one handkerchief. At this time, the Kapachors were not probably regarded as a separate clan, for the Hazarikhowas were expected to give a share of their collections to the Kapachors.[50]

But the inconvenience of allowing the tribesmen to come down to collect their dues was soon realised by the British authorities. David Scott was the first British officer to initiate the commutation of the system of collection of dues in kind by the tribes by a system of payment in cash. It was he who succeeded in making an agreement with the Akas by which they agreed to forego their right to direct collection in consideration of a payment of Rs. 175 per annum by the British Government.[51] But, as a result of the Balipara massacre of 1835 perpetrated by the Kapachor chief Taghi Raja, the payment of *posa* to the Hazarikhowas was stopped because they were also suspected to be involved in the affair.[52] In 1842, when settlement was made with the Kapachors, the *posa* of the Hazarikhowas was restored, but a new engagement was entered into with four of their chiefs. They promised to maintain peace in the Duars for a payment of Rs. 180 to be paid annually to them in lieu of the levy they used to collect from the Duars.[53]

The Kapachors had no relations with the British till 1842 when an engagement was entered into with them. Shortly before the annexation of Assam by the British they had murdered an official of Charduar, and for this David Scott had declared them outlaw and forbade them to enter Assam.[54] But they continued to collect their dues from the Duars evading the

British vigilance as though they were legally entitled to do so. In 1839, their leader Taghi Raja fled to Assam as a result of an inter-tribal dispute. He was captured by the British and sent to Gauhati jail. While at Gauhati he became a disciple of a Hindu spiritual master and through his influence got release from the jail.[55] He went back to the hills and rallying his followers behind murdered all those who were connected with his capture in Assam in 1832. Thereafter to avenge his humiliation at Gauhati he came down in 1835 to Balipara and set fire to the frontier outpost there. Seventeen persons were killed including men, women and children.[56]

All efforts of the government to capture him proved abortive and he continued to raid Charduar repeatedly. In December 1837, he carried off several persons.[57] The government had to set up outposts at the foothills to check his forays and yet he succeeded in evading them and carried on his depredations. In 1838-39 and 1841 he raided the plains of Charduar.[58] At last through the Kotokis an offer of pardon and pension was made to him and he came to the plains to surrender to the British authorities. He was released on a solemn oath that he would not attack the ryots of the plains any more in consideration of a monthly pension for him and three of his chiefs—Seemkolee, Sooma and Nisul. An engagement was entered into in this regard in 1842.[59]

Subsequently other chiefs came down and accepted pensions from the government. In February 1844, Capt. Gordon, the Deputy Commissioner of Darrang, interviewed and granted annual pensions to Chengkolee, Singingkandor, Narsoo and Sarsoo. Again, in 1848, he further granted five more annual pensions to Srigi, Barsoo, Kangsoon, Pasoo, Deekoks and Dhenno.[60]

The British relations with the Aka tribes began to improve after the grant of these pensions or *posa* to the chiefs. The oaths taken by the chiefs to maintain peace and forego collection of dues from the Duars were generally observed though the amount of *posa* was gradually raised to Rs. 668 per annum through peaceful negotiations.[61] The Hazarikhowas had further received a grant of 18 puras of land for their temple in the Darrang district.[62] But in 1857 the Aka chiefs refused to receive their *posa* in protest for getting their *posa* raised. The government ordered to stop the payment of *posa* and closed the markets of the Duars to the Akas. Arrangement for keeping a sharp watch over the border of the hills was made to prevent any disturbance that might result. It had the desired effect of bringing the Aka chiefs to terms and gradually they began to come down for pardon. Some submitted in 1859, and in 1869 Taghi Raja himself submitted to the authorities. The Akas during these years had not committed any raid and therefore the Deputy Commissioner of Darrang recommended payment of their *posa* which was paid with all arrears.[63]

The relations with the Akas began to deteriorate from the seventies. They had been protesting for an increase of their *posa* as the prices of commodities had gone up. When the lands in the foothills were being brought within the boundary of the Darrang district by demarcation of the boundary by the Commissioner, Lt. Col. Graham, in 1872-73, the Kapachor chief objected to the boundary.[64] The Hazarikhowas petitioned for a further grant of revenue-free land and the Kapachors asked for a similar grant of 200 puras of land.[65] On the recommendation of the Deputy Commissioner of Darrang, 36 puras were granted to each clan which seemed to have reconciled them. The boundary line was demarcated in 1874-75.[66] Medhi, the Aka chief, even agreed to send two of his relations to schools in British territory where they would read at government expense.[67] But in 1878, his people gave trouble when they came down for their annual visits and three of them were whipped for theft.[68]

Discontent began to manifest itself from the early eighties. In 1882, Medhi's brother who was reading in school at Balipara left his school. It was reported that a large body of Akas and Daflas had come down and set up boundary marks in the forests of Potashali, Diju and Naminimukh which, they held, were within their side of the boundary. They declared that they would not allow anybody to go into their territory. It was known that they objected to the issue of passes to Nepalese coolies who under the passes intended to go to their hills to tap rubber. The matter was temporarily settled by denying passes to the Nepalese.[69]

But the matter did not end there. The Aka remained unsatisfied and continued to press for enhancement of *posa* and redrawing of the boundary. When a party went to their hills to collect some specimens for Calcutta exhibition, the guide of the party, Lakhidhar, with other two were detained by them in 1883. Lakhidhar died in detention.[70] In the cold season of 1883-84, Chandi, the brother of Medhi Raja, raided the Balipara forest range office, the first time after the grant of pensions to the Akas in 1842, and carried off the Ranger and his clerk together with a compass, some money and two guns.[71]

The government sanctioned an expedition to chastise the Akas and drive them back to their hills. The expedition left for the Aka hills under the PoliticalOfficer Capt. H. St. P. Maxwell, Deputy Commissioner of Garo Hills, with a force of 290 Frontier Police under W.B. Savi and Lt. E.H. Molesworth, 571 officers and men of the 43rd Native Infantry drawn from Shillong, 210 of the 12th Khelati Ghilzais from Cachar, 2 mountain guns and a party of Sappers under the command of Brigadier General Sale Hill. A flying column of 150 Rifles, the 43rd Light Infantry and 50 of the Dibrugarh Corps of the Assam Frontier Police started for Medhi's village under the command of Major Bresford.[72]

When the news of the expedition reached the hills, the Akas sent word that they would restore the captives. But when the force advanced into the hills some villages were evacuated and the vanguard was attacked. One sepoy was killed and another was wounded by the shot of poisonous arrow. The expeditionary force easily overpowered and dispersed the Aka force and advanced upon the village of Medhi. The village had already been deserted but the houses were destroyed together with stores and herds. The Aka chiefs sent back the captives together with the property they had seized in 1883-84 but did not come in for settlement.[73] Capt. Maxwell stayed inside the hills for some time but due to outbreak of fever among the force left the Aka hills considering the result of the expedition satisfactory. He had succeeded in obtaining a fine of 10 mithun valued between Rs. 700 to 1000 and release of the captives. Villages of the Kapachor Akas had been destroyed with stocks and grains which he considerded enough punishment for the offence they had committed.[74]

The Chief Commissioner receiving the reports of the expedition expressed disatisfaction for not staying longer in the hills to obtain the surrender of the chief Medhi. He instructed the Deputy Commissioner of Darrang to continue the blockade of the hills for getting the surrender of Medhi and also to continue negotiations with the Akas.[75] The Akas continued to represent for enhancement of their *posa* to Rs. 20,000, a grant of 200 puras of revenue-free land in the Duars, and rectification of the boundary of their territory. They represented that the prices of commodities had gone up and the money granted to them was quite insufficient for the articles they purchased from the Duars. The Akas held that they were already in good terms with the government and never meant to kill Lakhidhar who had died in captivity; they had detained him to get their complaints heard.[76] The Deputy Commissioner of Darrang wrote to the Chief Commissioner that really the Akas purchased goods from the Duars with their pension, and as the prices had gone up it was quite inadequate for their purchase.[77] But the authorities did not pay any heed to the solicitations of the Akas and the blockade continued.

At last, the chiefs tendered their submission in 1888 and the compass taken away in 1883 was returned. An agreement of good behaviour was executed with their chief Medhi wherein he accepted the foothills as the boundary between their hills and the British territory. It was stated that the *posa* would be restored after two years if they behaved well as per agreement.[78]

The relations with the Akas began to improve after 1890 when the *posa* was again restored. In 1896, a party of hillmen stayed in the house of Padu Miri near the Inner Line and in the night killed the host and his son and left with four other captives. It was found that the act was perpetrated by the Apa Tanis who lived in the valley of Hong within the Dafla hills. An expedition was sanctioned and sent to rescue the captives and punish the guilty persons under Capt. G.R. Row with 300 men of Lakhimpur Military Police Battalion and Lt. H.F. Norie of 42nd Gurkha Rifles. R.B. MacCabe of the I.C.S. as Political Officer led the team. The captives were rescued and the guilty were punished by releasing six of their slaves. The punishment was light but considered enough in view of the fact that Padu Miri had enmity with the tribe and the tribesmen had acted in the customary tribal way to avenge their wrong. The government accepted the report of MacCabe.[79]

But the question of rights in the forest brought the Akas into the plains again in 1900. A party of the Akas came to the Balipara market and demanded a sum of Rs. 3000 from a merchant for tapping rubber in their territory. When they were on their way back with the money, the Deputy Commissioner of Darrang arrived there and succeeded in capturing ten of them. He fined them Rs. 3000 for their conduct and released them after payment of the amount.[80] It was decided that to avoid any such occurrence in future, all agreements for rubber-tapping between the merchants and hillsmen would henceforth be executed in the presence of the Deputy Commissioner of Darrang and all payments would be made in his presence.[81]

The British relations with the Akas after this did not bring in any trouble. When the North-East Frontier Tracts were divided into three charges, the Aka Hills were included in the Western Section of the North-East Frontier.[82] In 1913, G.A. Nevill, Political Officer of Western Section led a promenade through the Aka hills with A.L.M. Molesworth as Assistant Political Officer in a party of 1032 officers and men under the command of A.M. Graham. The tour was peaceful except for an attack by the Daflas of Riang. Over 400 square miles of territory of the Miji and Aka hills were explored and surveyed by this promenade.[83] The Aka hills were brought under the control area from 1914 and there was no opposition from the people. Rather the Akas made representations for opening of posts within their hills.[84] Nevill opined that the Akas were an excellent people and capable of improvement; they were much more civilised than the neighbouring Daflas. He recommended to set up a post at Jamiri in the Aka hills.[85] But no steps were taken to implement the recommendations of Nevill. Capt. Lightfoot found the Akas exacting tribute from the Mompa and Sherdukpen villages of Dirangjog and Rupa, and an expedition was sent to punish the Miji Akas for raising tribute from their villages.[86] Practically the Akas were left to themselves till the end of the British rule.

THE DAFLAS

As already noted, occupying the hills in Darrang, north of Noaduar and Chaiduar in Lakhimpur, and between the rivers Bhorali on the west and Sundri to the east lived the Daflas who call themselves *Bangni*, meaning 'man'. They were not united as a tribe and were divided into several clans independent of each other; there were sometimes thirty to forty chiefs in the same clan.[87] The tribes on the borders of Darrang were generally called Paschim or western Daflas and those on the border of Lakhimpur, Tagin Daflas.

The Ahom king Pratap Singha had assigned them certain *paiks* to enable them to get supply of rice and other necessaries not available in the hills on condition of supplying him auxiliaries and paying tribute.[88] The *paiks* who satisfied their demands were granted a remission in their dues to the Ahom kings. Thus a *paik* of the Dafla Bhutia Khel, that is, a subject who paid dues to the Daflas, paid Rs. 3/- instead of Rs. 9/- to the Ahom kings. The difference was remitted to enable him to meet his Dafla engagement. The different Dafla clans did not interfere with each other on the plains, for they knew from which village they were to collect *posa*. But they claimed the *posa* from a *paik* even if he had migrated from one place to another and demanded full dues from the *paiks* without any consideration of their ability to pay.[89]

When the British authority was established over Assam, David Scott allowed the Daflas to collect their dues from the Duars.[90] But as time went on the British wanted to stop these savage tribes' collection from the plains which they wanted to bring within the settled districts. Lt. James Mathai, when he was officiating Magistrate and Collector in Darrang, wrote, "the mountain tribes on its (Darrang) northern frontier, *viz.* the Bhutias, Akas and Daflas, are allowed to collect blackmail from the ryots, and usually come down in February in large parties to collect articles of produce such as rice, sugar and clothes from each house. . . . If we still acknowledge their right to a portion of our revenue, it should be paid in cash for so long as the present system remains in force. I conceive, after what I have witnessed, that the realisation of the government demand is doubtful, and the lives and property of our subjects left in great jeopardy".[91] The Government of India wrote to Robertson, the Commissioner of Assam, that the 'blackmail' collected by the hill tribes should not be stopped but negotiations for commutation of their rights in the Duars might be carried on by Capt. White, the Political Agent of Upper Assam.[92] Capt. White recommended that money payments should be made instead of the 'blackmail'.[93] Thereupon Capt. Mathai, the Collector and Magistrate of Darrang, began negotiations with the chiefs for commutation of their rights in the Duars.[94]

At first, the Daflas seemed to be reluctant.[95] In 1835, some Daflas were suspected of complicity with Aka raiders. The Daflas were then forbidden to enter the plains whereupon they raided Charduar and carried off several persons. An expedition was sent to the hills to rescue the captives and the party brought down the culprits as prisoners. Capt. Mathai then opened negotiations to stop collection of blackmail; eight out of thirteen of the Dafla clans of Charduar came to terms.[96] They refused to accept money instead of articles but agreed to resign the right of collection from individual ryots. In case of any dispute they agreed to refer the matter to the Magistrate; further, they engaged not to aid the enemies of the British and to help in the capture of offenders. The *posa* was fixed now at one coarse askhut sheet, one long cotton handkerchief, two seers of salt, one dao and one goat for every ten houses.[97] After this, five more clans also came to agreement on similar terms. The Government of India felt gratified at this course of action and not only approved of the action of Mathai but praised him as well.[98]

After this, the Daflas of Nao Duar consented to receive their dues also through the village revenue officer. But they insisted on payment of two-thirds of all the revenues paid by the *paiks* of the Dafla Bhutia Khels as they considered them to be their hereditary slaves.[99] In 1838-39, they became very troublesome and the collection of *posa* was entirely stopped. This brought the clans to terms and agreements were entered upon to pay them through the village revenue officer.[100]

But it was only in 1852 that the *posa* was finally commuted for monetary payment. The Court of Directors had ordered that if the local officers could substitute monetary payment in lieu of 'blackmail' without any disturbance, they had no objection.[101] There were four Mahals in which there were nine Duars from which the Daflas collected dues. The Chaiduar Mahal consisted of Nakrang, Boranga and Bar Duars; the Banskata Mahal comprised Kaudarahat, Dalahat Malahat and Ohat Duars; the Lakhimpur Mahal comprised the Manomati Duar; and in Boodoloni Mahal was included Phulpani Duars.[102] A list of the ryots who paid Dafla dues in these Duars showing the chiefs who received them was prepared by Brajanath Bharali Baruah in 1841. Capt. Gordon's letter of 13 February 1844 states that Rs. 2494-0-1 was paid to the Daflas commuting the Dafla chiefs' right to make collection in the Duars. In 1852, Col. Dalton and Lt. Biver modified the list excluding those who did not claim their *posa*, and a list was prepared by the former showing that there were 238 Gams or chiefs who received Rs. 2543. But in 1853-54, the total amount of *posa* reached Rs. 4129-15-0; besides 234 maunds of salt in lieu of 'hat' (weekly market) dues and rights of fishing and gold washing, a diet allowance of Rs. 5 and 26 bottles of rum were also paid.[103]

The relations with the Daflas thereupon began to improve and there was no cause of anxiety till 1870. After this the Daflas raided two Dafla settlements within the Darrang district. In one case the raid was directed to recover an absconding slave and it did not indicate any ill-feeling towards the British authority. But nevertheless they committed an act of violence within the British territory. So all annual allowances were withheld and a reward was declared for the capture of the offenders.[104] In the other case, some Daflas who had submitted a case for settlement to the British authorities became tired of the delay in British justice and they swooped upon their offending brethren and secured justice in their customary way. The case was as follows. One Dafla chief arranged the marriage of his son with the daugther of another chief and gave some presents. But the father of the girl did not honour his word and even did not return the presents to the party to whom he had refused the marriage of his daugther. The offended party filed a complaint with the Deputy Commissioner of Darrang, but being tired of delay and failing to obtain satisfaction, it made a night attack, recovered the presents and took to custody some hostages. In this case also, the allowances were stopped and a reward was announced for the capture of the ringleader.[105] Yet a third raid occurred within the British territory in 1872-73 when some Daflas from the hills carried off some Daflas as they believed that a Dafla of that village was the cause of an epidemic which took serveral lives. An expedition was sent for the recovery of these British subjects in 1874-75. When the closure of the market proved ineffectual for the recovery of the captives, an expedition was sent and the guilty villagers were punished for their misconduct.[106] Subsequently in 1877 again there occurred a robbery in a Kaya Shop in Lalukadolonee. Lt. Maxwell pursued the Daflas and under threat of closing the market, succeeded in recovering the looted property. The action was approved of by the Chief Commissioner.[107]

Disposition of the Daflas after this was not found to be hostile towards the British. All the raids that occurred subsequently arose out of either inter-tribal disputes or disputes over collection of forest produce by British subjects. In 1887, a party of the Daflas raided the house of the Dafla named Tarang beyond the Inner Line as the latter had quarrelled with hill Daflas. The Government did not take upon itself the burden of punishing the offenders.[108] In 1888, again, another subject Dafla was murdered 10 miles beyond the Inner Line. Again, the authorities declined to punish the criminals as it was not certain whether the British subject was forcibly taken away from his home within the settled district and whether he had quarrels with them.[109] In 1881, the Daflas captured some plain Daflas as they had crossed the Inner Line without passes to tap rubber.[110] Through negotiation the captives were released. In 1896 again the Daflas captured some run-away coolies of a tea garden when they crossed the Inner Line. The British authorities did not send any punitive expedition as the capture did not take place as a result of any raid. When negotiations to release the coolies were conducted the Daflas asked for the restitution of two of their slaves who had escaped into the British territory. The restitution of the slaves was denied and the release of the coolies was purchased by the owner of the garden.[111] In 1899[112] and 1900[113] again the Daflas captured the agents of the Mahaldars; captives were released in the first case, and in the second case the captives were released after the payment of their dues. Two Dafla raids in 1904[114] and 1908[115] are also recorded in the

Administration Reports and these show that they had begun to violate the terms of their engagement with the British.

As a part of the general policy of the Government of India, in the North-East Frontier a mission was sent to the hills beyond the Inner Line to increase knowledge of the tribes, establish friendly relations with them, and explore and survey the region between the Subansiri and Bhutan which would enable the Government of India to fix up a boundary between India and Tibet. The party started from Lakhimpur on 11 November 1911 with 75 Rifles under Kerwood, the Sub-divisional Officer of Lakhimpur, as Political Officer. Escorts numbered 150, Officers and men, under Assistant Commandant Capt. A.M. Graham. The party, which went up the Subansiri to survey the Khru valley, was attacked but when Capt. Graham opened fire, the Dafla opposition melted and the party came back doing its job successfully.[116]

We have observed that subsequent to the explorations and survey by the Miri mission in 1911, the North-East Frontier was divided into three sections and Capt. G.A. Nevill took charge of the Western Section, in which was included the Dafla hills. Nevill was attacked by the Daflas while he was leading the Aka promenade in 1913 at Riang.[117] He observed from his experience that the Daflas as a tribe had not yet recognised the British authority which was evident from their treacherous attacks and petty aggressions on the plains of Assam. In 1918, Miripathar Daflas raided the Dafla villages of Gaigaon and Boranipathar in the plains and carried off 59 persons. Nineteen of the captives escaped but 20 had to be released by the Political Officer who imposed fine on the Miripathar Daflas for the raid.[118] Again, in 1926, the Runganadi Daflas raided Jorum Dafla village and, killing three, escaped with three captives. Again, Nevill with armed escorts visited Runganadi to punish the raiders. He recommended to establish a post in the Dafla hills at Miripathar with a dispensary to bring them under effective control.[119]

Things began to change with the introduction of 'loose political control' from 1914 onwards. Nevill writes in his Administration Report for the year 1927-28, "As years have passed by, the Akas, the Daflas and other tribes have gained confidence and learnt to appreciate the benefits of the new order.... The growing friendliness has brought about the desire for a still closer relationship. Now a days constant request from all sections of the hills is to establish a garrison in their country.... Daflas realise the benefits of peace but owing to their entire lack of combination they are unable to make a united effort to stop this anarchy."[120] But arrangement for direct administration or setting up of Assam Rifles posts in the Dafla hills had not been made during the British regime and the petty inter-tribal raids or raids on the plains continued till almost the end of the British period. In 1931-32, N.L. Bor had to lead three expeditions to punish Chemgung for imprisoning British subjects;[121] in another case to punish the Daflas for visiting Senmara within 5 miles of the Inner Line;[122] the third expedition to punish Midpu for raiding Luluk in the plains of Lakhmipur.[123] The Administration Report for the year 1938-39 shows that the Daflas of Kabeng raided Pinji in which 8 persons were carried off. An expedition succeeded in releasing the captives and a fine of 10 mithuns was imposed on the Daflas which of course had good effect on the Eastern Daflas.[124]

THE ABORS AND THE MIRIS

To the east of the Daflas and west of the Mishmis and between the rivers Dihang and Dibang live the cognate tribes of the Abors and Miris. Originally one and the same tribe, the Miris came down the hills and in course of time became plain-dwellers. They engaged themselves in permanent cultivation on the plains and acted as go-between in trade between the Assamese and Abor traders.[125] But the Abors continued to live in the hills and regarded their co-tribe, the Miris, as their slaves on the plains and exacted some tribute from them. The exact nature of this tribute is not known, but the Miris did not decline to pay this impost and their relations with the Abors were constant and intimate.[126]

In the *Assam Buranji*, it is recorded that king Pratap Singha had given some villages to the Abors for the cultivation of paddy and the ryots who cultivated for the Abors were exempted from revenue payment to the Ahom authorities. Besides, some persons were assigned to catch fish from certain *beels* (marshes) for the Abors. But the Abors also paid tribute to the Ahom kings.'[127] With the establishment of the British authority in Assam the Miris became British subjects in all respects; they paid poll-tax for cultivating lands and subjected themselves to the regular jurisdiction of the civil and criminal courts of the British Government.[128] As such, their relations with the government need not be studied separately.

In between the Abors of the uphills and the Miris of the plains lived the so-called Hill Miris. In the hills west of Dirjimo and to the north of Sisi and Dhamaji lived the so-called Ghesi Miris: north of Bordoloni and on the course of the Subansiri lived the Sarak Miris; and on the same river lived the Panibatia and Tarbatia Miris and all other tribes of the Hill Miris. They were in no way subordinate to the Abors of the upper hills. These Hill Miris collected *posa* from the mouzas of Sisi, Dhamaji and Bordoloni of Lakhimpur.[129] The Abors did not collect *posa*, but the Miris of the plains who saved the Abors were exempted from payment to the Ahoms.[130]

The British authorities seemed to have commuted the right of the Ghesi Miris, Sarak Miris, Panibatia, Tarbatia Miris and the Bormithuns by granting *posa* to be paid to each as in the case of the Bhutias, Akas and Daflas. It appears from a resolution of the Chief Commissioner of Assam of 1884 that the afore-mentioned clans of the Hill Miris were in receipt of annual *posa* of Rs. 218-7-5, Rs. 930-4-9 and Rs. 25/- respectively, in lieu of their rights of collection in Sisi, Dhamaji and Bordoloni mouzas.[131] No such arrangement or conciliation, however, was made initially with the Abors who were considered distinct from the Hill Miris and who did not collect any impost from the plains.

The British took note of the Abors in 1830 when Capt. Neufville had recommended to David Scott to erect buildings for setting up guard houses as the Abors had come down to reclaim the Miris of the plains. David Scott proposed to the government construction of 8 such posts for the protection of plains people, as the proposed measure of Neufville seemed to him highly expedient. He had recommended to recover the expenses from the villagers who were to be benefited by the proposed measure.[132] But in the later part of the same year Neufville wrote again that the Abors were best disposed of all the hill tribes of the North-East Frontier and they had never been known to have committed any act of unprovoked ravage or violence on the villages of the plains.[133] Subsequently, in 1840, when the Khamptis rebelled against the British, the Abors took side with the government.[134] As late as 1847, the Abors remained friendly towards the British; when Capt. Vetch, Political Agent of Upper Assam, paid a visit to their hills, they voluntarily released the captives whom they had carried off from the plains as a gesture of friendship.[135]

Till the middle of the nineteenth century, the Abors claimed and received levies from the gold-washers known as Beehas and fishermen on the Dihang and Dibang rivers and the islands of the Brahmaputra as also from the Miris who had settled down within the Lakhimpur district of the Brahmaputra valley.[136] But in the later half of the century the gold-washers and fishermen and the Miris, encouraged by the attitude of the new authorities, that is the British, and feeling a sense of security and protection, began to defy the Abors; some even moved down to remote places beyond the easy access of the Abors.[137] That led to a change of attitude on the part of the Abors; rather, the Abors had to coerce the refractory subjects whom they regarded as their hereditary slaves and thus violated the law of the British which they did not know and considered unnecessary to observe. Thus, began the strife between the Abors and the British.

The friction began on the issue of jurisdiction over the gold-washers. In 1848, Capt. Vetch went to the Abor hills to get release of some gold-washers. The captives, who were detained for non-payment of dues, were released but the camp of Capt. Vetch was attacked in the night and the Abors were sent back after hard fighting. To punish the guilty, Capt. Vetch burnt the villages of the Abors,[138] but this tended to strain the good relation that subsisted between these tribes and the government. The government which began to farm out the right of gold-washing felt an obligation to protect the gold-washers. Escorts were sent to accompany the gold-washers to Dihang and orders were given to station a guard house at the mouth of that river.[139] To conciliate with the Abors, a proposal to start an annual fair was mooted and the proposal to tax the Miris near Dihang was negatived as it would annoy the Abors further. But the fair did not come to pass and the guard remained on the Dihang for one season only. In the turmoil of the Second Anglo-Burmese War the Abor frontier was forgotten and guarding of the Abor frontier lost sight of.[140]

Meanwhile the Abors thought of teaching a lesson to the refractory Beehas; in January 1858 the Beeha settlement of Sengajan only six miles from Dibrugarh, to the north of the river Brahmaputra, was massacred by the Kebang clan of the Bor Meyong Abors.[141] The authorities made an attempt to follow up the raiders to the hills, but owing to the inaccessible character of the hills the troops could not overtake the Abors and with discredit they returned to Dibrugarh. Emboldened by their success, the Abors now took up an advanced position and threatened the plains below the hills.[142]

The government now was required to prove that it was in a position to accord protection to its subjects and chastise those who threatened their security. Therefore, an expedition to punish the perpetrators of the crime of Sengajan was sanctioned by the government. One European officer of the Navy with fifteen gunners; an Indian officer of Artillery with 12 pounds howitzers, with 50 rounds per gun, and 15 privates; and a contingent of Native Infantry under three Indian officers; an European medical man, 11 non-commissioned officers, 3 Buglers and 88 Sepoys, with the Deputy Commissioner of Dibrugarh left for the Abor hills. But even with such a big preparation, the party returned to Dibrugarh in ignominy without imposing upon the Abors the might of the British Administration, once again losing face.[143] Another expedition was sanctioned on a much larger scale in 1859 to retrieve the lost prestige. It consisted of 4 European officers of the Indian Navy with two Buglers and 60 men; a contingent of Native Artillery under one European officer, three Havildars, two Naiks, one Bugler and 50 men with 12 pounder howitzers and 24 2.5 masters; and a Regiment of Assam Light Infantry consisting of an European officer, one European non-Commissioned officer, 13 Havildars, 14 Naiks, 5 Buglers and 211Sepoys. This expedition succeeded in destroying Kebang and its allies.[144] Moreover, the government now took up a proposal to establish a number of posts from Sisi to Pobah Mukh to guard the Abor frontier. Later, in 1859, a strong reconnoitring party passed along the entire Abor frontier. This made an impression upon the Abors and some Gams or Chiefs came in 1860 for peace and friendship.[145] Major Biver, the Principal Assistant of the Lakhimpur district, received the chiefs courteously and asked them to see him next year and referred the matter to the authorities.[146]

But in 1861, the Miyong Abors once again cut up another Beeha settlement, 15 miles away from Dibrugarh but on the south bank of the Brahmaputra. These Beehas had left the north bank of the Brahmaputra after the massacre of Sengajan and settled with a sense of impunity on the south bank.[147] The Abors raid of 1861 proved that unless they were held up within the hills, no place in the district was too distant for them. Biver proposed to construct a number of posts along the foot of the Abor hills:[148] The government thereupon took up a scheme of restraining the Abors by means of roads, forts and effective military command of the whole Abor frontier.[149]

The Abors now began to come in for settlement with the government. As for the proposal of peace, the Government of India wrote to the Commissioner of Assam that peace negotiations might be carried on provided the Abors recognised British jurisdiction up to the foothills and entered into engagements not to molest the British subjects of the plains, to refer all disputes to the Deputy Commissioner of Lakhimpur and to allow free communication of persons between the Assam plains and the Abor hills.[150] Biver opened negotiations with the Abor chiefs. At first, the attempt at agreement seemed far from success. The Abors claimed sovereignty over the lands up to the Brahmaputra and rights over the Miris and Beehas. But Major Biver succeeded in impresssing upon the Abors the futility of such claims and benefits of peace and friendship. He told them that if they came to terms with the British the country below their hills would be cultivated and communications would improve whereupon population and market would expand. These would benefit the Abors.[151] He, however, promised to pay them in kind some stipend for he understood that money payment would not be welcomed. He thought that payment in kind extending to all individuals would give all of them a direct interest in maintaining peace, for otherwise everybody would suffer from the loss of the *posa*.[152]

The gesture of the government to protect the frontiers did not fail to impress upon the Abors the futility of fighting the British army with its dangerous fire arms. When they heard that the government was willing to compensate their losses by paying small subsidies they came up for a settlement. At length, in November 1862, eight Khels of Miyong Abors concluded agreement with the Deputy Commissioner of Lakhimpur. Major Biver undertook to provide for them their necessaries in kind in specific quantities, on condition of their maintaining peace along the border and handing over the criminal refugees who might take shelter in the Abor hills. Moreover, the British sovereignty up to the foot of the hills was recognised by the Abors who promised not to violate it and molest British subjects. Access to the Abor hills by British subjects for trade and to the British market by the Abors for marketing purposes was also granted.[153] The Kabeng Abors followed the Miyong Abors in 1863 when Capt. Comber, Deputy Commissioner of Lakhimpur, concluded an engagement with them.[154] The Bor Abors from remote parts of the hills then came in for similar agreements in 1866.[155]

After these agreements were concluded, the Abors tended to be conciliatory, but their discontent hardly passed away. In 1863, the Meybo Abors refused to accept the presents as the Deputy Commissioner refused to clasp hands with them;[156] in 1865 the Miyong Abors abstained from coming on the plea of outbreak of small-pox and cholera epidemic;[157] in 1866 again they insisted on the removal of the Poba Mukh guard post.[158] In 1876-77 hostility was shown upon the advance of the Trigonometrical Survey party into the hills.[159]

It was found that the Abors were collecting blackmail from the timber-cutters from forests of the foothills which were considered to be within British jurisdiction. The Chief Commissioner, Keatinge, was of opinion that the government must stop such collection and must assert its right over every square mile of territory in the plains.[160] Lt. R.G. Woodthrope of the Trigonometrical Survey party even asked to advance the frontier to show that the British were not afraid of the Abors.[161] J.B. Goad, who had accompanied Woodthrope, proposed that the *posa* to the Abors should be stopped because the Abors in lieu gave trouble only.[162]

The Deputy Commissioner of Lakhimpur, Graham, proposed to gradually substitute cash payment of *posa* for that in the shape of articles; he held that, to start with, money instead of tobacco and opium should be given.[163] It is found that in 1877 the payment in kind had ceased and cash payment had been fixed at existing market rate.[164] A guard-post was advanced to Nizamghat up the Dihang river and defences were arranged in 1878 to stop the Abors crossing the river for the other bank.[165] The Chief Commissioner, Sir Charles Elliot, while commenting upon the results of the advance of the post at Nizamghat, proposed to the Government of India to appoint an Assistant to the Deputy Commissioner of Lakhimpur to help him in conducting political relations with the Abors in particular and the other tribes in general.[166]

Jack Francis Needham of the Bengal Police was appointed Political Officer in 1882 and posted at Sadiya. When Needham visited Abor villages in 1884 they complained of the paucity of the *posa* and British authorities giving shelter to their run-away slaves. They pointed out that the government had been favouring the Miris and had built a *Namghar* for them. But there was none for the Abors. Moreover, there was no rest house for the Abors at Sadiya.[167]

In 1882, the Chief of Padu in a raid murdered a Sepoy of the guard house and killed two Miris.[168] In 1887, some Abors carried off four girls and some articles of domestic use from within the British territory. Subsequently, the captives and articles were recovered when payment of *posa* was stopped, but the guilty persons declined to come down.[169] In 1889, again, four Miris were taken away across the frontier for refusing to pay *posa* and were murdered. The authorities imposed a fine of 30 mithuns on the raiders, instituted a blockade on the Abor frontier and stopped payment of *posa* for a year.[170] Thereupon the Abors came down with mithuns as fine whereupon *posa* was restored and blockade withdrawn.

Early in the last decade of the century, the Abors became most restive in their hills and all combined for concerted action against the British. Several police parties were attacked and in 1893, three Sepoys were ambushed and cut with *dao* and their rifles were taken away.[171] A Miri village within the British jurisdiction had been attacked and some persons were carried off by the Pasi and Miyong Abors. The usual negotiation for the restoration of the captives proved of no avail, and the government ultimately sanctioned an expedition to chastise the criminals of the hills.[172]

The expedition under the command of Capt. R.M. Maxwell and Political Officer Needham started its journey in January 1894. The force consisted of 100 men of 44th Gurkha Rifles under Lts. J.A. Wilson and G.L.S. Ward; 300 men of Lakhimpur Military Police and 100 men of Naga Hills Military Police under Capt. W.R. Little and 711 guns. The Abors began to retreat and Bomjur was taken without any opposition. The next place Dambuk was stockaded; it was taken after some fight when the Abors further retreated. The villages of Mingsipu and Silluk were destroyed and the party advanced upon Damrah, leaving Bordak as the base of supply with a small guard. The attempt to storm Damrah proved of no avail, and supplies being cut off from behind the force began to retreat without achieving its object. The Abors intercepted the retreat and harassed the force; the base of Bordak was burnt by the Abors and the guards there were cut to pieces by the Membu and Padu Abors. But no expedition to either burn or destroy the village of Damrah was sanctioned by the Government of India. Though they agreed to the blockade and withdrawal of *posa* deportation of Dambuk and Silluk Gams was refused.[173]

Relations with the Abors did not improve after the expedition of 1894. In 1898, again, some Abors from Silluk came down to Sibyamukh about 3 miles from the Inner Line, with a view to settling there. Needham was ordered to send them back and as they refused to go back, he destroyed their houses and crops and sent them back.[174] In 1899, the Ghesi Miris raided a village called Chouldhoa and escaped with a girl Yapi. A general blockade of the Abor frontier was now resorted to and in 1900 the Abors were compelled to submit to the British authorities.[175]

But the spectre of Abor hostility continued to haunt the officials; they wanted to bring the Abors under direct and complete control. Noel Williamson, the Assistant Political Officer who had succeeded Needham in 1905, crossed the boundary of the British territory without any escort and succeeded in generating a good feeling among some of them.[176] In March 1908 Williamson made a tour from Pasighat through the foothills south-west to Ledum and then on through Pasi Meyond and the Gallong hills to the Sinyeng River at Dijmur. He proposed a forward policy and establishment of advance posts beyond the frontiers.[177] The Lt. Governor of Eastern Bengal and Assam forwarded the proposal to the Government of India and submitted a scheme of his own. He held that the territories within the Inner Line but up to the foothills should be assessed and a system of presents instead of fixed *posa* in cash should be substituted. The Government of India rejected his proposal entirely; instructions were issued for further exploration of the Abor tracts with a view to ascertaining the reaction of the tribal people to assessment.[178]

In 1911 Noel Williamson and Gregorson went across the British jurisdiction and were murdered by the Kebang Abors. The government could not view the murder as an ordinary crime outside British jurisdiction. An expedition under Major-General Bower to punish the murderers was sanctioned.[179] The expedition was to punish the offending villages, explore the territories and survey the hills on the Dehang. The ringleaders were arrested; the murderer of Williamson was tried under the Frontier Tract Regulation of 1880 and hanged, and that of Gregorson was court martialled.[180]

What Williamson wanted to do in his life time, i.e. to bring the Abor hills under direct British control, he was able to accomplish it only by his death. Major-General Bower, who led the Abor expedition, recommended the division of the Frontier territories into three charges to be placed under separate officers who would directly control the tribes from within the tribal territories under their respective jurisdictions.[181] Accordingly, the entire tracts were divided into three sections in 1912 and separate officers were posted for each. In 1911, an Assistant Political Officer was posted at Pasighat within the territory of the Abor hills and in 1914 the Abor hills were made part of the Central and Eastern Section of the North-East Frontier.[182]

The Government of Iadia formulated the new policy of 'loose political control' over the frontier tribes as recommended by the Government of Eastern Bengal and Assam. Subsequent to the creation of the new charge of the Central and Eastern Sections of the Frontier administrative posts were gradually opened within the Abor territories and Political Officers began to tour the hills up to the international border. The Administration Report for the year 1917-18 submitted by W.C.M. Dundas, the Political Officer, states that the Abor villages had been brought under direct administration; but a large area to the north but south of the McMahon Line remained outside the control of the Political Officer of the Abor hills. There was no hostility against the new order, rather inter-tribal disputes were brought before him for settlement. The people were contented and under the new administration it was hardly felt that the conditions were ever different.[183] In 1838, Godfrey, the new Political Officer, wrote that the Tibetans intruded into the Abor territory and it was necessary to prevent them. On his recommendation, posts were opened at Karko and Riga to stop Tibetan incursions south of the McMahon Line.[184] Thus, the control area was extended to cover up the entire Abor hills or the Siang valley, and the Abors were subjected to the jurisdiction of the British Government.

THE MISHMIS

To the eastward of the Abors from the Dibang river up to the Indian borders on the Talok pass to Burma lay the extensive Mishmi hills. The Mishmis, of all the North-Eastern Frontier tribes, did not exact any levy from the people of the plains. Perhaps because of the existence of the Khampti settlement below their hills they could not come down, as the Khamptis were powerful and were in a position to protect their people against any encroachment. During the Ahom times, no formal relation seems to have existed between the Ahoms and the Mishmis. The *Ahom Buranji* mentions that the Mishmis killed four persons of the Ahom kingdom in 1674. The Mishmis produced the murderers to the Sadiya Khowa Gohain and paid some tribute.[185] Again the *Ahom Buranji* mentions that two

Mishmis paid tribute to the Ahoms; no *posa*, however, was granted to them by the Ahoms.[186]

At the beginning of British rule, the Mishmis were found divided into three divisions; each of these was ruled by the hereditary chief of the clan. There was no love lost between these clans and the Mishmis were not united. They were engaged in extensive trade with the outside world, the Digaru or Tains had trade intercourse with Tibet and the Chulikatas traded with the plains of Assam.[187] But they did not realise any blackmail from the plains of Assam.

The Mishmis from the very beginning were averse to receive the foreigners, observed Lt. Barlton after he had visited the Mishmi hills to explore the course of the Brahmaputra in 1825.[188] In 1827, Wilcox could persuade them to permit him to go across Tain territory to the Idu tracts. But he escaped from an attack by a retreat overnight.[189] In 1826, Dr. Griffith was hospitably received by the Tains, but they refused to allow him to go to the Miju country, stating that they had a quarrel with them. Tains were anxious to trade, says Dr. Griffith, with Assam.[190]

The unfriendly disposition of the Mishmis is evident from the murder of an Indian *fakir*, Permanand Acharya, who tried to travel to Tibet across the Mishmi hills, and the murder of the French missionary M. Krick. The British authorities, though they did not have any regular intercourse with the Mishmis, could not view the murders silently. In the case of Permanand, a reward was declared for the capture of the murderers, but it was reported that the Tibetan authorities had punished the culprit.[191] M. Krick first visited the Mishmi country in 1851 in the company of the Khampti Chief of Sadiya, Choking Gohain. In 1854, he went again to the Mishmi hills with a colleague, M. Bourri, and crossed the Mishmi country for Tibet. A Miju chief named Kai-en-Shah by name followed them. He murdered both of them and carried off their property in disregard of the Tibetan authorities. Lord Dalhousie, the Governor General, authorised an expedition to punish Kai-en-Shah. In 1855, a party of 20 Assam Light Infantry personnel with 40 Khampti volunteers and a few hill porters marched from Sadiya under the command of Lt. Eden. After an eight-day journey the party surprised Kai-en-Shah in his village on the river Du and captured him. His elder sons were killed in the fight. The tribal people around were dispersed and awad. Kai-an-Shah was tried at Dibrugarh by the Deputy Commissioner and hanged for murdering the Frenchmen.[192]

But it was with the Chulikatas that the British found difficulty. Between Sadiya and their hills lay about twenty to thirty miles of dense forest through which hillmen came to the markets of the plain. The Chulikatas, who lived in their border hills, took advantage of their situation, surprised the travellers and border villages, and carried off captives from the British territories.

In April 1855, the Apelong Clan of the Chulikatas took away three servants of Lt. Eden from Sadiya. A blockade was instituted against all Mishmi tribes and markets were closed. The other clans who began to suffer as a result brought forth the captives and delivered them to the authorities.[193] Again, towards the close of the same year, the Apelongs attacked a village near Sadiya and, killing two, took off others. Again, the rival clans rescued the captives and this time they punished the criminals.[194] A third time, in 1857, the Apelongs cut up a village in the vicinity of Sadiya. Capt. A.S. Biver, Assistant to the Governor General's Agent, wrote that the prestige of the government would be lost if the raid went unpunished. The authorities planned a punitive expedition but the outbreak of the Sepoy Mutiny kept such petty affairs out of consideration for the time being.[195] At the end of the year again the Chulikatas massacred the women and children of the village of a Khampti Chief, Chauking Gohain, on the plea that some of their clan members had died of cholera after visiting the Gohian. Col. Hannay, who was in charge of the Sadiya stockade, held the view that punitive expeditions into the Mishmi hills were useless; instead, to stop future raids, guard houses should be set up on the Dikrang, and roads along the foothills for patrolling should be constructed.[196]

The raid on the Khampti village roused the spirit of the Khampti people and they armed themselves for their own defence. The government now promised to supply arms and pay one rupee to each Khampti cultivator who would settle to the north of the Brahmaputra. This policy proved to be a success;

a strong colony soon developed on the Dikrang. It succeeded in driving back the Mishmi raids in 1861 and 1866.[197]

The sequel of screening the Mishmis was interesting. In 1868, a Chulikata Chief, Kalood by name, came to Dibrugarh to meet the Deputy Commissioner and to seek permission to settle under British protection in the valleys of Dikrang, Koondil and Diphoo in the neighbourhood of Sadiya. The Deputy Commissioner wrote to the government and was instructed that immigration should be encouraged. The Deputy Commissioner allowed Kalood to settle at Habba in the Koondil Valley where they would be under British supervision. He came to settle with his families and later on some 200 followed.[198] In 1880, another Chief, Kaladoi, formally professed allegiance to the British while visiting the Sadiya fair.[199] The Mishmis henceforth began to visit the Sadiya fair in large numbers and began to take to peaceful pursuits.

But the Bebejia clan of the Mishmis became very restive. They were described as "a fierce race of cannibals, a very savage, blood-thirsty and dangerous race." In the cold season of 1878-79, they committed two small raids. In one case, they attacked the house of an Assamese ryot in Patia Pathar and killed two persons. The reason behind the raid was known to be an old feud dating back to 1865 when some Mishmis had been killed by British subjects.[200] In the other case, the Mishmis killed two Khamptis and captured four others for tapping rubber 20 miles away from Sadiya in Mishmi tracts. The raiders were pursued by the Frontier Police, but they could not overtake the raiders.[201] In 1884, again, the Bebejias murdered an Assamese ryot in a Dikrang village. A fine of Rs. 2,000 was imposed on them and the Sadiya market was closed to them till they cleared off the dues. The money, however, was paid and the blockade was withdrawn.[202] In 1893, three Sepoys of the Military Police while patrolling near Bomjur outpost were killed again.[203] In 1899, again they made a daring attack on an outlying Khampti village sixteen miles north-east of Sadiya, very near the administrative border. They killed three persons and ran away with four children and three guns.[204]

After the murder of the Sepoy in 1893, Needham wanted to go into the Mishmi hills to punish the offending village; a blockade was imposed on the Mishmi frontier as the Government refused permission for expedition and sanctioned blockade. But after the attack on the Khampti village of Mighaigaon, a punitive expedition was sent to the offending Bebejia village. Needham, with 290 rifles, left for the Mishmi hills under Col. Molesworth. The village was burnt and two Mishmis were captured, but the culprits could not be arrested as they had fled into the interior hills. The captives and one gun were recovered. The British suffered a loss of 34 coolies who died and Rs. 16,000 by way of expenditure. Five Chulikata Mishmis, who acted as interpreters and guides, were given presents of a muzzle gun each and Chulikata Chief Grambon was given an additional reward of Rs. 200 by the Chief Commissioner. One of the raiders, ChenChen, was captured later and given up by the Miris; a reward of Rs. 500 was given to them. ChenChen was tried and hanged at Sadiya.[205] Still in 1905 the Bebejias committed another murderous outrage on the Chulikata Mishmis within the British territory to avenge the collaborators of the expedition 1899, and again blockade had to be resorted to.[206]

A new factor was introduced in tribal politics by the advent of the Chinese on the Indo-Tibetan border and the murder of Noel Williamson. Two exploratory missions were sent in 1911-12 and 1912-13 for survey and exploration of the Mishmi hills and to tell the Mishmis that they were under British protection.[207] The last mission succeeded in surveying the entire Mishmi country including the course of the Dibang. The Mishmi hills were included in the Central and Eastern Sections of the Frontier in 1914 when the Frontier Tracts were divided. From 1914, 'loose political control' over the entire Mishmi hills began to be exercised.

The change in policy, that is, the policy of bringing the tribes under direct political control, was not welcomed by all the clans of the Mishmis; the attitude of the Bebejia Mishmis continued to be hostile. In 1918, a Sepoy was murdered at Nizamghat to avenge again the death of one of their members in the outrage of 1905 by three men of Elapoin Mishmi. An expedition was sent to punish the culprits in 1920 under O'Callaghan. It notonly punished the guilty but also settled many local disputes following the new policy.[208] The disposition of the Mishmis began to change. The British Museum party visiting the Mishmi hills in 1933-34 attested the fact that the Mishmis were friendly. Unfortunately the Chulikatas of the administered area committed an outrage in 1933 in a village within one march, killing four children and injuring others. A promenade was sent in 1934 under a Police Officer from Nizamghat to exact retribution and settle disputes between tax-paying and non-tax-paying villages.[209] This proved successful. Mr. Calvert in 1937-38 toured the unadministered areas on the Du Valley to renew contact with the Taraon Miju clans.[210] In 1940, Godfrey visited Rima, renewed contacts with the Taraon and Miju Mishmis, and succeeded in bringing them under British influence. The extension of the control area thus gradually brought peace and contentment among the Mishmis.[211]

THE KHAMPTIS

Below the Mishmi hills to the south on the Brahmaputra and between them and the Singphos lived the Khamptis. The British came into contact with them when they came to Assam during the Anglo-Burmese War of 1824-26. The Khamptis were immigrants from the land called Bar-Khampti between the eastern extremity of Assam and the river Irrawaddy. At first they had settled around Tengapani in Upper Assam. In 1797-1800, the Barasiriagis revolted in Sadiya; the Khamptis along with other tribes joined them and crossed the Brahmaputra and ousted the Assamese governor of Sadiya.[212] The *Tungkhungia Buranji* records that they occupied Sadiya in 1797, and the title and dignity of the Ahom governor were assumed by the Khampti Chief.[213] The Ahom kings had no formal relation with the Khamptis, nor had any of the Ahom kings granted any *posa* to them. The Khampti Chief ruled like an independent prince.

He had succeeded in keeping his tract free from the Anglo-Assamese turmoil. When Scott, the Agent to the Governor General, came to Upper Assam in 1824, the Khamptis rendered him good service. Therefore, Scott recognised the Khampti Chief 'Chousalan Sadiya Khowa Gohain' as the Chief and permitted him to collect taxes from the Assamese people within his jurisdiction. The Khampti Chief himself did not pay any tax and instead undertook to maintain a contingent of 200 men to be armed by the British, as per terms of an agreement entered into in this regard. But he was required to obey orders of the British Government sent through the Political Officer of Upper Assam to whom they were to bring all serious crimes for trial.[214]

The relation between the Khampti Chief and the British remained friendly and peaceful till 1839 though rumours of Khampti intrigue were reported occasionally.[215] As late as 1838 Capt. White, Political Agent of Sadiya, wrote that they were faithful to their engagements and gave no cause for anxiety,[216] though a report of the year shows that the Khamptis had become disgusted at the long continuance of the British supremacy over Sadiya which they considered to be their own territory.[217] In 1835, a fresh batch of immigrants from the Bor-Khampti land entered Assam and sought permission to settle under the British Government. They asked for remission of taxes for ten years and fire arms. The British were anxious to settle them as barrier between Assam and Burma, because still they were haunted by a dread of fresh Burmese invasion. Therefore, the Khamptis were allowed to settle without payment of taxes for three years, but no fire arms were supplied to them.[218]

In 1838, a dispute arose between the Khampti Chief of Sadiya and the Bor Senapati of Muttack, the Moamaria Chief of Upper Assam, in regard to a tract of land on the south bank of the Brahmaputra. The Political Officer at Sadiya asked both the parties to appear before him. The Khampti Chief took possession of the land in defiance of the order whereupon the Political Agent in vindication of his authority attached the land in dispute. He ordered first the suspension and then the removal of the Khampti Chief from the post of Khawa Gohain. The Khawa Gohain was thereafter removed to a distant station down the river out of the reach of easy intrigue and his post was abolished. His territories were brought under the administration of the British Officer at Sadiya who collected taxes from the Assamese people and administered justice to them. But the Khamptis and Singphos of this territory were left under their own chiefs; no tax was levied upon them.[219]

Apparently the Khamptis seemed content and during the Singpho rising of 1838 they rendered good help to the British.

The ex-Khawa Gohain was allowed to return to Sadiya in his private capacity in recognition of the Khampti service.[220] But their hatred of the British and fear of being brought under regular jurisdiction of the British administration resulted in a premeditated outbreak on 19 January 1839, when about 500 Khamptis in arms attacked the British post at Sadiya, butchered Col. White and his men, and burnt the lines to the ground. The Khamptis on the south bank of the Brahmaputra also rose; but they were put down by the British troops. The successful Khamptis on the north bank, however, retreated with their adherents and took refuge among the Dibang Mishmis. Compelled by distress in their jungle refuge one chief, Chouking Gohain, surrendered and then led a British force to compel others to follow him.[221] In 1839-40, more expeditions were sent to disperse the Khamptis from the hills, and finally in 1843 all the Khamptis surrendered to the British under agreement of good behaviour.[222]

The Khamptis were divided as suggested by Capt. Vetch who suppressed the Khampti rebellion; with a view to weakening them they were dispersed by the British in four divisions.[223] One body was settled at Choonpura, above Sadiya under Captain Gohain, cousin of the late Khawa Gohain. Another division which was formerly near Tengapani was now settled near Saikhowa to the south of the Brahmaputra. A third party under Chowtang Gohain was settled at Dhemaji and the fourth sent to Bhodia, west of Lakhimpur, under the son of late Khawa Gohain. Since then they could not be united and as a result failed to acquire any political importance. They took to agricultural pursuits. Those who settled in Chorapoorah and below Saikhowa did not pay revenues; the rest in Bhodia and Dhemaji paid regular taxes.[224]

The British relations with the Khamptis did not face any strain thereafter. Rather henceforth the Khamptis and their Chiefs always acted as guides of the British officers in their tours in the Mishmis and Singpho hills. Needham, Williamson and Dundas took Khampti Gohains in their tours.[225] The Khampti Chief of Chowkham was granted a pension and a gun in recognition of British favour to him. As late as 1916 he claimed restitution of his independence and title; though the request was turned down, his pension was increased to Rs. 50/-

from Rs. 30/- and his people were exempted from taxation when poll-taxes began to be levied in the Central to Eastern Sections of the North-East Frontier in which some Khamptis were included after 1914.[226]

THE SINGPHOS

Of the North-East Frontier tribes, the British had to come to some sort of relation with the Singphos first. The Singphos were immigrants from a tract of land on the eastern bank of the Irrawaddy whence they gradually crossed the Patkai. In the troublesome reign of Gouri Singha in 1797 the Singphos, together with the Moamarias, began to attack the Assamese villages and gradually occupied the whole territories lying between Upper Assam and Bhamo, driving out the Khamptis beyond the Brahmaputra.[227] When the Burmese invaded Assam in 1817 they set in an era of plunder and misrule. The Singphos began to take advantage of the situation and carried off hundreds of Assamese as slaves.[228] Further, the Singphos were believed to be preparing for an attack over the territories of the Bor Senapati of Muttack and the Khampti Chief of Sadiya. These chiefs now appealed for help to the British. The British succeeded in driving out the Burmese in course of the war, but apprehending another Burmese invasion concluded engagements with the Bor Senapati of Muttack and the Khamptis of Sadiya. Now they were required to come to terms with the Singphos who bordered on the tracts of these two chiefs and Burma.

The British were harbouring an idea of creating a buffer z ne to be inhabited by friendly tribes between Upper Assam and Burma. Therefore, the British officer at Sadiya was given strict instructions to give assistance to the Muttack and Sadiya Chiefs only for defensive purposes and not to advance into the tracts inhabited by the Singpho tribe.[229] Meanwhile the Singphos, becoming anxious to protect themselves against possible attack from the Burma side, made overtures of friendship to the British who now realised that to create a tract of tribal territory to defend the Burma border was impractical as the tribe itself was afraid of Burmese invasion and wanted their protection. Besides, the question of restoration of the slaves and the booty of plunder stood on the way of settlement with them.[230]

Early in 1825, the British informed four Singpho Chiefs that they would be allowed quiet possession of their lands if they surrendered the Assamese slaves, recognised the British supremacy and agreed to inform them of the Burmese activities on the borders.[231] Shortly afterwards, the Burmese appeared on the borders and the Singpho chiefs made over their stockades to them and sided with the Burmese, expressing contempt for the English. But they had also sent message to the British expressing their anxiety to be rid of the Burmese.[232] In June, Capt. Neufville advanced up the Nao Dihing and by a series of attacks expelled the Burmese from the Assam side. During the operations, many Singpho Chiefs who had taken sides with the Burmese were attacked by the English. The Chiefs fled into the hills and their Assamese slaves were set free by Neufville. Bisa Gam, during these operations, moved from his original site on the Nao Dihing to a place called Borhat on the Buri Dihing.[233]

After these raids in June 1826, Scott, the Governor-General's Agent, visited the Singpho territories and entered into engagements with sixteen of their chiefs who set free the Assamese slaves and promised to help the British in case of future need and refer all disputes of inter-tribal nature and heinous crimes to the arbitration of the British Officer at Sadiya. Hostages were given for the due fufilment of these engagements.[234]

But the loss of slave labour had impoverished the Singphos who had become lazy and idlers and dependent on slavery. Therefore, to provide some sort of engagement and income to these Singphos, the British tried to open up a trade route through the Singpho territories wherein the Singphos would act as middlemen in trade.[235] But these attempts did not continue for long as the Company's servants found work elsewhere and the matter was forgotten. Moreover, some Singhpho Chiefs were aggrieved by the recognition of Bisa Gam as the paramount Chief and held aloof from the British. One of these Chiefs, Duffa Gam, was a rival of Bisa Gam and he continued to raid Bisa Gam and his dependent villages. In 1830, they, with some Khamptis and Singphos from across the broder, attacked the villages of Luttora Gam on the Tengapani river. Capt. Neufville drove them out with the aid of the friendly Singhphos and those who had aided him were rewarded. After this incident, the Singphos gradually settled down in agriculture and many took to elephant-catching and hunting.[236] In 1834, an European Officer was posted at Sadiya permanently to conduct relations with these chiefs and gradually the slaves began to be released.[237]

But the raids of the hostile Singpho Chiefs, particularly of Duffa Gam, continued to trouble the Singphos on this side of the border. In 1835, again Duffa Gam made a sudden foray from across the border and took many prisoners including women and children, after killing many. He appeared again from Burma and drew to his side many Chiefs who had owed allegiance to Bisa Gam.[238] A British force was despatched; they dispersed the Singphos, who came from Burma, and all the Chiefs save Luttora Gam, once again came to the side of the English. In 1837, Luttora also resubmitted to the British.[239]

Now the British Government wanted to restrain the raids from the Burma side by pressing the Burmese Government to check their subjects. The Burmese Government agreed to depute the governor of Mogoung to accompany Capt. Hannay to visit the borders and see what could be done. But the issue became delicate when the trouble-maker Duffa was received with honour by the Court of Ava, after he had submitted to the Burmese.[240] The Government of India again insisted on sending a second deputation to the borders to close the issue of border trouble and the Burmese reluctantly agreed to it. But settlement became difficult on account of the Burmese claim of sovereignty over tracts of Upper Assam up to Joypore. The British officers rejected the claim as ridiculous and thereupon a military post was established on the Buri Dehing for the protection of the Singpho borders.[241]

Meanwhile, from 1838 the Singphos themselves began to quarrel among themselves and attacked each other. Some even joined the Khampti rebellion in 1839 against the British and the British officers reported that all the Singphos were in a most agitated and discontented condition.[242] At about this time, a strong force of British troops was sent through the

Singpho tracts and this had a singular effect upon the Singphos who now were awed and had now some respect for the British arms. Many now became friendly and in recognition of their friendship revealed the existence of a brass cannon left by the Mughal force of Mir Jumla as a token of their fidelity.[243] An attempt was made by the government after this to bring the Singpho settlements within the reach of surveillance of British posts.[244] In 1841-42, Capt. Vetch visited the Singpho tracts and found them quiet; thereafter the management of the Singphos was transferred from the Political Department to the Revenue and Judicial Department of the Bengal Government.[245]

But peace on the Singpho border did not last long. In 1843, a fresh raid by Singphos from across the border took place. Simultaneously, the Singphos attacked the British post at Nigroo and the guard post at Bisa. A large body of Singphos and Khamptis threatened the British post at Sadiya; all the Singphos rebelled against the British and sided with the invaders. The Tippum Raja of Hookoom was said to have inspired this movement.[246] British troops were quickly despatched and many chiefs quickly came back to the British side. Ningroota soon resubmitted and Bisa followed him. They protested their inncence and offered to act in future against the Burmese Singphos. The British Government acceped their overtures and agreed to pardon their offences as they had not succeeded in providing them adequate safeguard against the Burmese invasion.[247]

The government now wanted to have a thorough probe into the Singpho affairs and appointed Col. Lloyd and Stainforth to enquire into the causes of the Singpho rebellion.[248] As they were unable to do the job, Capt. Jenkins was appointed to do it.[249] He reported that the causes of the rebellion were three, viz., (1) encroachment on the lands and privileges of the Singphos; (2) the seizure and punishment by local officers of some members of the tribes; (3) the orders of the Tippum Raja who was the Chief of the Hookoom province of Burma. The Governor-General in Council, while reviewing the report, set aside the last two causes and accepted the first cause as valid.[250] In the final report, it was held that the main reason behind the Singpho rebellion was the loss of their Assamese slaves; the loss of land had nothing to do with it as no land had ever been granted to the Singphos or was claimed by the Singphos as theirs. It was concluded that after the loss of their slaves they would be compelled to take to agriculture and they might be left alone for the time being. The government accepted this report.[251]

Gradually the Singphos became peaceful and obedient. The main reason behind their reversion to peace was that after the Second Anglo-Burmese War, when Upper Burma was annexed to British Empire, the Singphos in India did not get either any insinuation or hope of assistance from Burma, and they were ultimately compelled to take to agriculture and hunting. No other Singpho rebellion is mentioned after the Anglo-Burmese War of 1851, when the first Assistant Political Officer of Sadiya, J.F. Michell, pushed up to the Huking valley.[252] He repeated his visit in 1891. On both occasions, he was assisted by the Singphos and no symptoms of hostility were shown to the party.[253] In 1909, Noel Williamson, who succeeded Needham, visited these tracts. He, too, was assisted by the Singphos and they did not oppose the move of the Political Officer.[254] In 1914, when the Frontier Tracts were divided, the Singpho tracts were brought within the Eastern Section of the North-East Frontier, and gradually all the Singphos were brought under the 'loose political control' and purview of the Rules for the Administration of Justice in the Frontier Tracts. Poll-tax began to be introduced and collected from the Singpho villages henceforward.[255]

In 1917-18, Dundas, the Political Officer, recorded in his annual report that all the Singpho tribes had been brought under direct administration and all of them paid poll-tax. They were found contented, "hardly realising that the conditions were ever different."[256] In 1943, the Singpho tracts were divided when the Tirap Frontier Tract was created; some were brought within the new charge while others continued to be within the jurisdiction of the Political Officer of Sadiya.[257] The Singphos posed no problem for the British till their withdrawal from India in 1947.

TRIBES OF THE PATKAI HILLS

Though the British penetrated into Upper Assam in the

wake of the First Anglo-Burmese War (1824-26) and proceeded up to Joypur where a garrison post was established after the war, no notice was taken by them of the inhabitants living in the hills beyond. These inhabitants were the Nagas who had been living over and along the spurs and foothills of the Patkai range even before the Ahom advent in Assam in 1226. The Ahoms are said to have crossed the Patkai while marching towards Assam, and they followed a route along the banks of the Noa Dihing and Buri Dihing close by the Patkai. On their way to Assam they first encountered the Naga tribes and, defeating them, established administrative posts before they marched further towards the Assam plains.[258] Later on, as the Ahom became rulers of Assam, they had to grant concessions to the western Naga tribes in the form of *posa*.[259] Land grants were made to the Nagas to enable them to procure paddy and other articles which were not available in their hills. Salt wells which abound along the foot of the Naga hills were also shared by the Naga tribes and the Ahoms successively every year.[260] The Nagas visited the Ahom kings with presents, which Mackenzie holds might be supposed to be tribute.[261] It can be safely assumed that during the troublesome days of the Moamaria rebellion and the Burmese invasion, many tribes attacked the Ahom kingdom; the Abors, Daflas, Khamptis and Singphos swooped upon the Ahom kingdom. But the Nagas did not encroach upon the Ahom territories and attack Assamese villages; no such account is available in either the *Buranjis* or in the British records.

That the Nagas were living in the Patkai hills is evident from the British records of the 1830s. It is recorded in the correspondence of 1835 that the Nagas were raiding villages within the British jurisdiction along with the Singphos and the Burmese. But soon it became clear to the British officers that such raids were reprisals for raids on their villages, mostly perpetrated by the Singphos.[262] In 1837, Capt. Hannay, while marching through the spurs and valley of the Patkai in pursuit of the Singphos, found the Singphos taking the Naga people in captivity in gangs.[263] The Singphos were compelled by the British to surrender the Assamese slaves and the former found alternatives in the Nagas. The British had not yet claimed rights over the Naga territories and did not intervene on behalf of the Nagas. A proposal, however, was mooted to accord protection at this time to the Nagas and to establish a post under a European officer to take effective political charge of the Singpho-Naga tracts.[264] But it was found inexpedient to take charge of such a sparsely populated area, 90 miles long and 40 miles deep, and do it under an officer. As Capt. Hannay reported, it was not possible to accord protection to the Nagas unless they established themselves near the military posts. Then it was decided to leave the Nagas under the care of an officer who would visit the area as and when necessary.[265] Subsequently, the Singphos reduced many Naga villages to subjection to them and levies were imposed on them.

The Nagas did not realise any blackmail or *posa* from the villages of the Assam plains and, therefore, the British were not required to commute their rights over the villages. What caught the attention of the Company's servants was the salt wells of the Naga hills.[266] These hills were within the jurisdiction of the Principal Assistant of Sibsagar. From 1840, the Naga relations with the government were chiefly conducted by this officer; he maintained contact with the Nagas of the western hills which is beyond the jurisdiction of the Principal Assistant of Lakhimpur. Capt. Bordie, the Principal Assistant of Sibsagar, proposed to levy tribute on the villages in recognition of British paramountcy and mediate in the inter-tribal disputes of the Naga hills. He also went to their hills several times between 1840-47 to settle some such disputes. But the government soon decided to follow the policy of leaving the tribes 'alone', and Bordie's proposal as such came to naught.[267]

The eastern hills, or the Patkai hills within the jurisdiction of the North-East Frontier Agency, were initially under the Political Agent of Upper Assam posted at Sadiya and then under the Principal Assistant of the Lakhimpur district when the Political Agent of Upper Assam shifted his headquarters to Gauhati.[268] An Assistant Commissioner from his headquarters at Joypur now conducted relations with the eastern Nagas and occasionally paid visits to Margherita and adjacent areas, as it was decided after the receipt of Capt. Hannay's reports. The Nagas of the eastern hills or of the Patkai caught attention of the government in the last quarter of the nineteenth century when Naga raids consequent upon the encroachment of the tea planters became imminent after the quarrel between a tea planter and the Changnoi Nagas beyond the Lakhimpur frontier.[269] Subsequently, the massacre of Borlangia of 1872 perpetrated by Kamsangias forced the government to establish some link with some chiefs of the Nagas who had leased out lands to these tea planters.[270]

In 1873-74, the government executed agreements with the chiefs of Borduarias and the Namsangias to pay them Rs. 25/- and Rs. 450 on account of the lands taken by Minto and Company for the Tawrouck and Hukanjuri tea gardens near Joypur on the Delli river.[271] The object was to bring these chiefs into direct dealings with the government which would enable the government to exert pressure on them in case of raid or any misbehaviour by the Nagas under these chiefs. The Government of Assam, of course, had settlements with the tea garden-owners for realising revenue from them. At the time of specification of the Inner Line boundary of the Lakhimpur district, the line was stretched to bring the tea gardens within the district of Lakhimpur.[272] It is worth remembering that the government held the view that the crest of the Patkai was the boundary between Assam and Burma and the claims of the Burmese over tracts of territory up to Joypur on the foothills of the Patkai was turned down. Yet the government avoided the responsibility to administer the Naga hills of the Patkai range and usually murders and atrocities committed beyond the Inner Line were ignored by them.

The opening of the coal mines in Joypur, Margherita, Ledo and the adjacent areas, extension of railheads to the coal-fields and tea garden areas and exploration of petroleum in Upper Assam brought the government close to the Nagas and roused their suspicion. In 1875, an attempt was made to survey the Eastern Naga hills and that led to a serious clash. The Assistant Commissioner of Joypur, Lt. Holcombe, accompanied by a survey party under Capt. Badgeley, went inside the Patkai range in February 1875. After four days' march beyond Joypur, they were attacked at a village called Ninu by the Nagas (Rangpangs). Lt. Holcombe with 80 men was butchered; Capt. Badgeley with 50 men escaped but was wounded. An expedition was immediately sent to punish the village of Ninu. It destroyed the village, but succeeded in recovering the arms lost and the heads of the men who were murdered in February.[273] In 1876, another expedition was sent to punish the village as it had refused to surrender some more men connected with the massacre of February 1875. The village of Ninu was burnt again.[274]

Meanwhile, in September 1875, the Lakhimpur Inner Line was notified and the Naga area of the Patkai range beyond Joypur was kept beyond the Inner Line. No raid by the Nagas of the hills beyond the Inner Line is reported before 1888 when the chief of Borduarias raided a Delli village near Joypur and took away a British subject. The British subject was killed subsequently together with another hillman whereupon the Deputy Commissioner of Dibrugarh detained the brother of the chief who was in the plains and stopped the payment of *posa* due to the Borduaria chief until he came for trial under the Deputy Commissioner. The chief was fined Rs. 2000 and 15 guns in the customary way; he paid off the fine.[275] The Chief Commissioner commenting upon the report held the view that the punishment was too light in consideration of the crime; but as the measure had already been adopted it was approved of by him.[276]

The government followed a policy of non-interference in Naga affairs from the beginning of the nineteenth century. This minimised the chance of government involvement in Naga affairs. But we find that the tribes beyond Joypur in the Lakhimpur Frontier Tract brought their inter-tribal disputes for settlement to the Deputy Commissioner of Dibrugarh. The boundary dispute between the Namsangias and Borduarias was settled by the Deputy Commissioner in 1905.[277] Henceforth, the main problem faced by the government was that of frequent thefts committed by the Naga tribes. The tribes required iron to make spears and other domestic implements. For the purpose, scrap iron from the mines or workshop of Railways were stolen. In case of theft by the Nagas of the hills beyond the Inner Line they were punished with fines. The offending villages readily submitted to the fines imposed on them. In 1904-05 some Rangpangs had committed a theft in the Ledo colliery and escaped with two captives and a gun with other stolen property. On their way back, some 30 persons of the party were arrested by a Harkara with the help of Sarkari

Nagas. These people were detained in jail till their villagers came for their release. The Deputy Commissioner punished them with fine of Rs. 200 after the captives and stolen properties were restored.[278] Subsequently, another theft occurred there and this time the Sarkari Nagas were suspected. The Deputy Commissioner proposed to fine all Sarkari Nagas within 10 miles of Ledo with an amount of Rs. 300; the Chief Commissioner, however, declined to approve of the measure, pointing out that the culprits who were British subjects should be duly tried and the whole community could not be punished.[279] Theft of iron scrap cases by the Nagas of unadministered areas are reported as late as 1936[280] and 1937 when Rangpangs took away from Lekhapani Colliery some scrap.[281]

The opening of coal mines, extension of railways and development of Plantation industries had benefited the Naga tribes of the Lakhimpur frontier greatly. Many of the tribesmen came down to the plains during winter season and, serving in the industries, earned wages. Many got employment in the reserve forests and jungle clearings. These facilities kept the Nagas quiet. Yet sometimes raids occurred in the Frontier Tracts and in the hills beyond the Inner Line. In 1905, Borduarias were attacked by Kunlungas under the Bormithunia chief, 4 miles within the British territory.[282] Again, in 1907, the Rangpang Nagas committed a raid in the Wakpong village within the Frontier Tract, and in 1908 some Rangpangs attacked and murdered some Longhangs who were going back to their villages beyond the Inner Line after serving in the plains for some time.[283] They later complained to the British for the redress of their grievances. In 1909 Noel Williamson, Assistant Political Officer from Sadiya, went to the Rangpang hills to punish the offenders of the Wakpong raid of 1907 and obtain satisfaction for the Longhang massacre. Williamson's party of 554 persons, consisting of 2 British, 3 Native officers and 142 rank and file of the Assam Rifles, with a Hospital Assistant and one Surveyor and his servants and some privates, together with Naga Singpho and Nepali coolies, left for the village of Rashi in November 1909. They reached the village on the 29th and set fire to the village. On December 1, again, the remnant of the village was burnt and the party returned after destroying the village with stock and property.[284] Thereafter no serious raid on British territory was reported from the Rangpang Nagas.

From the beginning of the twentieth century, the government began to bring the Naga villages within the Frontier Tracts and impose taxes upon them. In 1909, Sarkari Naga villages beyond Ledo were annexed to the British territories, and the Assam Frontier Tracts Regulation of 1880 was extended to the Tract. Poll-tax was collected through the chiefs of the villages. In the Lakhimpur Frontier Tract areas, Political Jamadar seems to have disposed of the petty cases, referring serious ones to the Deputy Commissioner.[285] The Naga villages were visited by the Political Jamadar who sometimes went with Harkaras under him to visit the villages and apprehend criminals. The government usually did not provide any welfare measure until late twenties of the present century when one primary school in the Lakhimpur Frontier Tract was taken over by the government.[286] But an agricultural demonstrator was appointed to instruct the Nagas in imoroved methods of cultivation and some seeds were provided to the villagers.[287]

In 1914, some of the Naga areas were brought within the Eastern Section of the North-East Frontier and others were included in the Lakhimpur Frontier Tract to be administered by the Deputy Commissioner of the Lakhimpur district. In 1937, the transfer of the hill areas of the Lakhimpur Frontier charge to the Central and Eastern Sections was mooted inspite of the protest of the[288] Hill Nagas, but the proposal was, however, dropped. In 1943, again a new charge was created under the name of the Tirap Frontier Tract during the war taking portions of the Eastern Section of the North-East Frontier and the Lakhimpur Frontier Tract.[289] No opposition seems to have come this time from the Nagas.

CONCLUSION

Thus a survey of the British relations with the North-East Frontier tribes leads one to conclude that the first concern of the British was to dislodge the tribes from the Assam plains where they had established themselves before the advent of the British in Assam. Gradually the rights and privileges of the tribal people over the plains of Assam were abrogated by following a policy of what may be called in the words of Col. Henry Hopkinson, the Commissioner of Assam, "Gold" and "Steel". This means that they were to be conciliated by granting 'gold' or cash payment in lieu of the customary '*posa*' of the Ahom regime; but when they declined to accept the new terms of the new rulers, 'steel', that is to say, armed force, was to be employed to compel them to accept the offer. Till 1910, the British Government was quite unwilling to burden itself with the responsibility of administering the tribes of the Frontier; they followed a policy of what is called "let alone", that is, to leave the tribes to themselves. But if they (tribes) violated the terms of engagements imposed on them by the British Government, punishments were meted out to them. After 1910, beginning with 'loose political control', direct control and administration were imposed on the tribes, and their territories were tagged to the province of Assam. But then the tribes were lagging so much behind the people of the plains as a result of neglect for such a long time that the Government of Assam had no alternative except to write to the Government of India in 1931: "what is needed for the future is a policy of development and unification on lines suited to the genius of the hill people."[290]

REFERENCES

1. (Buragohain) Padmeswar Sing, *Ahom Buranji*, transcript No. 109, vol. IX, p. 569.
2. Revenue Proceedings, 11 August, 1834, No. 5.
3. A. Mackenzie, *History*, p. 6.
4. Foreign Proceedings, March 1885, No. 40.
5. *Ibid.*
6. *Ibid.*
7. *Ibid.*
8. *Ibid.*
9. L. Devi, *Ahom Tribal Relations*, p. 199.
10. *Ibid.*
11. Foreign Political (India), 12 September 1838, Nos. 64-85.
12. *Ibid.*
13. *Ibid.*
14. Foreign Political (India), 6 June 1838, No. 48.
15. *Ibid*, 18 July 1836, Nos. 76-78.
16. C. U. Aitchison, A Collection of *Treaties, Engagements and Sanads*, Related to India and Neighbouring Countries, vol. I, p. 143.
17. A. Mackenzie, *History*, p. 17.

18. *Ibid.*
19. *Ibid.*
20. *Ibid.*
21. *Ibid.*
22. *Ibid.*
23. *Ibid.*
24. Political Proceedings (Bengal), October 1864, Nos. 18-21.
25. Foreign Proceedings (Assam), March 1885, No. 40.
26. *Ibid.*
27. *Ibid.*
28. L. Devi, *op. cit.*, p. 199.
29. A. Mackenzie, *Memorandum on the North-East Frontier of Bengal*, henceforth referred to as Memorandum., p. 5.
30. Foreign Political (India), 20 February 1834, Nos. 23-24.
31. *Ibid.*
32. *Ibid.*
33. Foreign Proceedings (Assam), November 1875, Nos. 3-4.
34. Foreign Proceedings (Assam), March 1885, No. 40.
35. J.A.M. Mills' Report, p. xcv.
36. Foreign Proceedings (Assam), March 1885, No. 40.
37. Foreign Proceedings (Assam), March 1885, No. 40.
38. *Ibid.*
39. Lakhimpur Deputy Commissioner's Collection, No. XVII of 1915-16, F. 7.
40. Foreign Proceedings (Assam), November 1875, Nos. 3-4.
41. File No. 309 of 1873, Sl. 15 (Bengal Papers) in Assam Archives.
42. Foreign Proceedings (Assam), April 1878, Nos. 8-12; July 1878, No.1.
43. *Ibid.*
44. Political Proceedings (Assam), December 1914, Nos. 1-37.
45. Proceedings of Governor's Secretariat, Tribal Affairs Deptt., June 1940, Nos. 535-626.
46. *Ibid.*
47. Revenue Proceedings (Bengal), 21 August 1834, No. 5.
48. H. Barua, *op. cit.*, p. 40; Singh, P., *op. cit.*, p. 569.
49. David Scott, son of Archibald Scott was born in August, 1786 in England. He joined the East India Company's service and served as a Judge and Magistrate between 1812-1813 at Purnea (Bihar) and Rangpur and became Commissioner in 1823 in the latter place. In 1824 he was appointed Agent to the Governor-General on the North-East Frontier and Commissioner of Revenue and Circuit in the districts of Assam, North-East Rangpur, Shirpur and Sylhet. He encouraged the Christian missionaries in the Garo hills. He escaped the massacre of April 4-5 of 1831 of Nungklow and established a Sanitarium at Cherrapunjee. He died on August 20, 1831. See C. E. Buckland, *Dictionary of Indian Biography*, pp. 378-79.
50. Political Proceedings (Bengal), 5 February 1825.
51. Foreign Proceedings (Assam), March 1885, No. 40.

52. *Ibid.*
53. *Ibid.*
54. Political Proceedings (Bengal), 13 March 1835, Nos. 7-8.
55. *Ibid.*
56. *Ibid.*
57. Political Proceedings (Bengal), 16 January 1838, Nos. 41-48.
58. *Ibid*, 19 April 1841, Nos. 80-81; 27 September 1841, Nos. 95-96.
59. Foreign Proceedings (Assam), March 1885, No. 40.
60. *Ibid.* In 1944, Capt. Gordon had granted Rs. 32 each to Chengkolee, Singingkandor and Sarsoo and Rs. 24 to Narsco; and in 1848 he further granted Rs. 40 to Srigi and Rs. 32 each to Barsoo, Kangsoon and Rs. 22 each to Pasoo, Deekoks and Dhenno.
61. Foreign Proceedings (Assam), March 1885, No. 4o.
62. *Ibid.*
63. Political Proceedings (Assam), June 1880, Nos. 55-56.
64. Bengal Papers in Assam Archives, File No. 309 of 1873, Sl. 15.
65. *Ibid*, April 1874, No. 11.
66. *Ibid*, June 1874, Nos. 23-24.
67. A. Mackenzie, *History*, p. 26.
68. *Ibid.*
69. Foreign Proceedings (Assam), December 1884, Nos. 7-9.
70. Judicial Proceedings, File No. 1545 of 1883, Nos. 1-18.
71. Judicial Papers (Assam), File No. 116J of 1884, Nos. 1-26.
72. Judicial Papers (Assam), File No. 116J of 1884, Nos. 1-26.
73. *Ibid.*
74. *Ibid.*
75. *Ibid.*
76. Foreign Proceedings (Assam), March 1885, No. 34.
77. *Ibid.*
78. Foreign Proceedings (Assam), January 1888, No. 8.
79. Foreign Political (India), November 1897, Nos. 15-104.
80. Foreign Proceedings (Assam), July 1900, No. 40.
81. *Ibid.*
82. Political Proceedings (Assam), December 1914, Nos. 1-37.
83. Political Proceedings (Assam), December 1914, Nos. 1-37.
84. *Ibid.*
85. Administration Report, 1924-25.
86. *Ibid.*, 1938-39.
87. Bengal Papers in Assam Archives, File No. 309 of 1873, Sl. 15.
88. H. Barua, *op. cit.*, p. 40; P. Sing, *op. cit.*, p. 569.
89. Revenue Proceedings (Bengal), 11 August 1834, No. 5.
90. Foreign Political (India), 20 February 1834, Nos. 22-24.
91. Bengal Papers (Assam), F. No. 298 BG. of 1835.
92. Foreign Political (India), 20 February 1834, Nos. 22-24.
93. *Ibid.*
94. *Ibid*, 18 July 1836, Nos. 76-78.
95. *Ibid.*

96. Political Proceedings, 8 May 1837, Nos. 62-63, 15 May 1837, Nos. 10-11.
97. Foreign Political Proceedings (India), 18 July 1836, Nos. 76-78.
98. *Ibid.*
99. A. Mackenzie, *History*, p. 28.
100. *Ibid.*
101. Foreign Political (India), 20 February 1834, Nos. 23-24.
102. Lakhimpur Deputy Commissioner's Collection, No. XII, F. 7, 1884.
103. *Ibid.*
104. *Ibid*, February, 1870, Nos. 1-2.
105. Political Proceedings (Bengal), June 1871, No. 28.
106. *Ibid*, May 1877, No. 11.
107. *Ibid.*
108. Foreign Proceedings (Assam), June 1888.
109. *Ibid*, March 1888, Nos. 11-24.
110. *Ibid*, May 1899, Nos. 24-25.
111. *Ibid*, March 1900, Nos. 18-24.
112. *Ibid*, March 1900, Nos. 18-24.
113. *Ibid*, March 1900, Nos. 18-24; April 1899, Nos. 1-7; May 1899, Nos. 24-26.
114. Political Proceedings (Assam), August, 1910, No. 25.
115. *Ibid*, February 1911, Nos. 77-84; March 1911, Nos. 5-70.
116. Political Proceedings (East Bengal and Assam), March 1912, Nos. 149-197.
117. Political Proceedings (Assam), December 1914, Nos. 1-37.
118. R. Reid, *History of the Frontier Areas Bordering on Assam*, from 1883-1941.
119. Political Proceedings (Assam), June 1926, Nos. 587-603.
120. Administration Report, 1924-25.
121. R. Reid, *op. cit.*, p. 294.
122. *Ibid.*
123. *Ibid.*
124. Administration Report, 1938-39.
125. A. Mackenzie, *History*, p. 35.
126. *Ibid.*
127. H. Barua, *op. cit.*, p. 40; P. Sing, *op. cit.*, p. 569.
128. Political Proceedings (EBA), May 1906, Nos. 1-11.
129. A. Mackenzie, *History*, p. 36.
130. *Ibid.*
131. Lakhimpur Deputy Commissioner's Collection, No. XII, F. 7, 1884.
132. Foreign Secret Proceedings, 26 February 1830, Nos. 5-6.
133. *Ibid*, 7 May 1830, Nos. 47-48.
134. Political Proceedings (Bengal), 16 March 1840, No. 112.
135. *Ibid*, 28 April 1848, Nos. 104-06.
136. A. Mackenzie, *History*, p. 36.
137. *Ibid.*
138. Political Proceedings (Bengal), June 23, 1849, Nos. 23-29.

139. Revenue Proceedings (Bengal), 12 March 1851, Nos. 61-62.
140. *Ibid.*
141. Judicial Proceedings (Bengal), 19 August 1858, Nos. 262-89.
142. *Ibid.*
143. *Ibid.*
144. *Ibid*, 25 January 1859, Nos. 88-100.
145. *Ibid*, August 1860, Nos. 417-19.
146. Judicial Proceedings (Bengal), August 1860, Nos. 417-19.
147. *Ibid.*
148. Judicial Proceedings (Bengal), January 1862, Nos. 305-308.
149. *Ibid*, May 1865, Nos. 119-21.
150. *Ibid*, October, 1862, No. 176.
151. *Ibid*, January 1863, Nos. 310-11.
152. *Ibid.*
153. *Ibid.*
154. Judicial Proceedings (Bengal), March 1863, No. 248.
155. C. U. Aitchison, *op. cit.*, p. 299.
156. Judicial Proceedings (Bengal), May 1865, Nos. 119-21.
157. *Ibid*, November 1863, No. 166.
158. *Ibid*, June 1866, Nos. 6-7.
159. A. Mackenzie, *History*, p. 42.
160. Foreign Proceedings (Assam), January 1878, No. 7.
161. *Ibid*, October 1878, No. 12.
162. *Ibid* , No. 6.
163. Foreign Proceedings (Assam), November 1878, No. 14.
164. *Ibid*, September 1887, Nos. 35-38; June 1916, No. 37.
165. Foreign Proceedings (Assam), January 1880, Nos. 4-5.
166. Lakhimpur Deputy Commissioner's Collection, No. XII of 1904-8 F. 6.
167. Foreign Proceedings (Assam), February 1885, Nos. 2-6.
168. Lakhimpur Deputy Commissioner's Collection, No. XII of 1906, F. 6.
169. Foreign Proceedings (Assam), September 1887, Nos. 35-38.
170. *Ibid*, June 1890, No. 15.
171. Foreign Proceedings (Assam), July 1894, Nos. 34-371.
172. *Ibid.*
173. *Ibid.*
174. R. Reid, *op. cit.*, p. 199.
175. Foreign Proceedings (Assam), January 1901, Nos. 37-40.
176. *Ibid.* 177.
177. Lakhimpur Deputy Commissioner's Collection, No. XV of 1908-10, F. 32.
178. *Ibid*, No. XII of 1907-08, F. 59.
179. Political Proceedings (Assam), March 1912, Nos. 149-197.
180. *Ibid*, June 1912, Nos. 140-200.
181. *Ibid.*
182. *Ibid*, December 1914, Nos. 19-54.

183. Administration Report of the Central and Eastern Section, 1917-18.
184. Proceedings of the Governor's Secretariat, Tribal Affairs Deptt., June 1940, Nos. 535-626.
185. G. Barua, *Ahom Buranji*, pp. 231-33.
186. H. Barua, *op. cit.*, p. 185.
187. A. Mackenzie, *History*, p. 47.
188. Secret Proceedings, 29 April 1825, No. 2.
189. Bengal Papers, 23.
190. Political Proceedings (Bengal), 6 March 1837, No. 67.
191. *Ibid.*
192. Foreign Proceedings (Assam), July 1899, Nos. 32-49.
193. Judicial Proceedings (Bengal), 16 July 1857, Nos. 168-72.
194. *Ibid*, 10 September 1857, Nos. 120-23.
195. *Ibid*, 31 December 1857, Nos. 182-84; 25 February 1861, Nos. 351-60.
196. *Ibid*, 16 July 1857, Nos. 168-72.
197. Political Proceedings (Bengal), February 1866, Nos. 11-15.
198. *Ibid*, May 1868, Nos. 56-57.
199. A. Mackenzie, *History*, p. 52.
200. *Ibid.*
201. *Ibid.*
202. Foreign Proceedings (Assam), January 1907, Nos. 13-70.
203. *Ibid*, August 1900, Nos. 46-60.
204. *Ibid.*
205. *Ibid*, July 1899, Nos. 32-49.
206. Political Proceedings (East Bengal & Assam), January 1907, Nos. 13-70.
207. *Ibid*, March 1912, Nos. 47-148.
208. Political Proceedings (Assam), April 1921, Nos. 243-268.
209. *Ibid*, June 1934, Nos. 1300-1329.
210. Administration Report, 1937-38.
211. *Ibid*, 1939-40.
212. G. Barua, *op cit.*, p. 364-65.
213. S.K. Bhuyan, *Tungkhungia Buranji*, p. 120.
214. Political Proceedings (Bengal), 13 March 1835, Nos. 1-8.
215. Political Consultations (India), 15 May 1837, Nos. 12-13.
216. Foreign Political (India), 18 April 1838, Nos. 56-57.
217. *Ibid*, 15 May 1837, Nos. 12-13.
218. Political Proceedings (Bengal), 24 November 1835, No. 11.
219. *Ibid*, 13 March 1835, Nos. 1-8.
220. *Ibid*, 20 February 1839, Nos. 105-110.
221. *Ibid.*
222. *Ibid*, 20 January 1844, No. 61.
223. Foreign Political Proceedings (India), 20 January 1844, Nos. 61-66.
224. Foreign Political Proceedings (Assam), June 1917, Nos. 5-6.
225. *Ibid*, November 1916, Nos. 3-5.
226. *Ibid*, June 1917, Nos. 5-6.

227. S,K. Bhuyan, *op. cit.*, pp. 150-207.
228. A. Mackenzie, *History*, p. 62.
229. *Ibid*, p. 63.
230. *Ibid.*
231. *Ibid.*
232. *Ibid*, p. 64.
233. *Ibid.*
234. *Ibid.*
235. *Ibid.*
236. Political Proceedings (Bengal), 7 May 1830, Nos. 7-8.
237. A. Mackenzie, *History*, p. 66.
238. Political Proceedings (Bengal), September 25/26 1835, Nos. 1-48.
239. *Ibid*, 6 March 1837, Nos. 33-34.
240. A. Mackenzie, *History*, p. 67.
241. *Ibid*, p. 68.
242. Political Proceedings (Bengal), 4 April 1838, Nos. 103-4.
243. *Ibid*, 27 January 1841, Nos. 59-60.
244. *Ibid.*
245. *Ibid*, 7 August 1841, Nos. 187-89.
246. *Ibid*, 1 February 1843, Nos. 162-63.
247. A. Mackenzie, *History*, p. 69.
248. *Ibid*, p. 70.
249. *Ibid*, 9 March 1844, No. 142; 28 April 1848, Nos. 103-4.
250. *Ibid.*
251. *Ibid*, March 1844, Nos. 89-91.
252. Assam Secretariat, File No. 547J of 1887.
253. *Ibid.*, File No. 613J of 1888.
254. Political Proceedings (East Bengal and Assam), May 1910, Nos. 13-40.
255. *Ibid* (Assam), December 1914, Nos. 1-3.
256. Administration Report, 1917-18.
257. *Ibid.*
258. H. Barua, *op. cit.*, pp. 11-12.
259. *Ibid.*
260. A. Mackenzie, *History*, p. 91.
261. *Ibid.*
262. *Ibid*, 24 November, 1835, Nos. 32-33.
263. Political Proceedings (Bengal), 10 April 1837, Nos. 120-123.
264. *Ibid*, 8 May 1837, Nos. 64-66.
265. A. Mackenzie, *History*, p. 89.
266. Revenue Proceedings (Bengal), 8 August 1842, Nos. 125-26.
267. A. Mackenzie, *History*, p. 95.
268. A J.M. Mills' Report, p. ixxxiv.
269. February 1870, Nos. 110-111.
270. A. Mackenzie, *History*, p. 99.
271. Political Proceedings (Assam), August 1874, No. 18.
272. *Ibid*, April 1874, No. 14.

273. A. Mackenzie, *History*, p. 99.
274. *Ibid.*
275 Lakhimpur Deputy Commissioner's Collection, No. XII of 1888, No. 10.
276. *Ibid.*
277. Lakhimpur Deputy Commissioner's Collection, No. XII, F. 8, 1904-08.
278. Lakhimpur Deputy Commissioner's Collection, No. XII of 1904-08; Political Report of 1904-05.
279. *Ibid.*
280. *Ibid*, Collection IX-5 of 1836, sl. 1.
281. *Ibid*, Collection IX-2 of 1937, sl. 1.
282. *Ibid*, Collection No. XII of 1905, F. 1.
283. *Ibid*, Collection XVII of 1915-16, F. 19.
284. Political Proceedings (East Bengal and Assam), April 1910, Nos. 13-40.
285. Lakhimpur Deputy Commissioner's Collection, No. IX of 1937, F. 10.
286. *Ibid*, Collection IX of 1939, F. 15.
287. *Ibid*, Collection IX of 1935, F. 2.
288. *Ibid*, Collection No. IX of 1936, F. 1.
289. Administrative Jurisdiction, p. 1.
290. Political Proceedings (Assam), September, 1931, No. 135.

3

The Inner Line, the Outer Line and the McMahon Line

DRAWING OF BOUNDARY

THE BRITISH came to Assam during the Anglo-Burmese War of 1824-26 and occupied it as a conquered territory. The treaty of Yandabu (1826) did not define the boundary of Assam; it simply stipulated that the Burmese would not interfere in Assam and its dependencies.[1] The Ahom kings whose place the British stepped in did not possess any map to show the boundary of their kingdom, nor did they possess any documentary records giving descriptions of their frontiers. Therefore, the new rulers of Assam did not know the bounds of their newly acquired territories.

The study of the British relations with the hill tribes shows that the extent of the territory of Assam and the hills was not known definitely. The hill tribes, whether dependent on Assam or independent of any political master, claimed tributary payment not on the basis of lands the peasants cultivated but on the very ground of their living in the certain areas.[2] Whether the villages from which the hill chiefs collected levies were within Assam or had been taken possession of by them during the troublesome days of war cannot be definitely ascertained.[3] Then again, these hill tribes in many cases were still in a nomadic state; they were moving from place to place in pursuit of their livelihood.[4]

Yet another problem of the relation of the hill tribes with the Ahom princes remains. The Ahom prince Pratap Singh had granted the right of *posa* to the Bhutias, Akas, Daflas and

Abors. But whether these tribes were independent of or subordinate to the Ahoms cannot be categorically said. We know that during the reign of Gauri Singh an army was sent to punish the Daflas and many were brought down as captives.[5] If we assume that the Daflas were vassals of the Ahom kings (which is, of course, not probable) then also we face another problem, that of the boundary of the Dafla territory.[6] The same problem arises in regard to the territories of the other hill tribes, *e.g.*, the Bhutias, Akas and Abors. Indeed, we do not know the extent of the territories of the different tribes of the North-East Frontier.

The attention of the British was drawn at first towards the boundary between Assam and Burma and between Manipur and Burma. Till the second Anglo-Burmese war the British were anxious to check the Burmese invasion of Assam and, therefore, they came to an agreement with regard to the boundary between Assam and Manipur on the one hand and Burma and Manipur on the other hand. The Burmese claim upon the territories west of the Patkai range extending to Upper Assam and Joypur was turned down, but the Kubo Valley was restored to the Burmese giving a compensation to the ruler of Manipur. The British stressed upon the watershed of the Patkai range as the boundary between Assam and Burma and held fast to this contention till Burma was absorbed in the British Empire after the third Anglo-Burmese war.[7] The boundary between Assam and Burma, however, was not demarcated; in 1967 the Governments of India and Burma entered into an agreement regarding the border between the two countries.[8]

The question of settling the boundary in the north-west between Assam and Bhutan was taken up after the annexation of the Duars to British India. At the time of annexation of the Duars, the boundary between Bhutan and Assam was not defined or demarcated. The Bhutia chiefs sometimes came down and laid claims upon the British territories; at least in some cases they claimed jurisdiction within the British area. The British authorities now decided to settle the boundary problem and delegated Lt. Col. Graham, the Deputy Commissioner of Darrang, to demarcate the boundary between Assam and Bhutan. He completed the task in 1872-73, but he went up to the river Deoshan, beyond the boundary of Assam and

Bhutan, in the Dafla hills.[9] The boundary between Assam and Bhutan was agreed upon by the Bhutia and English authorities, but the boundary beyond was not an international boundary as the tribes living there were neither paramount nor vassals of any sovereign master.[10] Therefore, the boundary of Assam in the north on the side of Tibet remained to be agreed upon between the two countries.

It has been observed in the preceding chapter that the British authorities had resumed the territories of the different tribes on the foot of their hills on condition of paying them some blackmail. The tribes withdrew within the hills but then where the territory of the hill tribes began was not known. Lt. Col. Graham had demarcated the southern boundary of those tribes who came down and agreed to accept the line as the dividing line between Assam and their territories. But the question of jurisdiction of the British authorities was not settled. E.J. Monahan, the Secretary to the Chief Commissioner of Assam, wrote to the Government of India that the Boundary Commissioner Lt. Col. Graham had demarcated the boundary of Assam up to the river Baroe but the boundary beyond Deoshan could not be regarded as valid as no treaty was entered into in this regard. He observed, "the agreement which we have with the Bhutias of Towang, who are dependent on Tibet, and with the independent Bhutias and Akas, do not provide for any delimitation of the territory nor have we any such agreement with the Dafla tribes further east. There exist some treaties with some of the Abor tribes which distinctly mention that British territory extends to the foot of the hills. The Chief Commissioner has ascertained that the frontage of the Abor territory covered by their agreements extends from a point near Mesaki on the west to Nizamghat on the Dibong on the east. After crossing the Brahmaputra, it follows approximately the Daphabum range to the south and then turning south-west follows the crest to Patkai range as far as the north-east corner of Manipur territory. But the Chief Commissioner can find no definite authority for the adoption of Daphabum range and the crest of the Patkai range as the 'outer line' of British India."[11]

THE INNER LINE

The problem of the boundary was further complicated by the specification of the Inner Line from 1875. By the beginning of the seventies of the nineteenth century, the economy of Assam had become promising and trade and industry had made a good start. Tea, petroleum, coal, rubber and wood became flourishing industries and elephant-catching and ivory were engaging growing attention. Besides, the revenue of the Assam valley increased so as to provide for good surplus and huge fallow lands could yield more if tenants were invited to take them up. But the economy depended upon the Administration's capacity to maintain law and order in the province. All the districts of the Assam valley bordered on some hills inhabited by the tribes. The unrestricted intercourse between the people who had come for commerce and who knew very little about the tribes led to many disputes and sometimes these took violent dimensions.[12] Moreover, the tribes driven into the hills sometimes had to fall upon the plains to draw their supplies. The problem of regulation of the intercourse between the tribes and ryots and businessmen of the Assam plains, therefore, drew the attention of the Administration. The hill tribes problem forced them to create a barrier between the hills and the plains which would reduce contact and consequently friction between the civilised valley-dwellers and the primitive hill tribes. This was done by a Regulation in 1873.[13]

Regulation I of 1873, called a "Regulation for the peace and Good Government of certain districts on the Eastern Frontier," commonly known as the Inner Line Regulation of 1873, authorised the Local Government, with the previous approval of the Governor-General in Council, to prescribe and from time to time alter, a line, to be called the 'Inner Line', in each or any of the districts of Assam.[14] The term 'Inner Line', however, originated from the suggestion of Arthur Hobhouse who observed in his draft for the Regulation of 1873 that the line to be prescribed under the Regulation might be called 'Inner Line'.[15] The Local Government was also empowered to prohibit all British subjects, or any class of British subjects, or any person residing in or passing through such districts, from going beyond such Line without a pass under the hand and seal of the executive officer or such officer as might be authorised to grant such pass. The Local Government, however, was given the power to suspend or vary this prohibition from time to time. Any person who went beyond the Inner Line fixed according to the above process, without a pass, was liable to conviction before a Magistrate of first or second class and to a fine not exceeding Rs. 100 for the first offence; for each subsequent offence there could be a fine not exceeding Rs. 500 or simple or rigorous imprisonment for a term not exceeding three months or both.[16]

The object of the Inner Line Regulation was to keep outside the boundary all "tracts over which semi-savage tribes wandered or in which they lived", for their free intercourse with the people of the plains might lead to complications. It was clearly expressed that Government of India would not be responsible for life and property of the people beyond such Line and, if necessary, people might not be allowed to go beyond the Line. The Government of India had suggested to the Government of Bengal that while prescribing such Line, they should see that the Line corresponded to the natural features of the country, and if there was no such feature it was to coincide with obligatory points like crossing of a road. The place where a road crossed the Line was to be clearly shown in maps, and if the area where it ran had not been mapped, arrangement should be made for topographical survey as well. If any tea garden was there on the frontier, that should be brought within the Line, if possible, for avoiding possible complications.[17] Commerce beyond the Inner Line could be carried on pass basis, that is, people desirous of capturing elephants, cutting wood, collecting forest products like rubber could carry on their trade in the tribal area getting pass from the government, but they would be subject to payment of tolls to the tribes inhabiting the region where such trade was to be carried on.[18]

Some conclusions may be drawn from an examination of the provisions of the Inner Line Regulation of 1873. In the first place, the British government defined a boundary up to which it would exercise its authority and uphold law and order; it would decline responsibility beyond, and there the tribes would be left to themselves. Secondly, it did not mention whether the tribes living beyond the Inner Line were under its political control; nor did it accept any paramount power of exercising control over them. Finally, free intercourse of the people of British India with the tribes was restricted, but no restriction upon the movement of the tribes was imposed. The tribes were allowed to fish and hunt on both sides of the Inner Line.[19] People from within the administered districts of Assam were allowed to go within the Inner Line and even beyond with pass, but the businessmen had to pay blackmail or tolls to the tribes for collection of wood or other forest products from the territories which were regarded as outside the so-called boundary of Assam.[20] The Miju Mishmis even collected tolls from the Hindu pilgrims visiting the Parasuram Kund as it was regarded as lying outside the administered area.[21]

For the first time, the Inner Line was notified for the Lakhimpur district on 3 September 1875, applying Regulation I of 1873.[22] The Deputy Commissioner of Lakhimpur, Major W.S. Clarke, submitted his final proposal, after revising his original proposal of 1873, on 22 May 1875.[23] In his original proposal of December 1873 for the south-eastern and eastern part of the Inner Line of the Lakhimpur district he had proposed to include within the Line the three tea gardens of Taurack, Hukanjuri and Namsang which were held by M/s. Minto & Company on a lease from the Namsangia Naga Chief and which were considered to be outside British territory; those were intended to be brought within the British jurisdiction on agreement by the Government from the Nagas and then leased to Messers Minto & Company. But then the Line would cut off a tongue of the hilly country lying between the Disang (Dilli) and Namsang rivers. The Line running down the Namsang river to its mouth, or its confluence with the Boori Dihing, would go up the course of the Boori Dihing as far as the mouth of the Makumpani, which ran southward from the hills into the Dihing; it would then deviate from the natural boundary, but it was supposed to be the most practicable line. The Line was then to run down the course of the Tirap to where it fell into the Boori Dihing, and then be marked by the Boori Dihing to where the Kherampani fell into it, then up the Kherampani to the Noa Dihing, and along that stream to the Brahmaputra.[24]

To the north the Line should take the course of the Rajghur Ali, from the Darrang boundary to the Sisi river; thence by as direct a line as practicable to the Dimu guard. Thence it should be marked by a frontier path as straight as circumstances might allow as far as the Poba military guard; thence by a frontier path running along the line of the Brahmaputra to Lallimukh; thence by a line to Dibongmukh by the Debong to the Debong guard; thence by the path communicating between the Debong and the Dikrang guards; thence, by the general line of the frontier guards, to the revenue survey masonry pillar on the Brahmaputra.[25]

But the Chief Commissioner of Assam instructed Major Clarke to redraw his proposal keeping in view that the boundary should be as far as practicable coterminous with the revenue survey, and the boundary between ordinary and political jurisdiction should be consistent.[26] It was practically impossible to suggest a line through a natural line in a country unsurveyed, practically uninhabited and covered by dense jungle. Therefore, in his revised proposal, Clarke suggested small modifications. The Line which he finally drew up would take the course of the Dihing, in the south-eastern section, as it was a good natural boundary though it kept outside the Inner Line the coal-fields of Tirap and Namdang, situated in the neighbourhood of peaceful and small Naga villages. The tea gardens of Namsang, Hukanjuri and Taurack, however, were brought within the Inner Line as an agreement with the Namsangia chief was being processed to bring the latter under direct agreement with the government, and arrangement for revenue survey was provided for. The tea gardens of Joyhing and Harmati were also brought within the Inner Line. In the original proposal the Line was to adhere to the boundary of the ordinary jurisdiction, and deviation from such boundary was proposed under the orders of the Commissioner. The new line thus would pass from Dimu guard to the Debong river; the revenue survey boundary, and the boundary between ordinary and political jurisdiction, ran from Dimu to Boori Sooti, and down the Sooti to the Brahmaputra, and then along the right bank of the Brahmaputra to the mouth of the Debong.[27]

The revised proposal of Major Clarke was forwarded and recommended to the Government of India by the Chief

Commissioner of Assam and the Government of India notified the Line on 3 September 1875 in the *Gazetteer of India.* The Line as notified ran as follows :—[28]

> Commencing on the south-east of the district at the Desang (Dilli), from the Taurack garden, on the Desang river, along the path leading to Hukanjuri garden on the Namsang river; thence along the Namsang river, to its junction with the Boori Dihing along the course of the Boori Dihing to where the Kherampani runs into it; thence along the Kherampani to its junction with the Noa Dihing; along the Noa Dihing to where it joins the Brahmaputra.
>
> North of the Brahmaputra, commencing from the Darrang boundary, along the Rajgurh Ali to where it meets the Dihing to where it is met on its other or left bank by the Rajgurh Ali, to the Rangadi; thence including within the line the Joyhing tea-garden, along the Rajgurh Ali, so far as it is practicable; and thence along the base of the Abor Miri hills to the Sisi river; and thence to be marked by as straight a line as may be practicable to the Dimu guard; thence by a frontier path, taken as straight as practicable, to the Poba guard; and from thence by a frontier path to Lallimukh, where the Lalli falls into the Brahmaputra; thence along the Brahmaputra river to Debongmukh, along the Debong to the Debong guard; thence by the path connecting the Debong and Dikrang guards; thence along the general line of frontier guards and the boundary of the revenue survey to the revenue survey masonry pillar on the Brahmaputra, and thence by the Brahmaputra to Noadihingmukh, the termination of the Inner Line on the east.

The drawing of the Inner Line of the Darrang district did not prove as difficult as the case was with the Lakhimpur Inner Line. The boundary of the district and the hill tribes had already been demarcated by Col. Graham in 1873 along the Daflagurh which was a continuation of the Rajgurh Ali of Lakhimpur. The Deputy Commissioner proposed the same line, stretching it a little between boundary pillar No. 160 and the Daflagurh so as to include within the Inner Line the tea garden of Singlijan which was held under waste land grant No. 18

in Darrang district. The Line commenced from the eastern boundary of the district of Kamrup, that is, from pillar No. 98 on the Bor Nadi, and then followed in an easterly direction the southern boundaries of Bhutan (including the tracts of Kuriapara and Charduar Bhutia), and of the Aka and Dafla Hills, as defined by the revenue survey in the years 1872-73-74-75, and demarcated by pillars Nos. 98 to 160, inclusive. From pillar No. 160 the Line ran in a south-easterly direction to the point where the Balum river cut the northern boundary of the Singlijan tea waste land grant No. 18. Thence the line followed the eastern boundary of the Singlijan grant No. 18 to the point where the boundary cut the Daflagurh. Thence the Line followed the Daflagurh to a point on the More Sessa river being the north-westerly extremity of the Inner Line of the Lakhimpur district, as notified on 30 September 1875 in the *Gazetteer of India.*[29] The Line was notified on 8 March 1876.[30]

THE OUTER LINE

The origin of the term Outer Line, unlike that of the Inner Line, is vague and could not be traced. A note of the Foreign Department, Political Branch, goes like this: "The limits of the district were at first thrown very far forward, too far to enable us to exercise jurisdiction all the way up to them; so it became necessary to draw a line up to which we intend to work. This was the Inner Line. The limits of the district as originally proposed became the Outer Line...."[31] So the Inner Line passed through the British territory and marked the boundary of the ordinary and political jurisdictions of the district officers. But the Outer Line was purposely kept undefined so as to enable them to bring any tract of territory within the jurisdiction of the district officers as and when necessary. "The Outer Line is purposely left indefinite, so that we can advance the Inner Line to any extent circumstances may render necessary."[32] So far as the international border is concerned, the British authorities did not care at all till the advent of the Chinese across Rima in 1910.

Thus the Inner Line was the line up to which the British officers exercised regular jurisdiction. Between that Inner Line and the originally accepted boundary of Assam which in course of time began to be called Outer Line, the British government claimed some sort of sovereignty, but did not exercise any regular jurisdiction except some sort of personal influence. Beyond it lay the territories of the tribes over which they did not acknowledge any paramount power. The limits of this Outer Line were purposely kept undefined and indefinite so that the Line could be advanced to any extent that circumstances might render necessary. The Lt. Governor of Eastern Bengal and Assam, Sir Lancelot Hare, wrote to the Government of India that the boundary of the Lakhimpur district was wholly undefnied and unknown till 1875 and it was impossible to say how far the British jurisdiction extended.[33] While proposing the Inner Line in 1873 the Deputy Commissioner of Lakhimpur tried to include all the existing lands granted under the Waste Land Grant Rules and proposed a line beyond which British jurisdiction should not be extended at that time. But he made it clear in his notes that over all territories beyond that Line the British authority would be indefinite but sufficient for all purposes, and there could be no dispute as to British authority beyond the Inner Line. He did not, of course, like to propose any Outer Line.[34]

The issue of the Outer Line was very nicely put in Lord Hardinge's despatch of December 22, 1910. He wrote, "I think I hardly brought out with sufficient distinctness one important consideration which should induce us to press forward beyond the limits by which under a self-denying ordinance our frontier is at present limited. We only now claim suzerainty up to the foot of the hills. We have an Inner Line and an Outer Line. Up to the Inner Line we administer in the ordinary way. Between the Inner Line and the Outer Line we only administer politically. That is our Political Officers exercise very loose iurisdiction, and to prevent troubles with frontier tribes passes are required for our subjects who want to cross the Inner Line. The country between the two lines is very sparsely inhabited and is mostly dense jungle."[35]

But the jurisdiction of the Chief Commissionership of Assam was never defined specifically nor was it ever demarcated. The Inner Line which was specified from time to time in different districts by applying Regulation I of 1873 did not in any way solve the problem of the boundary. The Inner Line was jurisdictional, and not a territorial limit. Godfrey, the Deputy Commissioner of Lakhimpur, wrote : "I don't know that the limits of the Chief Commissionership have ever been specified so that we know precisely what the area within which the acts of the Governor General in Council are in force. I have been inclined to think that the Inner Line marked the boundary of our regular jurisdiction, that is, our courts of law . . . but the Inner Line Regulation is not one that defines jurisdiction. The Chief Commissionership of Assam extends up to the borders of China and Tibet and Burma."[36] He further writes, "We have, of course, got an admitted political control over the border tribes which emanate from, and is dependent upon, our being possessed of superior force, and so we command obedience to such orders as may be passed by our officers in their political capacity: it has accordingly been my opinion that the Deputy Commissioner has beyond the Inner Line a general political authority resting upon force, but no law as such can be enforced upon the inhabitants of those tracts."[37]

The relations of the British Government with the border tribes bear out the reality of the situation. We have seen that though the Brititish authority did not penetrate into the territories of the Bhutias of the present Kameng district, the British pursued the Aka, Dafla, Abor, Mishmi, Khampti and Singpho tribes as and when necessary. Troops were sent beyond the Outer Line and the Government exacted fines, arrested criminals, destroyed villages of the tribes and were thus free to deal with them. The Dalai Lama and his ministers gave the Government of India to understand that these tribes were under the British by their consent.[38] Of course, the government always shrunk from the responsibility of administering these tribal tracts as it was expensive. Several officers advocated the imposition as direct administration on these hill tracts. Col. Hopkinson clearly wrote to the Government of India that by the anexation of Assam the British Government had undertaken an obligation to administer and civilise these tribes.[39] But the Government scrupulously avoided the responsibility.

The issue of the delineation of the border and assertion of paramountcy over the border tribes became imperative after the appearance of the Chinese on the other side of the border. The Chinese general Chao Exh-feng having consolidated his imperial power in Szechuan and Sikiang province of China made thrust into Tibet through the eastern marshes. A report of Chinese concentration beyond the Abor hills was reported as early as 1908. Then a fresh force appeared beyond the Mishmi hills in 1910. Though the recommendations of the Local Government for bringing the frontier tribes under administration on humanitarian and logical grounds could be flouted for pecuniary considerations, the prospect of a Chinese thrust into the valley of the Brahmaputra, full of British capitalist enterprise, could not be ignored. The hill of the tribes under Chinese control, influence or occupation would render the plains below vulnerable, and if the Dragon was to be resisted at all that should be done before it crossed the hills and came down to the plains. The unspecified and undemarcated nature of the North-East Frontier boundary made the title over the range of the Eastern Himalayas disputed. Therefore, the whole frontier policy came under fresh examination and orientation.

The Political Officer at Sadiya, on receiving the information of the Chinese crossing the border, sent a message to the Government and sought permission to declare that the Mishmis were under the political control of the British Government. As a matter of fact, the Mishmis looked towards the British as their masters and from time to time sought permission to settle on the plain land below their hills. The British officers also had from time to time gone to the Mishmi Hills and taken prisoners from among the offending tribes. Yet the Administration had avoided responsibility for the Mishmis. So when Kugno, the Mishmi Chief, approached the Assistant Political Officer and reported that the Chinese had asked them to construct a bridle path down the valley through their hills, the latter sought permission from the Government to declare that Mishmis were under British control. The Lt. Governor of Eastern Bengal and Assam saw wisdom in his report and recommended to the Government of India the proposal of the Assistant Political Officer, though the Commissioner of the Assam Valley districts had declared in 1907 that the Mishmis were never under the control of the government.[40] The Government of India, though much concerned at the advent of the Chinese, was hesitant.

Meanwhile the Chinese had withdrawn, the Tibetans had declared their independence of China, and China herself was in the throes of a revolutionary upsurge. Williamson, who visited the Mishmi Hills along the Lohit valley and proceeded up to Walong, recommended to open up the hills to Walong by constructing a bridle path along the Lohit valley and to appoint for each of the tribes in the Mishmi and Abor Hills some influential man as British agent to report on the developments on the borders and look after the upkeep of the proposed bridle tracks. He recommended the name of the Mishmi men who were to be appointed and the Government accepted his proposal.[41]

But the unsettled state of the boundary could no longer be neglected. Younghusband had laid emphasis on the settlement of the boundary between India and Tibet.[42] The success of the Russians in Mongolia and reports of their activities in Tibet further highlighted the problems of the frontier. It was also apprehended that China under a Republican Government would be more powerful and aggressive than under the Manchus. The Political Officer at Kalimpong, Charles Bell, in his report on the developments in Tibet spelled out the consequences of the rise of the Chinese power and suggested the settlement of the India-Tibet boundary and bringing of the border tribes within the Indian side of the frontier under the jurisdiction of the British Government.[43]

Bell clearly pointed out that the Government of India could no longer avoid the problem of the North-East Frontier. The military reports on the North-East Frontier made it clear that the Government of India never apprehended the slightest chance of invasion of Assam by a civilised military power and consequently no strategic plan, no defence arrangement and no organisation whatseover were ever provided to repel such an invasion. As it would not be possible to keep China out of Tibet, it would be of vital importance to keep China and other powers out of the narrow strip of territory between India and Tibet.[44]

The natural corollary of such a policy as contemplated by Bell was that the Government of India should maintain inviolate the territory that intervened between Assam and Tibet. Two things, he thought, would be essential to implement this policy. First, China should not be allowed to enter into the territory. Secondly, no Indian or British vested interest should be allowed inside the territory as far as possible. But he did not advocate the assumption by the Government of the responsibility of internal administration of the territory of the tribes at all. The reason for not allowing the Indian or British vested interests in the region was that by allowing such interests to grow up in the zone, the Government would assume some sort of obligation to protect them. Again, such a course would destory the buffer which the Government of India should maintain between the two countries and create those difficulties which the Government wanted to remove. Moreover, the management of tribal affairs by the tribes themselves was very much prized by the tribal people. A guarantee that there would be no interference in the internal affairs would win the hearts of the tribal communities as in the case of Bhutan.[45]

Bell in his letter cited the reports of the growing public concern for the developments in the North-East Frontier. He quoted from the newspaper *Englishman* of August 1910 which wrote that while the "Secretary of State for Foreign Affairs and the Secretary of State for India were content with philosophising along the lines of radical thought"...the growing pressure on North-East subjected India to serious dangers". "There is a vast region of forests, hills and rolling downs inhabited by the Daflas, Miris, Abors and Mishmis through which access can be had into the Assam valley without too much difficulty. It will not be long before Chinese activities and ambition manifest themselves in that region at present practically unregarded by us.[46]

Bell had gathered intelligence from the Tibetan ministers in Darjeeling that they regarded the northern and north-eastern tribes of the Assam frontiers as under British suzerainty rather than under Chinese or Tibetan subjection. They thought that the tribes had been conquered by the British. He apprehended that the Chinese would not be content with such a view as they were making claims of suzerainty and sovereignty where ever possible. Therefore, explorations, survey, cultivation of friendship with the tribal chiefs and arrangements of political control over the area which were claimed by the British were imperative. Control through the Deputy Commissioners of the Assam valley districts over the tribal territories would not be sufficient. He held that separate Political Officers who would serve for a long period should be appointed.[47]

The lines of action proposed by the Political Officer, Charles Bell, were similar to those recommended by the General Staff of the Army regarding military policy on the North-East Frontier from the Bhutan border to the west of Burma as set forth in their Memorandum. It admitted that under an improved administration or in alliance with some Western country, China might in future become a formidable military power, and she appeared to have wished to regain effective control over her dominions bordering on India. They were afraid that China might wish to recover Burma which she considered as a Chinese province and which they thought, had been forcibly taken away from her. In case of the Chinese move to India, she would exert pressure on the North-East Frontier and with a view to carrying out that policy, she must first open out some of the undeveloped territory in her possession up to the Indian border. (This was surprisingly found to be true in 1962). They apprehended that this could be done either by working through Tibet towards Nepal but more likely through Uunan towards Burma and Assam, as the latter seemed to offer greater advantage and less difficulties.[48]

Under such circumstances, the Army General Staff recommended that the first concern of the Indian Government should be to obtain such a frontier as would render incursion into India by the Chinese as difficult as possible. For that purpose, the mountainous region and the almost impassable mountains on the North-East of Assam and Burma would offer the greatest advantage. The natural mountain frontier, they suggested, was the watershed of the Brahmaputra and Irrawaddy valleys extending from Bhutan in the west to the Salween-Irrawaddy divide. The Memorandum recommended extension of the Government's hold and control over the tribes inhabiting the region and effective occupation of the valley of the Zyul-chu as far as the Chinese outpost near Rima. If the Government of India did not do that, the Chinese would gradually occupy these valleys and with the aid of the industrious population obtain in time a base of supplies on this side of the watershed which would greatly facilitate their further advance into India. The Memorandum also recommended to inform China that the Indian frontier lay across the natural line of the Himalayas from the border of Bhutan to Burma. It further suggested the setting up of Military Intelligence posts all along the Frontier.[49]

The Staff Memorandum, on strategic grounds, opposed the proposal of railway link with China through the Mishmi Hills from Sadiya to Batang in the Chinese province of Szechuan or any plan of connecting China through Upper Burma as these would ultimately facilitate the movement of the Chinese troops.[50]

Meanwhile another development had occurred which to some extent influenced the course of action in regard to the frontier to be followed as per suggestion of Charles Bell, the General Staff of the Army and the Government of Eastern Bengal and Assam. Noel Williamson, who had crossed the Outer Line and penetrated into the interior of the Abor Hills contrary to the orders of the government, was murdered together with his companion Dr. Gregorson. This revealed the enmity of the Abors towards the British which again meant the possibility of easy Chinese penetration into the Abor Hills, through the Khams province of Tibet across Tum-La and Shoka-La. Therefore, with a view to punishing the offending Abor hills to delineate the boundary between India and China-Tibet, an expedition was sent to the Abor hills. Almost simultaneously, teams were sent to the Mishmi and Dafla hills for survey and exploration.[51]

Meanwhile the Government of Lord Minto had addressed a letter to the Secretary of State urging the settlement of the India-Tibetan border. They suggested that a "representation should be made at Peking pointing out that disorders on our border would not be viewed with indifference by us" and "subject to further information being obtained in regard to the nature and extent of the territories of the tribes and their position *vis-a-vis* China and Tibet, etc., that the external boundary should run, approximately from the east of the wedge-shaped portion of Tibetan territory known as the Towang district which runs down to the British frontier north of Odalguri in a north-easterly direction to latitude 29° longitude 94°, thence along latitude 29° to longitude 96°, thence in a south-easterly direction the Zayul Chu valley to the Zayul Chu-Irrawaddy watershed, and then along that watershed until it joins Irrawaddy-Salween watershed."[52]

The results of the surveys and explorations carried on by the Abor expedition, the Mishmi Mission and the Miri Mission were the basis of the recommendations of the Political Officers of the Western Section and the Central and Eastern Sections, G.A. Nevill and W.C.M. Dundas respectively, as well as the Chief of the General Staff. All unanimously recommended that the boundary between the two countries should be the water-parting of the Sanpo (Brahmaputra) and the Subansiri and their tributaries which were co-terminus with the traditional, customary and geographical boundaries between India and Tibet. The Chief of the General Staff pointed out that the results of the survey of the Miri Mission were unsatisfactory and could not be the basis of a proposal for fixing a boundary between the two countries. But then the results of the survey could be combined with the data collected from the traders and other sources and on the basis of that he suggested that the high snow mountain range between Longitude 94°, Latitude 28°25″ to Longitude 93°, Latitude 28°20″ without break, with peaks rising from 13000 to 16000 feet, could be a well-defined boundary between India and Tibet beyond the Western Section of the North-East Frontier.[53] It may be pointed out here that this line was later on pushed back further towards the north-west to include the Tawang tracts after the explorations and surveys conducted by Bailey and Nevill in 1913-14, as pointed out by Lamb.[54] For the Central and Eastern Sections of the North-East Frontier, the Chief of Staff suggested the Pemakai range and the Dibong and the Lohit watersheds, together with their tributaries respectively, as the boundary between India and Tibet.[55]

Recommendations of G.A. Nevill for the Western Section of the North-East Frontier boundary between India and Tibet was the Miri Section boundary suggested by the Chief of the General Staff. Nevill suggsted a line south of Se La and he was supported by W.C.M. Dundas.[56] Both of them suggested the line south of Se La as shown in the map of Alaister Lamb. The line recommended by Nevill commenced from Dho Shong La on the headwaters of the Siyom in the neighbourhood of Lungu La to the mountain range Sha Gam La through the peaks, 19423, 18056, 18813, 17279, 19026, 21276, 20950, 21488 and 20860 to Saila pass (Se-La) and then following mountain range to 13550 to Bhutan border.[57]

For the boundary between the Central and Eastern Sections of the North-East Frontier (the Abor and Mishmi Sections of the General Staff Note) and Tibet, W.C.M. Dundas recommended a line, beginning from the tri-junction of India, Burma and China at Talok La in the west, through the Dichu to its confluence with the Lohit : thence down the Lohit to the confluence of the Tor Chu : thence up the Tor Chu to its lowest sources : thence in a north-westerly direction along the range which forms the watershed between the Rong Thod Chu and the rivers flowing into Assam, that is to say, the Dou, Delei, Tiding, Ithun, Tangon, Dri, and tributaries past the Glei Dakhru, Hadigra, Dakhru, Kaya and Aguia passes to peak 19557 at Latitude 29°27″ approximately: thence along the same range in south-westerly direction to and the head of the Andhra and its tributaries and past Yonggypla Andhra La to peak 13838 at the source of the southern tributary of the Chimdru Chu : thence north along the subsidiary feature forming the watershed between the Chimdru Chu and the smaller streams training into the Dihong as far as the confluence of the Chimdru Chu : thence up the Dihong to the confluence of the Nyalam chu (also called the Nyalam Thangpo) : thence up the Nyalam chu to its source below the Nam La on the main Himalayan range : thence in south-westerly direction along the main range which was the watershed between the Taang Po and the rivers flowing into the Dihong past the Doshang La, Deyan La, Lushe La and Lungma La.[58]

The Line suggested by Dundas included some villages established in recent times by some Tibetan Monbas (Menbas). Therefore he proposed an alternative line if the government wanted to exclude the Memba tracts. The line commencing from "peak No. 13838 in a westerly direction round the source of the Nyigong (also known as the Yen-sangchu) and down to the spur between Korbo and Mongku villages to the Dihong ; up in Dihong to the confluence of the Nugong; thence up that stream to the Deyanla on this main Himalayan range, past the Damnyala, Lushela Nungmala and around the headwaters of the Siyom, the point where it was suggested that the boundary between Tivet and the W. Sati of the North-East Frontier should begin."[59]

Meanwhile Chao had occupied Lhasa but failed to subjugate Tibet. Active resistance to the Chinese continued in the south-east while in Lhasa the people resisted the Chinese in every way they could. The Tibetan National Assembly adopted a sullen and sometimes hostile attitude towards the Chinese forces.[60] The Dalai Lama in exile in India tried to obtain British and even Russian help against the Chinese, but to no effect.[61] But before the Chinese could come to any conclusion on the Tibetan issue, the Emperor and the Manchu dynasty were swept away by the Chinese Revolution of 1911. The effect of the Revolution was immediately felt in Tibet. The Chinese garrison in Lhasa mutinied and broke up into unruly mobs. The Tibetans rose against the disorganised Chinese and with a zeal of hatred and vengeance slaughtered thousands of them.[62] The Dalai Lama returned to reassert his authority in Tibet and declared his independence of China.[63] The Mongols had also declared their independence similarly and concluded a convention of mutual help and cooperation for meeting internal and external dangers with Russia which was confirmed by the Russo-Chinese agreement of 1913. This was followed by a Mongol-Tibet treaty.[64]

On the other hand the Anglo-Tibetan Treaty of 1904 concluded after the Younghusband Mission was made ineffective by the Anglo-Chinese Adhesion Agreement of 1906 and the Anglo-Russian Convention of 1907. "A disorganised Tibet has already proved a direct menace to India and to our broader imperial interests", writes Henry McMahon.[65] The Japanese subjects were in intimate relations with the high authorities in Lhasa. Russian consular students were receiving training in Kumbum Monastery on the Tibetan frontier; a Russian Buriat and a Japanese were training the Tibetan troops.[66] The collapse of Chinese power and the prospect of Russian intervention and intrigue changed the whole situation. The Mongol-Tibet treaty and the Urga Convention gave the Russians an indirect but real basis of intervention in Tibetan affairs. The chance of Tibet undergoing the fate of Outer Mongolia was imminent.[67]

The British were in a dialemma. They could either convert Tibet into a thinly veiled British protectorate as was the case with Nepal, Bhutan and Sikkim as requested by the Dalai Lama when he was in India.[68] But the British had declined the offer for two reasons. It would have extended the boundary by 2000 miles or so, enclosing 500,000 square miles of territory mostly high ranges and unpopulated, lacking utterly in communication, and brought her face to face with China and Russia. It would also have given the Russians a chance to modify the Anglo-Russian Convention of 1907 and to put forward inconvenient demands. Secondly, the British could have helped Tibet to be an independent country. But it was quite certain that Tibet could not stand alone without the help of any foreign power and would fall an easy victim to Chinese aggression. There was also a risk of Tibet throwing herself into the arms of the Russians which it was the primary aim of the British policy to resist and eliminate. Therefore, a message was given to the Dalai Lama on his return to Tibet that the Government of India desired him to regain internal autonomy under the Chinese suzerainty.[69] A third alternative was to allow China to re-conquer Tibet and constitute it into a Chinese province. But that would have left the possibility of intrigues and incursions into British territories in India and Burma.

Therefore neither China's policy of considering Tibet as a province nor the Dalai Lama's rejection of Chinese suzerainty suited the British. They wanted to keep the fiction of China's position of suzerain as the Russians had done in Outer Mongolia because it provided China with some legal primacy while depriving her of any effective control.[70] Therefore, on 17 August 1912 they proposed to the new Republic of China that Tibet's status be negotiated on the basis of the situation which had existed before the Younghusband Mission.[71] The Chinese were disturbed by the success of the Russians in Mongolia and the weakness of their own Government; further, the prospect of direct British negotiation with Tibet ultimately force them after much reluctance not only to negotiate Tibet's status with the British but to accept a representative of Lhasa as a co-equal plenipotentiary in the negotiations.[72] The acceptance of an equal representative was in fact an important part of the British diplomatic plan. It was calculated that Tibet's full participation in the negotiations would constitute evidence of its autonomy.

MACMAHON LINE

The conference began at Simla, the summer capital of India on 6 October 1913. Sir Henry McMahon was the British plenipotentiary and was assisted by Charles A. Bell who had a thorough knowledge of the Tibetan affairs and the Indo-Tibetan border. China was represented by Ivan Chen. Tibet sent Lonchen Shatra, a leading minister of the Government of the Dalai Lama.[73] The Tibetan concern at the conference was to get an admission of their independence which they had declared after the eviction of the Chinese troops and officials. They wanted the cancellation of the Anglo-Chinese Convention of 1906; they also desired to have a fresh Trade Regulation. At the same time, they proposed a re-definition of the Sino-Tibetan frontier so as to include all Tibetan people within the Tibetan boundary. Lonchen Shatra put forward a stupendous mass of materials in support of his claims: revenue records; list of houses, officials and headmen; charters, agreements and other materials relating to disputed districts.[74] In reply, Iban Chen in utter panic ignored all historical records and practices and emphasized only conquest of Tibet by Chingiz Khan and the last victory of Chao in support of his claims. In recognition of the claim to sovereignty over Tibet, Ivan Chen demanded the right to station an Amban with 2000 troops in Tibet and to control military and foreign affairs of the country. As for the frontier, the Chinese claimed a line only some sixty miles east of Lhasa.[75]

Under the circumstances both Iban Chen and Lonchen Shatra requested McMahon to suggest some definite solution of the problem, which they would refer to their governments without delay. McMahon had anticipated this impasse; he had already worked out in consultation with London a solution which was likely to afford satisfaction to the contending parties and at the same time accord with Indian interest. This solution envisaged the division of Tibet into two zones, to be called Inner and Outer Tibet (as viewed from China), on the lines of Inner and Outer Mongolia created by Russians. Outer Tibet was to be the wider area to the east of the historic Yangtse frontier, over which the Tibetan Government had for many centuries exercised complete jurisdiction. Here, the Chinese were not to send their troops, nor station any civil or military personnel, nor establish any colonies. But as a symbol of their suzerainty, they might install at Lhasa an Amban to look after the Chinese interests. Inner Tibet was to be the broad peripheral area of Tibet extending in the north to the Atlya Tagh range and in the east to the old provincial borders of Kansu and Szechuan in which the population was mainly Tibetan by race and religion. China would have full administrative authority over this zone, subject to the provision that it could not be made a Chinese province and, in the selection and appointment of high priests of the monasteries control was to be vested in the Lhasa authorities. McMahon spelt out this solution in the form of a draft convention and the proposed boundaries of Outer and Inner Tibet were shown on the accompanying map.[76]

Both the parties were dissatisfied with this solution; but the atmosphere was one of strain and anxiety, and it was considered desirable to avoid an immediate break down. All the three plenipotentiaries accepted the draft convention prepared by McMahon and initialled the revised convention on 27 April, 1914.[77] The map signed by both the Chinese and Tibetan representatives was initialled by McMahon who congratulated the delegates on the excellent work they had done.[78] The Chinese Government, however, disavowed the action of its plenipotentiary on 29 April and declined to recognise the settlement.[79]

Simultaneously with the tripartite negotiations, two other bipartite negotiations were conducted between Great Britain and Tibet during the Simla Conference. The first related to the delineation of a boundary alignment between India and Tibet to the north of Assam, and the second to a new Trade Agreement between these two countries.[80] On the Indian side, C.A. Bell, the Political Officer of Sikkim, was entrusted with a task of conducting negotiations with Lonchen Shatra on the border issue. The broad principle followed in the delineation of the Indo-Tibetan border was the principle of watershed usually followed in demarcating borders in inaccessible mountainous regions, which was followed in suggesting the boundary of the North-East Frontier by the Chief of the General Staff, Nevill and Dundas.[81] In determining the Sikkim-Tibet frontier in 1890, the crest of the mountain range separating the waters flowing into the Sikkim Tista and its affluents from the waters flowing into the Tibetan Mochu and northward into other rivers of Tibet was the determinant.[82] The same principle of watershed was accepted as the basis of demarcating the border between Inner Tibet and Outer Tibet by Ivan Chen.[83]

Although watershed was generally kept in view in determining the alignment, a multiplicity of factors—historical, ethnic, geographical and strategic—were also considered. While anxious to secure a frontier which would be consistent with India's strategic requirements, Henry McMahon and Charles Bell tried to exclude what was undisputedly Tibetan territory. Moreover, in Subansiri region, the two holy places of Tibetan pilgrimage, Tso Sharpo and Tsari Sharpo, together with the village of Migyitun, wherefrom the pilgrimage started, were kept north of the McMahon Line to enable the Tibetan pilgrims[84] smooth and unrestricted entry into those places disregarding the watershed principle. Therefore, though based principally on watershed, the boundary line as it emerged in the Simla Agreement was drawn "on a combination of ridge, watershed and high crest," as aptly pointed out by Ekelen.[85]

To protect the Tibetan private ownership in some estates south of the McMahon Line, Lonchen Shatra said to Bell : "The Potala Trung-Yik Chenpo and the Loseling college of Drepung monastery each get 10 Dotse (1 Dotse—Rs. 84) from Tawang for the right to send Agents to manage the land of the Tawang monastery, which right they farm out to them considered as the right of private individuals. The Lebrang and Nyetsang get a share of about Rs. 500 together, out of the subsidy paid by the British Government annually for the Kuriapara Duar. This, Lonchen requests, may be continued to be paid to them. The families of Shewo and Sam-drup Po-trang have also private estates in Tawang which, he requests that they may be allowed to retain. The Tawang monastery, established by the 5th Dalai Lama, has got about 300 monks, although its oficial strength is about 500. This monastery has got private estates at Dhirang and Takla Jongs which he requests that they may be allowed to retain with the monastery's other income". Charles Bell agreed that "all proprietory rights (Dak-top) of the individual Tibetans on the British side of the frontier will be retained by those who at present enjoy them.[86]

The Tibetan Government, on reference by Lonchen Shatra, agreed to the transfer without prejudice. So the agreement drawn up at Simla was agreed to by Lonchen Shatra.[87] The Chinese were not invited to take part in the discussions about the Indo-Tibetan frontier and their specific acceptance was not sought; but they were provided with information about it. The Indo-Tibetan boundary alignment, on a reduced scale, was shown in the map showing the boundaries of Inner Tibet and Outer Tibet, which was enclosed with the Simla Convention and was duly initialled by all the three plenipotentiaries.[88]

The boundary line, which was named in India as the McMahon Line after the name of the Indian plenipotentiary at the conference, as it emerged from the Indo-Tibetan Boundary Agreement of 1914, runs over a distance of 820 miles of which 640 miles are between India and Tibet from the tri-junction of Bhutan, Tibet and the Kameng district of the present Arunachal Pradesh of India through the crest of the Himalayas to the Diphuk Pass (Talok-La) to the north-west of Burma where India, Burma and Tibet meet. Commencing from a point to the east of Bhutan at 92°40″ E, 27°48″N, it crosses the Namjang river and follows the eastern range of the Great Himalayas, which is also the watershed between the Chayul Chu in Tibet and the Kameng, Kamla and Kru rivers in India, and then proceeds east and north-east and crosses the Subansiri river and then the Tsari river just south of Migyitun. From this point it takes a north-eastern direction, crosses the Tunga pass (approximately Longitude 94°10″ E and Latitude 28°59″N), continues eastward again, crosses the Dihang (Siang) and ascends the watershed between Chimdru Chu and Rongta Chu in Tibet and the Dibang and its tributaries in India. Thereafter it runs south to a point, just below Latitude 28°30″ and just west of Longitude 96°30″, continues in easterly direction, crosses the Lohit river a few miles to the north of Kahas and a few miles to the south of Rima and joins the tri-junction of India, Burma and Tibetan boundaries near the Diphuk or Talok pass.[89]

With regard to the inclusion of Tawang and Walong inside the Indian side of the border, there were disputes and authorities expressed different views. Alaister Lamb holds the view that although the British did not recognise any paramount power over the north-eastern tribes, Tawang was undoubtedly Tibetan territory.[90] Again, he says that the Indo-Tibetan Agreement involved a nominal transfer of territory from Tibet to India.[91] As for the situation and inclusion of Walong, the Government of India at first was hesitant, but subsequently it was found to be outside the Tibetan province of Zayul Chu till the advent of the Chinese and inside the Indian side of the frontier, from watershed, geographical and historical points of view. Walong is situated on the left bank of the Lohit which forms the Indo-Tibetan boundary there. The area was at one time inhabited by the Mishmis but later on abandoned by them. In 1914, the area was largely uninhabited, but the Mishmi occupation of the region was still testified by the Miju names of the places, hills, flats and rivers.

W.C.M. Dundas wrote to the Chief Commissioner regarding Walong :

> There was no question about this strip of land until the Chinese came and arbitrarily fixed their boundary at Menilkrai.
>
> Sati is the last Miju village on the right bank of the Lohit, and Sama the first old established Tibetan village. Almost midway between the two is one Tibetan house at Walong which in the past was allowed to remain through the forbearance of the Mijus to whom this family of Tibetans was useful, as a halting place on the journey to Rima, and also because they kept and pastured the Mijus cattle, beyond Walong north of the Namti and between that stream and the Kraoti. There are remains of terraced fields which shows that there was once a Tibetan village on the site. These people, it is said, were driven north by disease, and also on account of continual atttacks by Mijus who once raided as far as Rima itself, besieging that place. The absence of Miju habitations is accounted for by the fact that there is no soil suitable for Jhum cultivation. That Mijus jhumed the land years ago and occupied it, I have

no doubt. The appearance of the land gives colour to this belief. All the cultivable patches are denuded of trees and covered with short san grass, while the steep slopes are thick with pine forests, proving to my thinking that the barer flats are the sites of Miju cultivation, which have been abandoned as, owing to the lack of timber, the soil cannot recover enough even to be jhumed again.

The names of places, hills, flats, and streams are Miju and these are the names used by Tibetans who have none of their own for the Yepuk, Namti, Kraoti, Dunai, etc. The first Tibetan name met on the right bank of the Lohit, proceeding north, is Tor Chu. Sama has neither cultivation nor any claims to land south of that stream.

As a matter of fact the whole area is uninhabited (except for one house of Walong) from Sati stream to the Tor Chu and is a kind of Tom Tiddlers ground, belonging actually to the Mijus who, however, for many years have had no use for it.

I went into this question carefully when I was in charge of the Mishmi Mission. Just the one visit of the Chinese to Menlikrai and the planting there of their flags which indicate no boundary line, and the notification has given rise to the belief that the land above as far as the Tor Chu cannot be claimed by us.

Across the Tor Chu, it is very different; Sama and Singor are undoubtedly Tibetan and very long established communities.

For the left bank of the Lohit, I have proposed the Dri Ti as our boundary with Tibet. The last Miju village is Wati, and the first old established Tibetan village Kahao (or Kahap). In between, there is one Tibetan house at Tine (or Tinai) opposite Walong, and two at Dong about 1½ miles further north. The arguments given above all apply even to the Miju names of all places including the Kri Ti which is pure Miju. Kahao village has no cultivation or land south of the Kri Ti.[92]

Ivan Chen held that the Tibetan Government did not possess any control over the Zayul which, he held, was inhabited by independent tribes called Miris, Abors and Mishmis.

Tawang, it has been held, was an undisputed Tibetan territory. This part of territory is separated from the Tibetan plateau by a range of rugged mountains averaging 16000 feet in height and is known as Monyul or low country by the Tibetans.[93] The people of the tract are known as Mompas who, it has been shown by T.S. Murty, who was Political Officer in the NEFA, are racially, linguistically and culturally different from the main stream of the Tibetan population.[94] But it cannot be gainsaid that the Tawang monastery is an off-shoot of the Drepung monastery of Lhasa and was founded in the 5th century as a daughter institution of the same. It was, however, an independent institution. Pandit Nain Sing of the Trigonometrical Survey of India, who visited the monastery in 1874-75, on his way back to Assam from Lhasa found that the affairs of the Tawang district were managed by a sort of Parliament termed Kato, which assembled in public to manage business and administer justice. The Kato was composed entirely of Lamas, chief officials of the principal monastery. "The Tawang monastery", he says, "is entirely independent of the Dzongpon (of Tsona) and of the Lhasa Government."[95] Almost 50 years later, G.A. Nevill, who visited Tawang in 1914, stated the same thing.[96] It is significant to note that Lonchen Shatra told Bell at Simla about the temporal authority of the Tawang monastery in the area and existence of private estates only. Be that as it may, the McMahon Line was first published by Charles Bell in his book on Tibet in 1924. The Government of India soon after the Simla Conference was engaged in the First World War and Sir Henry McMahon was transferred to Egypt. It was not before 1929 that the map was incorporated in the volume of Aitchison's work entitled *Treaties, Engagements and Sanads* etc. Thereafter it was published in 1962 by the Government of India after the Sino-Indian border clashes of 1962.[97]

After the delineation of the North-East Frontier in the Simla Conference of 1914, the Government of India took effective measures to exercise control over the area stretching up to the McMahon Line. By a Notification dated 25 September 1924, the Frontier Tracts were constituted into three political charges : (*i*) Central and Eastern Sections consisting of the hills inhabitated by the Nagas, Khamptis, and Singphos; (*ii*) the Lakhimpur Frontier Tract, and (*iii*) the Western Section. The first was to be administered by three Assistant Political Officers at Sadiya; the second and the third were left under the Assistant Political Officer of Charduar. By another Notification, the Assam Frontier Tract Regulation of 1880 was promulgated in these tracts; it was amended in subsequent years.[98] But control over outlying areas was extended only gradually over the years as we have already noted in studying the relations of the tribes with the government.

Government of India equated the frontier with a buffer as it was believed by McMahon. He held that frontier or buffer meant a tract of neutral territory separating two potentially antagonistic neighbours; but a boundary was a specific line, either delimited by precise map description or demarcated by ground surveys. To him, it was the frontier buffer zone which had the greatest importance, and the boundary was comparatively less significant, particularly when it ran through uninhabitable mountain or desert terrain. Hence, the delay in establishing administration and control over the border region.[99]

The position of the North-East Frontier was well expressed in the words of a well-known Foreign Secretary of the Government of India, Sir Olaf Caroe: "In the early days of British rule, the external frontiers of India were conceived as lying at the limits of the territory of India where the British writ ran. But on the North-East, as on the belt known as the North-West Frontier, there lay beyond the limits of administered territory an agglomeration of tribes owning no master. In such cases, it became the practice of the early British administration to exercise in the region beyond the administered border what was known as a loose political control. Trans-border agencies were set up, but it was not until later that the need was felt to show the tribes so politically controlled as excluded from the neighbouring states and included in India."[100]

INDO-CHINESE BORDER CONTROVERSY

After 1954, when relations between India and China began to be strained on the score of the so-called border incidents and when the Chinese troops began to violate the North-East Frontier of India from January 1959, Prime Minister

J. L. Nehru addressed a letter to the Chinese Prime Minister Chou Enlai. Good humouring the Chinese Prime Minister on the progress made by China in agricultural developments, he pointed out that the Chinese Prime Minister had recognised the North-East boundary of India during his last visit to India though he did not approve of the method the British had adopted in settling the issue.[101] The letters that followed from the Chinese Prime Minister and the memoranda that came from the Chinese Government thereafter regarding the Indo-Tibetan border alleged that the McMahon Line was a product of the British policy of aggression against the Tibetan region of China; juridically too the Line could not be regarded as valid as it was discussed only secretly between India and Tibet behind the back of China, and the question had never been formally raised at the Simla Conference. Moreover, the Boundary Agreement was agreed between India and Tibet by a secret exchange of notes between Lonchen Shatra and Charles Bell, and China never ratified the Simla Convention of 1914.[102] Further Chinese arguments ran as follows :

(i) "Tibet is part of Chinese territory. China has full sovereignty over Tibet". The Chinese representative made it clear on 30 October 1913 that Tibet was an integral part of Chinese territory. Tibet had no right to conclude treaties with foreign countries independently of the Chinese Central Government, unless authorised by and consented to by the Chinese Central Government.[103]

(ii) The treaties of 1842, 1856 and 1904 which Tibet had concluded with Kashmir, Nepal and India respectively were all entered into with the prior or *ex-post facto* approval of the Chinese Central Government.[104] The Boundary Agreement of 1 March 1914, the Simla Convention of July 1914 and the Trade Regulation of 1914 were illegal as China had never ratified them. The Anglo-Tibetan negotiations of 1921-27 were of a local nature.[105] But the delimitation of the Indo-Tibetan boundary was a problem concerning a major internal administrative division of China, and since the McMahon Line was widely at variance with the traditional customary boundary, Great Britain was not competent to change it unilaterly.[106]

(iii) "The Chinese Government holds that the so-called McMahon Line is wholly illegal . . . it is known to the world that the Simla Convention itself is void of legal validity". China made it clear in three statements made in 1914 on 21 April, 3 July and 7 July that the Convention could not be recognised by her.[107]

(iv) The Simla Conference did not deal with the question of Sino-Indian (Indo-Tibetan) boundary, "the Simla Conference only discussed the boundary between so-called Outer and Inner Tibet, it never discussed the boundary between China and India.'' No such discussions were reported to the Chinese representative as well. The only map that was presented to the Conference showing the Indo-Tibetan boundary showed all of Tibet's external boundaries and not those with India alone. Even this map was not referred to in the Agreement of March 1914 and the Convention of July 1914.[108]

(v) The Simla Conference of 1914 was a part of the British plan to separate Tibet from China, make Tibet an independent State, and bring it completely under the British control. The aggressive intentions of Britain towards Tibet were given out in Lord Curzon's letter dated 11 June 1901 addressed to the Secretary of State for India and in the Memorandum of the British Government proposing a tripartite conference.[109] China expressed her regret and dissatisfaction with it. These aggressive intentions of Britain were recognised by Prime Minister Nehru also in his statement of 30 March 1959.

(vi) On 15 April 1914, the Chinese representative objected to Tibet being given an equal status with China in the preamble to the draft Simla Convention. As such, the question of China accepting Tibet's equal status did not arise.[110] The communication from Great Britain to China, dated 26 June 1914, should not be regarded as indicating acceptance by China of Tibet's status since it was a position forced on China by Great

Britain.[111] On 17 March 1959, Prime Minister Nehru said in the Lok Sabha that no country had recognised the independence of Tibet.

(vii) "Besides even the local authorities of Tibet did not regard as reasonable the so-called McMahon Line . . ." as can be seen from a letter dated 18 April 1945 to the Political Officer, Sikkim, regarding withdrawal of British troops from Kalkatang and Walong.[112]

(viii) The equivocal nature of the Simla Agreement of 25 March 1914 can be seen from the fact that the British Government did not dare publish—till 1929—either the letters or the map constituting a part of the Agreement.[113]

The Government of India to refute the Chinese allegations put forward the following points :

(i) Tibet was competent to settle her own boundaries with India and Chinese adherence or recognition of the Anglo-Tibetan Boundary Agreement of March 1914 or the Anglo-Tibetan Convention of July 1914 was not relevant to the formalisation of the Indo-Tibetan boundary. Tibet had signed treaties with Kashmir in 1852 and Nepal in 1842 and 1856. The Chinese had themselves agreed that Tibet was competent to conclude the Non-aggression pact in 1853. The treaty-making power of Tibet, as different from that of China, is evident in China's inability to enforce the Anglo-Chinese Convention of 1894 concerning Tibetan trade. This Convention had accepted the treaty-making power of Tibet by including the Anglo-Tibetan Convention of 1904 in the Anglo-Chinese Convention of 1906, and by abrogating the Nepal-Tibet Treaty of 1856 by the Sino-Nepalese Treaty of 1956. Extra-territorial rights, as in the Treaty of 1856, can be conferred only by sovereign nations. The Tibet Trade Regulations of 1914, signed independently of China, were also operative till their abrogation in 1954.[114] Tibet's competence to settle her own boundary with India, without consulting China, was further evident from the negotiations on her southern border which Tibet held with India in 1921, 1924 and 1926.[115]

(ii) Long before the Simla Conference, Sino-Tibetan relations had virtually ceased to exist. The Tibetans had issued a declaration of independence and resisted China's attempts to re-establish her authority. During 1940-44, Tibet even refused the combined request of China, Britain and America to allow Indian military supplies for China to pass through Tibet. The fact that in 1950 the Chinese Government considered it necessary to 'liberate' the Tibet region was further proof that areas contiguous with the Indian frontier were parts of Tibet and the power to confirm the boundaries of Tibet rested with the Tibetan Government at Lhasa.[116]

(iii) The British Memorandum of 17 August 1912 had envisaged Tibet taking part in the Simla Conference as an equal partner with China. This was reiterated, among other occasions, on 25 May, 28 July and 25 August, 1913.[117] China also recognised Tibet's right to participate on equal basis in the Simla Conference as "the Chinese representative accepted the credentials of the Tibetan representative as being in order." One of the causes for convening the Simla Conference was the Chinese Government's anxiety to re-establish its relation with Tibet.[118]

(iv) The Chinese were not intimidated into joining the Simla Conference. "The Foreign Minister of China wrote to the British representative on the 7th August 1913 that the Chinese plenipotentiary would proceed to India to open negotiations for a treaty jointly with the Tibetan and British plenipotentiaries." China was willing and eager to commence negotiations with Tibet. It is clear from the proceedings of the Conference that China took full and wholehearted part in the proceedings.[119]

(v) During the preliminaries to the Simla Conference, discussions were held on relations not only between Tibet and China but also between Tibet and India. The proceedings of the Simla Conference leading to the Indo-

Tibetan Boundary Agreement of March 1914 and the Convention of July 1914 were attended by India, China and Tibet in November 1913 in Delhi.[120] The British representative pointed out that the territorial limits of Tibet should be defined before her political status could be discussed. As a result, the Indo-Tibetan frontiers in the eastern region were shown in maps presented to the Conference on 17 February 1914 and 22 April 1914. If the Indo-Tibetan boundary shown in these maps was not discussed at the plenary session among all the three representatives, it was because the problem concerned India and Tibet only and not China. "The Chinese representative at the Simla Conference was fully aware of the McMahon Line boundary between India and Tibet."[121]

(vi) The Simla Agreement and the Simla Convention of 1914 were not kept as secrets. The boundary line accepted in those agreements was the same as that shown in several maps presented at the Simla Conference. The Agreement and the Convention were published in the very first edition of Aitchison's book which was issued after the Conference in 1929 (the last preceding edition was published in 1909) and also in Indian official maps. The British War Office map published in 1907 shows almost the entire area within India. "Sir Francis Younghusband's volume *India and Tibet* published in London in 1910 shows the Tribal area in India; and so does the map in Sir Charles Bell's book *Tibet—Past and Present* (Oxford 1924)."[122]

(vii) Under International Law, failure of ratification by one of the parties to a multilateral treaty cannot affect its binding force on other parties or the validity of the obligations assumed by them.[123] Throughout the proceedings of the Simla Conference and in the subsequent diplomatic communications from China on 30 May 1914, no objection was made by China to the boundaries between India and Tibet as shown in the maps presented to the Conference. China "suggested some modifications of the Simla Convention with a view to reaching a final settlement. These modifications related only to the boundaries between Inner Tibet and China and Inner Tibet and Outer Tibet".[124]

(viii) The Tibetan Foreign Office wrote to the Indian Government on 18 April 1945 reiterating its continuing adherence to the Boundary Agreements of 1914.[125]

(ix) The Indian Government announced publicly on several occasions during 1946-50 that it regarded China as continuing to accept the validity of the McMahon Line.[126]

Chinese Government and the Government of India regarding India taking over the former British responsibilities in Tibet shows that the then Government of China accepted the validity of the arrangements made in 1914 and since enforced. The present Chinese Government was the successor to the governments in power in Tibet during 1914-50. It was, therefore, bound to accept the obligations imposed on Tibet by Agreement of 1914. The present Chinese Government was similarly the successor of Nationalist Government of China, and it was not entitled to repudiate the actions of the Nationalist Government just because these did not suit its present purpose.[127]

The Simla Agreement only formalised the natural, customary, traditional boundary in this sector and did not set up a new boundary. The water parting formed by the crest of the Himalayas is the natural frontier which was accepted for centuries as the boundary by the peoples on both sides. The tribes inhabiting the area south of McMahon Line—the Mompas, Akas, Daflas, Miris, Abors, and Mishmis—are of the same stock as the other hill tribes of Assam and have no kinship with the Tibetans.[128]

It is evident from what we have seen in the foregoing paragraphs that the Indo-Tibetan border had remained unsettled till the advent of the Chinese across the traditional boundary of India in Tibet. The East India Company's Government was anxious first to stop the aggression into the Bengal Presidency through the north-east, and in quest of security for their newly founded empire in Bengal they had to come to Assam. First Assam was acquired not primarily for any material benefit other than the security of Bengal. But with the discovery of minerals and tea bushes the valley of the Brahmaputra assumed a new importance. To provide security to the tea plantations and the coal mines and oil fields which developed along the foothills, it was found necessary to keep away the hill tribes inhabiting the frontiers, for the Company's Government was reluctant to assume responsibility for them. Hence, the Inner Line.

The tribes of the frontier were kept aloof and no paramountcy was established over them excluding third-party influence over them as no such party posed any threat to British interests. The Outer Line was thus kept in abeyance and it was purposely left indefinite, unsettled and undemarcated. The British Crown which assumed the responsibility of Indian administration after the Sepoy Mutiny initially followed the same policy as did the Company's Government. But the Chinese invasion of Tibet in 1910 now opened the possibility of third-party influence over the frontier tribes. Therefore, it was now necessary to establish paramountcy over the tribes and settle the border. With a view to gaining knowledge of the territory, survey and explorations were undertaken and carried on between 1911-14.

Finally, it was now necessary to get approval of the border on the north-east from the countries beyond. Revolts in Tibet and China provided opportunity; and the Chinese and the Tibetans also wanted to formalise their relations with foreign powers following the revolutions in their respective countries. A Conference was convened in Simla where, during the negotiations between the Chinese and the Tibetans, the Indo-Tibetan boundary was settled: the McMahon Line was fixed by a Boundary Agreement between India and Tibet on 24/25 March 1914. The alignment of the border followed the principle of watershed usually followed in mountainous terrain, but ethnic, historic, and strategic considerations were also given due weight. The Sino-Indian border clashes followed in 1962. The unilateral cease-fire in the midst of their success by the Chinese and their withdrawal beyond th McMahon Line from all areas except Che Dong and Longju which the Chinese hold are south of that McMahon Line confirm India's North-East Frontier along the McMahon Line.

REFERENCES

1. C.U. Aitchison, *op. cit.*, vol. I.
2. A. Mackenzie, *History*, p. 27.
3. *Ibid.*
4. C. Von. Furer-Haimendorf, *op. cit.*, pp. 4-5.
5. W. Robinson, *op. cit.*, p. 354.
6. C. Von. Furer-Haimendorf, *op. cit.*, pp. 4-5.
7. Bengal Papers in Assam Archives, F. No. 308 of 1870, sl. 12.
8. All India Report, 1967.
9. Bengal Papers in Assam Archives, F. No. 309 of 1873, sl. 15.
10. Foreign Proceedings (Assam), December 1903, No. 14.
11. *Ibid.*
12. Bengal Papers in Assam Archives, F. No. 293/521 of 1873, sl. 10.
13. *Ibid.*
14. *Ibid.*
15. Foreign External Proceedings (India), October 1884, Nos. 366-75.
16. Bengal Papers in Assam Archives, F. No. 521 of 1873.
17. *Ibid*, F. No. 293, 1873, sl. 10.
18. Foreign External Proceedings (India), October 1884, Nos. 366-75.
19. Foreign Proceedings (Assam), January 1904, No. 5.
20. *Ibid*, No. 7.
21. Assam State Archives (Bengal Papers), F. No. 652, 1874, sl. 1.
22. Foreign External Proceedings (India), October 1884, Nos. 366-7 .
23. Foreign Proceedings (Assam), April 1874, No. 14.
24. *Ibid.*
25. *Ibid.*
26. *Ibid.*
27. *Ibid.*
28. *Ibid.*
29. *Ibid*, February 1875, No. 1.
30. Assam Administration Report, 1874-76, Part II B, para 8.
31. Foreign External Proceedings (India), October 1884, No. 366-75.
32. *Ibid.*
33. *Ibid.*
34. Foreign Political Proceedings (India), December 1873, Nos. 42-43.
35. R. Reid, *op. cit.*, p. 7.
36. Foreign Proceedings (Assam), July 1886, No. 5.
37. *Ibid*, December 1903, No. 14.
38. Foreign Political Proceedings (India), May 1912, No. 202.
39. *Ibid*, March 1886, No. 25.
40. Political Proceedings (East Bengal and Assam), 10 August 1910, No. 4.
41. Lakhimpur Deputy Commissioner's Collection, No. x, F. 16 of 1909.
42. F. Younghusband, *India and Tibet*, p. 488.
43. Foreign Proceedings (India), Secret 'E', January 1911, No. 211-240.
44. *Ibid*, No. 223.
45. *Ibid.*

46. *Ibid.*
47. *Ibid.*
48. *Ibid*, Nos. 5, 211-240.
49. *Ibid.*
50. *Ibid.*
51. Foreign Proceedings (India), Secret 'E', May 1912, Nos. 201-337.
52. Political Proceedings (Eastern Bengal and Assam), March 1912, Nos. 149-197.
53. Foreign Political Proceedings (India), November 1912, No. 619.
54. A. Lamb, *The McMahon Line: Study in the Relations between India, China and Tibet*, p. 537.
55. Foreign Political Proceedings (India), November 1912, No. 619.
56. Political Proceedings (Assam), May 1914, No. 74.
57. *Ibid*, No. 70.
58. *Ibid*, No. 74.
59. *Ibid.*
60. Foreign Political (Secret) Proceedings (India), October 1914, Nos. 134-396.
61. *Ibid.*
62. *Ibid.*
63. *Ibid.*
64. *Ibid.*
65. *Ibid*, May 1915, Nos. 36-50.
66. *Ibid.*
67. *Ibid.*
68. F. Younghusband, *op. cit.*, p. 395.
69. Foreign Political (Secret) Proceedings (India), October 1914, Nos. 134-396.
70. *Ibid.*
71. *Ibid.*
72. H.E. Richardson, *op. cit.*, p. 107.
73. Foreign Political (Secret) Proceedings (India), October 1914, Nos. 134-396.
74. *Ibid.*
75. *Ibid.*
76. *Ibid.*
77. *Ibid.*
78. *Ibid.*
79. *Ibid.*
80. *Ibid.*
81. Froeign Political.Proceedings (India), November 1912, Nos. 599-690.
82. Krishna K. Rao, "The Sino-Indian Boundary Question and International Law" Reprinted by the Ministry of External Affairs, New Delhi, 1963, from *International and Comparative Law Quarterly*, pp. 31-33.
83. Foreign Political (Secret) Proceedings (India), October 1914, Nos. 134-396.

84. *Ibid.*
85. P.C. Chakravarty, *Evolution of India's Northern Borders*, p. 75.
86. *Ibid*, p. 84.
87. Foreign Political (Secret) Proceedings (India), October 1914, Nos. 134-396.
88. *Ibid.*
89. P.C. Chakravarty, *op. cit.*, pp. 77-78.
90. A. Lamb, *op. cit.*, p. 310.
91. *Ibid*, p. 349.
92. Political Proceedings (Assam), May 1914, No. 66.
93. T.S. Murty, *op. cit* , pp. 527-28.
94. *Ibid.*
95. Survey of India Records, vol. VIII, Part I, p. 178.
96. Political Proceedings (Assam), December 1914, Nos. 1-37.
97. White Paper, vol. II, p. 41.
98. Political Proceedings (Assam), April 1914, Nos. 1-16.
99. Foreign Political (Secret) Proceedings (India), May 1915, Nos. 36-50.
100. P.C. Chakravarty, *India-China Relations*, p. 149.
101. White Paper, vol. I, p. 49.
102. *Ibid*, vol. I., p. 53.
103. *Ibid*, vol. IV., p. 14.
104. *Ibid.*
105. *Ibid*, vol. IV., p. 9.
106. *Ibid*,
107. *Ibid*, vol. III., pp. 63-64.
108. *Ibid.*
109. *Ibid.*
110. *Ibid.*
111. *Ibid.*
112. *Ibid.*
113. *Ibid.*
114. S.P. Sharma, *The India-China Border Dispute: An Indian Perspective.*
115. White Paper, vol. III, p. 94.
116. Report of the Officials of the Governments of India and the People's Republic of China on the Boundary Question, p. 17.
117. *Ibid*, Part III, p. 112.
118. White Paper, vol. III, p. 95.
119. *Ibid*, vol. II, p. 38.
120. Report of the Officials of the Government of India and the People's Republic of China on the Boundary Question, p. 112.
121. White Paper, vol. II, p. 38.
122. *Ibid*, vol. II, pp. 39-41.
123. *Ibid*, "Oppenheim points out that, according to the principle of rest-ransit cum Saononere, treaties of the extinct State concerning the boundary lines, repairing of the main roads, navigation on rivers and the like, remain valid and all rights and obligations accruing from such treaties of the exinct state devolve on the absorbing State". A

Appadorai, "Bases of India's Title on the North-East Frontier" *International Studies*, vol. I, No. 4, p. 370.

124. *Ibid*, vol. II, pp. 38-39.
125. Report of the Officials, etc., p. 115.
126. *Ibid*, p. 16.
127. *Ibid*, p. 18.
128. White Paper, vol. II, p. 40.

4

Administration of the North-East Frontier

AFTER THE annexation of Assam in 1826 the immediate task of the British was to provide for an administrative set-up for the new province as the Ahom system of government had collapsed completely during the Burmese depredations. In April 1826, a kind of dyarchy was brought into existence; David Scott was appointed Political Agent to the Governor-General and was entrusted with the management of the newly acquired territories while Col. Richards was entrusted with the administration of civil and criminal justice. The Political Agent, however, was forbidden to interfere with purely military affairs though he was to conduct negotiations with the border tribes and native princes of the rigion.[1] In 1828, when martial law was withdrawn from Assam, David Scott became the Commissioner of Assam as well as the Political Agent to the Governor-General for the North-East Frontier. In the latter capacity, he was entrusted with the management of the border tribes and conduct negotiations with them.[2]

SADIYA AGENCY

Meanwhile an Agency was established at Sadiya to conduct negotiations with the chiefs of the Moamarias of Mattack, the Khamptis of Sadiya and the Singphos of Upper Assam.[3] In 1832, the Supreme Government took the decision to restore an Ahom prince in Upper Assam and Purandar Singh was selected to rule as tributary king. The Political Agency of Sadiya was empowered to conduct negotiation with the Ahom prince.[4] Lower Assam was retained within the British territories. In 1835, the territory of Lower Assam was divided into three districts each of which was put under a Senior Assistant to the Commissioner whose title was later on changed to that of Principal Assistant to the Commissioner.[5] But for the management of the border and to conduct negotiations with the border tribes, the district officers were given the title of Assistant Agent to the Commissioner of Assam, as the Commissioner had the title of Agent to the Governor-General for North-East Frontier.[6] After the annexation of Upper Assam to the British territories, it may be recalled, Capt. Vetch, the district officer of Darrang, had initiated the negotiations with the tribes on the Darrang frontier for payment in cash or kind to the tribes stopping the system of direct collection by the tribes themselves.[7]

The district officer, entitled Assistant Agent to the Governor-General, maintained relations with the border tribes. It was the district officers who had to punish the tribes for violating the terms of their engagement with the British. When a punitive expedition was authorised to chastise any offending tribe, usually the district officer accompanied the expeditionary force as Political Officer and obtained satisfaction for the offence committed by the tribe of its member or members.[8] These Agents presented the annual *posa* to the tribes and heard their complaints and kept the higher authorities informed of what was happening in the hills, collecting information through the Kotokis.[9]

Intelligence Service

As for intelligence service, in the North-East Frontier the British did not bother very much except for a short period after the Anglo-Burmese War of 1824-26. For some time, the spectre of a Burmese invasion haunted them and a Political Agency was therefore set up, as already mentioned, at Sadiya. "Their duties consisted chiefly in keeping a watchful eye on the proceedings, journeying and communications with the tribes beyond the frontier, of all the clans, especially those situated near the Burmese frontier, and gaining through them intelligence, as early and accurate as possible, of all movements in Upper Burma."[10]

To oversee the proceedings and report on the movement of the tribes some watchers and interpreters were appointed in the Agency establishment at Sadiya. In the middle of the nineteenth century, when Mills submitted his report, one Jamadar, a Shan Interpreter and seven Harkaras were retained in the Agency which continued to function under the district officer of Dibrugarh, when tne Political Agent was withdrawn from Sadiya. All these officers were natives of Assam. The post of the Muharrir, that is the clerk, was held by a Khampti Chief, the post of Jamadar was filled up by an Assamese gentleman who was the head of the Doanies of Makum and knew frontier languages; the seven Harkaras were all local people who were well-versed in frontier tactics.[11] After the news of combined Mishmi and Singpho rebellion proved to be a mere rumour in 1866, the Agency establishment was subordinated to the police establishment of Sadiya.[12]

The duties of the Political Agent, however, consisted chiefly of the management of the Singpho and Khampti tribes who acknowledged the British supremacy and engaged to refer their inter-tribal disputes to the British officer. These tribes, by agreement, had bound themselves to obey all orders issued to them through the Political Agent and bring all heinous crimes for settlement to the Political Agent as they were not subject to the ordinary jurisdiction of the Magistrate of the Lakhimpur district. The Political Agent was required to mediate in their quarrels, keep peace between rival clans, and investigate into heinous crimes like murder and dacoity originating amongst these clans as also all complaints against them by other parties, whether British subjects or foreigners.[13]

Except at Sadiya, at no other place any regular intelligence establishment or agency was provided for. The states beyond the frontiers of Assam, Tibet and China were not considered powerful and were themselves in decaying condition in the nineteenth century. Therefore no possibility of invasion of Assam after the Second Anglo-Burmese War loomed large over the frontiers. The petty tribes of the frontier hills committed only petty raids for which no intelligence was thought necessary. But after the Bhutia raid of 1849, one Jamadar and 10 Chowkidars were appointed for watch and ward on the Darrang frontier: the Deputy Commissioner wanted to retain them permanently as he thought that by travelling on Duars and Mahals of Darrang they could provide useful intelligence regarding the border tribes.[14]

RULE IN ASSAM

With the consolidation of the British rule in Assam, the hands of the district officers of the Assam Commission were full with work. Assam was a Non-Regulation province; personal care and attention was more necessary for good administration here than in the Regulation provinces. Over and above their executive duties, the officers of the administration were also judges and registrars in Assam; as such they were required not only to maintain law and order in their respective jurisdictions, but as District Magistrates they were required to dispose of civil and criminal cases, register the transfer of land and try revenue cases.[15] It was now found necessary to have some sort of agency to maintain relation with the frontier tribes. Therefore, the office of native political agents called Kotokis was now revived to assist the district officers to conduct relation with the hill tribes of the frontiers.

KOTOKIS

The office of the Kotokis had its origin in the Ahom period. The Ahom kings appointed political officers to open negotiation with neighbouring princes and sometimes sent ambassadors to the courts of the Mughals. These political officers and ambassadors were styled as Kotokis. Usually high caste Brahmins, well-versed in the Shastras, intelligent, smart, with unusual common sense, were appointed to such offices. Naturally the respect they commanded was commensurate with their high office and bearings.[16]

The Kotokis who manned the frontier service were established throughout North Lakhimpur in connection with the Daflas, Chang Meeres (Abors) and other hill tribes in that quarter. There were Kotokis—one each—for Banskota Daflas and Chaiduar Dufla clans.[17] After the Aka expedition of 1882, Capt. Maxwell who had the expedition recommended the appointment of Kotokis in relation to the Akas in the Darrang frontier as well. On the recommendation of the Deputy Commissioner of Darrang, two Kotokis for the Hazarikhawa Akas and two for the Kapachars were appointed.[18] The Bhutias of Tawang conducted their intercourse directly with the Deputy

Commissioner, but the Bhutias of Rupa came through the Mauzadar of Orang and the Charduar Bhutias had two Kotokis. There were some eleven Kotokis for the Abor tribes known as Panibatia, Tarbatia, Charak and Ghasi Merees.[19] Kotokis were employed to carry on intercourse between the government and the hill tribes; a parwana of appointment was issued and a register giving details of the man who held the post together with his address was maintained at the headquarters.[20]

The duties of the Kotokis, wrote Capt. H.S. Biver, were to proceed to the hills on any occasion when required to do so in connection with the tribes and to render aid in furnishing information on the tribes and in interpreting any matter, as also to attend upon the Deputy Commissioner when he proceeded to the country bordering on the hills of the tribe to which they were attached.[21] Though the Kotokis were appointed by Government, they were also in close connection with the tribe for which they were appointed and accompanied them when the tribesmen came down to the plains. The government remunerated them by the grant of revenue-free land and paid them a paltry salary; they sometimes received some remuneration from the tribe as well. The Charduar Bhutias paid their Kotoki Rs. 10 per annum and stayed with him whenever they came down to the plains.[22]

But the Kotokis who began to be appointed for service in the frontier were practically a misnomer or a caricature of the Kotokis of the Ahom regime. No educational qualification was required for holding the appointment. The Kotokis were remunerated by allowing them to enjoy twelve *bighas* of revenue-free land for doing the hard and risky job of carrying on transactions with the savage tribes of the perilous hills or were paid a paltry sum of 5 to 15 rupees per annum.[23] Intelligent people who commanded respect in society for their accomplishments and wealth did not usually come forward to undertake the job.

INTELLIGENCE AT FRONTIERS

In 1903, after the Abor and Mishmi raids at the close of the preceding century, the Chief Commissioner of Assam opened the question of intelligence on the frontiers. He issued a circular to the Deputy Commissioners of Assam asking them to submit their opinions on the agency of intelligence to be employed for keeping themselves informed of the attitude of the tribesmen of the frontier, as also on the possibility of utilising effectively the Kotokis in the frontier service.[24]

The Deputy Commissioner of Darrang and Sibsagar suggested the abolition of these offices as useless but the Deputy Commissioner of Lakhimpur considered it useful.[25] Appreciation of the services of the Kotokis and recognition of their usefulness were brought to the notice of the local administration by P.G. Militus, the then Commissioner of the Assam valley districts. He wrote, "our Kotokis, if inefficient, are at any rate a cheap agency, and their inefficiency is, I think, to a great extent, due to bad system."[26] In 1884, the Deputy Commissioner of the Darrang district had suggested that the Kotokis be required to visit the hills they served at least once a year, preferably in the winter, and submit reports to the Deputy Commissioner.[27] As early as 1874, the officiating Superintendent of Police, Goad, had recommended to place the Kotokis under the Inspector of Police.[28] Nothing was done to give effect to these recommendations.

It is worth noting that Assam was a non-regulation province from the very beginning and it was only in 1837 that a system of code, drawn up in the spirit of Bengal Regulations, was prepared for a simple form of administration of the province.[29] The system continued to provide the basis of law in Assam, which was regarded as a Frontier province, till the end of the Sepoy Mutiny; the Civil Procedure Code (Act VIII) and the Criminal Procedure Code (Act XXV of 1861) were introduced in Assam on 26 April 1860 and in January 1862 respectively. In 1861, the designation of the district and subdivisional officers was changed, henceforth they were termed Deputy Commissioner and Assistant Commissioners and Extra-Assistant Commissioners instead of Principal Assistant, Senior Assistants and Junior Assistants respectively.[30] The officers of the Assam Commission consisted of chiefly the military officers of the Indian army who were deputed to civil service. Only some percentage of the vacancies were reserved for the Indian Civil Service, the rest being a monopoly of the Indian Army personnel. The first Commissioner was a civilian, but he had an Assistant from the Army. The Prinipal Assistant and Junior Assistants were selected from the military personnel.

The province was surrounded on all sides by hill tribes whom the British wanted to keep at arms length. This was done by deploying army under the civil authority. The duty of the civil administrators in such a province involved political intercourse tempered by armed force. The judicious employment of the army for civil purposes necessitated some knowledge of military tactics. Therefore, it was no wonder that the civil offices of the province, like the headship of districts and subdivisions, were filled up by army personnel on deputation to civil service. At the time of amalgamation of Assam with Eastern Bengal one-fourth of the membership of the Assam Commission was reserved for army personnel; one Commissionership and 8 posts of district officers were open to thm.[31]

But for the administration of the hills of the frontier the English did not employ any officer. They wanted to leave them (tribes) 'alone' but wanted to keep themselves abreast of the intentions or movements of the tribes.[32] Therefore, they provided for a hedge of outposts manned by units of Indian Army. At certain points, which were cross-roads of tribal movement, some intelligence establishment was set up. To convey the government policies and orders to the tribes as well as to act as guides and interpreters of the tribes some native agents termed Kotokis were attached to each tribe along the frontier.[33]

DEFENCE OF PLAINS

For the defence of the plains below the North-East Frontier hills, a chain of outposts were established. These posts, for the most part, governed the principal routes along which the tribal people moved or made inroads in the plains in the past.[34] The posts were held by the armed police and military guards. The army was employed because the police had an undue dread of the tribes and the army again lacked knowledge of the land, people and language of the tribes they had to guard against.[35] Therefore, the armed police who had knowledge of the territory of the tribes and their languages were employed in guarding the frontier along with the detachments of the army. In the event of a determined attack an outpost of a few persons could do little or nothing to protect the country around it; indeed, they could hardly defend the ground it stood on. But in case of a prowling enemy, the outpost was of much use, as the fear of being caught by a patrol or cut up on their return journey when burdened with plunder prevented raids on villages and robbery in the plains.[36] Behind the outposts, strong reserve was garrisoned and as and when called for they marched towards the frontiers. In 1861, at Kuriapara there were 70 men of military force to guard against possible attack of the Bhutias; at Balipara some 40 military personnel were stationed in dry season to guard against raids of the Akas, besides a reserve of 176 for general purpose.[37] To guard against the Daflas, a chain of posts along the frontiers were provided. Thus in 1874, guard posts were set up at Behali, Singlijan, Ghera, Gohpur, Katori, Barpathar, Ooahat, Sellonibari and at Joyhing.[38] To guard against the Abors and Mishmis posts were set up at Dimoh, Pobah, Sesei, Dibong, Dikrang, Disoi, Difoo and Sonpura; besides a reserve at Sadiya consisting of 210 military personnel and 69 armed police was quartered. These posts at Sadiya, Sesori, Dibong and Poba were held by the army and the rest were left with the armed police.[39]

Army

After martial law was withdrawn in 1828, British soldiers began to be withdrawn from Assam leaving the defence of the Brahmaputra valley to the Rungpore Light Infantry, named the Assam Light Infantry after three years of service in Assam and of the Surma Valley to the Sylhet Light Infantry.[40] Another corps of Sebundy troops was raised in 1835 to defend the Sadiya frontier. This was reorganised as the Second Assam Light Infantry in 1842.[41] But the defence of the frontier against the tribal incursions required a stronger force. In the Surma valley another corps known as the Cachar Levy was raised to defend the Cachar and Manipur frontier, and in Assam in 1840 a force known as the Jorhat Militia was raised.[42] Yet the regular army had to be quartered in Dibrugarh for defence of the Sadiya frontier against attack of the frontier tribes. In 1861, there were in Dibrugarh one European Artillery 100 strong and another Eurasian Light Infanty 100 strong, besides one Company of Native Local Artillery of 100 men. Besides, the 46th Regiment of Light Infantry was located at Dibrugarh with detachments at Sibsagar and the 47th Regiment of Native Infantry was stationed at Gauhati with detachments at Nowgong, Goalpara and Darrang. A total of 2300 men were thus employed in defence of the frontiers.[43]

Military Police

But the cost of the army was too high to be borne for defending the frontiers against possible attacks of petty and disorganised frontier tribes who practically possessed no fire arms. Therefore, the government considered the question of withdrawal of troops from Assam leaving the defence to the police. Lt. Col. A.H. Paterson, who was Inspector General of Police, Lower Provinces, recommended the withdrawal of military contingents leaving the defence of the Assam frontiers to a corps of 1860 Military Police to be organised for the purpose.[44] Lt. Col. Agnew, Commissioner of Assam, had proposed in 1871 to employ one Regiment of Native Infantry and a wing of regular troops with 300 Armed Police for the defence of the frontiers. And yet a third proposal of organising two local corps of Pioneers, each 700 strong, for the defence was mooted by reducing the number of the Armed Police.[45]

But the expediency of leaving the defence of the frontiers entirely to the military police was doubted. As early as 1861 Col. Henry Hopkinson, the then Commissioner of Assam, had suggested the disbandment of the three Native Regiments together with 400 Armed Police employed for the defence of the frontier and recommended to raise a force to be equipped specially for the peculiar duty in the frontiers under British officers. He, of course, would not agree to the withdrawal of the army altogether from the frontiers.[46] In 1862, the Police Commission had recommended to abolish the Military Police and organise Armed Police for the defence of the frontiers.[47] But Capt. J.R. Pughe, officiating Inspector General of Military Police, Lower Povinces, held that those who would be employed in defence of the frontiers would discharge quasi-military duties and as such it was inadvisable to abolish the Military Police.[48]

In 1873, the Bengal Government deputed Barker of the Bengal Police to recommend measures for frontier defence. He recommended to employ a separate force to be called Frontier Police, altogether separate from the Civil Police, for frontier duty. Accordingly, forces designated as the Surma Valley Frontier Police and Lakhimpur Armed Police Battalions were organised for the defence of the Surma valley and the Assam valley respectively.[49] On the creation of a Chief Commissionership, the issue of raising a separate force for guarding against the tribal incursions into Assam and punishing the raiders was again taken up. Consequently, as recommended by the Chief Commissioner of Assam, Keating, battalions of Military Police were raised in 1878 disbanding the Surma Valley Frontier Police and the Lakhimpur Armed Police battalions.[50] Units of these battalions were assigned to the border posts and a reserve was kept in readiness at the district headquarters to march to the frontier.

The year 1882 witnessed a further reorganisation. Sir Charles Elliot,[51] Chief Commissioner, recommended to form the Military Police into an essentially military body, altogether separate from the Civil Police. In the new organisation that was raised, the members of the force were drilled and equipped as soldiers, bore military designations and made into an armed force. The battalions were put under European officers of the Indian Army who had distinguished service records. The terms of service in the new force were assimilated with those of the Indian Army.[52]

During the First World War, the Indian Army was altogether withdrawn from Assam, leaving the defence of the frontiers to the Military Police. The designation of the Military Police was changed into Assam Rifles in 1919, as the police appellation seemed to be unpopular among the members of the corps.[53] The relations of the Assam Rifles with the Gorkha Regiment of the Indian Army had become so intimate that in 1924 the relations between the two were formalised by affiliating the battalions of the Assam Rifles with the Gorkha Regiments of the Indian Army.[54]

Recruits of the frontier forces of Military Police came largely from the Gorkhas recruited from Jalpaiguri and Darjeeling in Bengal and the battalions were put under the command of European officers of the Indian Army and the Bengal Police who were selected for their special qualifications and previous experience.[55] In 1905, the expediency of mixed enlistment, as in Burma, of servicemen of the battalions was mooted. But S.B. Chatterton expressed the opinion that mixed enlistment was not desirable for the recruitment of personnel of the Military Police as the Gorkhas were the best for service in the frontiers; they were rice-eaters and rice was available locally in sufficient quantity.[56] However, the Military Police force was originally regulated by the Police Act of 1861. But in 1882 the Assam Frontier Police Regulation was passed for enforcement of discipline and to assimilate the terms of the service with those prevailing in the Native Army—as already referred to. In 1890 and 1912, the terms were further modified; in 1919 the Assam Rifles Act was passed to govern their services without altering their status as a civil force while assimilating the form with the Indian Army.[57]

It is significant to note that for the tribal hills of the frontiers no police force was ever raised. In the sixties and seventies an attempt was made to provide guns to youngmen of some tribes to guard their own villages against the possible attack on them by the tribes of the interior hills. A little cash payment was also sanctioned.[58] But gradually the system fell into disuse and in the twentieth century we hear no more of those frontier wardens. The responsibility of watch and ward was regarded as a local responsibility and as in the Assam valley, no rural police operated in the frontier hills.[59] The village headmen maintained law and order in their respective hills.

The Military Police and the Assam Rifles, together with the Army, were employed mainly to check the tribesmen's propensity to raid the plains. The border posts indirectly influenced the villages in the vicinity. Any violence in the neighbourhood would have raised an alarm in the post and possibility of punitive expedition helped maintenance of law and order in the tribal villages. Moreover, the frontier force which discharged its duties with indefatigable energy and ruthless discipline and did not shrink from any kind of manual labour set examples before the tribes and this acted as a civilising agency in the frontiers.[60]

Reference has already been made in the preceding chapters to the Chief Commissioners of Assam.[61] The objects of separation of Assam from the Bengal Presidency was to provide security by invigorating the system of administration of the province.[62] The Jaintia rebellions of 1860 and 1862, the Bhutia raids of 1849, the necessity of waste land grant without survey to the European tea planters, the problem of immigrant labour for plantation and mining industries, construction of roads along the strategically important routes, distribution of armed forces in different strategically important places most economically—all these required an officer of sufficiently high rank on the spot to give quick decision and sanction. But the most important need was to formulate and follow an essentially uniform policy towards the extensive frontiers inhabited by savage tribes. The urgency of the last factor brought home the need for change in the system of administration of Assam. The Government of Bengal which was in charge of a very extensive area and a very large population, admitted the necessity of some relief.[63]

SEPARATION FROM BENGAL PRESIDENCY

APPOINTMENT OF CHIEF COMMISSIONER

The Governor-General in Council considered the issues involved and decided to separate the frontier province of Assam from the Bengal Presidency; it was to be put under a Chief Commisssioner who would be under the direct control and authority of the Government of India. But Sir William Grey, a member of the Governor-General's Council, differed as to the course of action to be taken to strengthen the Assam administration, though he too admitted the necessity of relieving the one-man Government of Bengal which could scarcely do justice to its heavy work and at the same time look after 1000 miles of frontiers. He suggested to provide the Lieutenant-Governor of Bengal with an Executive Council and leave the administrative departments of Assam independent of the central administration of Bengal, as Sind was administered from Bombay. Sir Henry Durand, another member of the Governor-General's Council, expressed doubt as to the efficiency of the proposed set up of Chief Commissionership. He pointed out, "Assam is so much connected with Bengal that it seems very inexpedient to separate it from that government, even though a Chief Commissioner be appointed as a panacea, which will not do much to restore its prospects unless the Bengal Government work cordially with him; and it is more likely to do so when under its own authority than if detached from it."[64]

But the Viceroy argued, "the object, I take it, is to strengthen the new administration and to bring it to a more forward state. The Government of India has far greater resources than the Government of Bengal command, both for assistance and encouragement. The new Chief Commissioner would be the man on whose personal exertion success would mainly depend, whoever be selected, he will assuredly prefer being under the Government of India and will thereby be in better heart and spirit." [65] Therefore, the Governor General addressed a despach to the Secretary of State for India proposing creation of a Chief Commissionership for Assam.

Administration under a Chief Commissioner was more personal than formal. As such, when newly acquired territories required an administration, a Chief Commissionership served as a convenient and useful machinery. Generally such a territory was governed in a rough and simple fashion by an executive partly civilian and partly military. The executive government accommodated all that was good in the indigenous institutions and in the local usages of the country in administering the territory. The head of the administration took quick decision on any issue depending upon the exigency of the situation.[66] Therefore, the Secretary of State for India observed, "I cannot doubt that when strength and directness of power are required in any subordinate administration, it is best to place that administration immediately under the Supreme Government so that it may, as directly as possible, enjoy the support and carry the authority of the Governor-General in Council. Assam and the eastern districts seem to be eminently a case requiring such an administration."[67] Receiving the approval of the Secretary of State for India, the Government of India constituted Assam into a Chief Commissionership on 7 February, 1874.[68]

The title of Chief Commissioner was first used in 1853 when John Lawrence was appointed head of the executive government in the Panjab in substitution of the Board of Administrators under a President. It was to distinguish the head of the Administration from the Financial and Judicial Commissioners who were also appointed at the same time. In earlier years, the title given to such a delegate entrusted with administrative functions in a new territory was Commissioner. For instance, Mountstuart Elphinstone was given this designation when he was appointed to administer the territories of the Deccan conquered from the Peshwa in 1818.[69] The Act of 1854, however, provided for the creation of Chief Commissionerships. It authorised the Governor-General in Council to take immediate authority and management by proclamation any territory and provide for its administration. But the title Chief Commissioner was not recognised by any Act of Parliament and as such the territories committed to the charge of a Chief Commissioner were theoretically under the immediate authority and management of the Governor-General in Council. Therefore, in official terminology, a Chief Commissionership was regarded as a Local Administration rather than a Local Government.[70]

DECLARATION OF SCHEDULED DISTRICTS

To provide for a simpler form of administration in the new province of Assam, the districts of Kamrup, Darrang, Nowgong, Sibsagar, Lakhimpur, Garo Hills, Khasi and Jaintia Hills, Naga Hills and Cachar were declared Scheduled Districts on 1 January, 1873, Goalpara on 15 December 1873, and Sylhet on 1 August 1874, as per resolutions of the Secretary of State in Council dated 15 September 1873 and 4 June 1874 respectively.[71] It was realised that the whole or parts of those districts were inhabited by hill tribes who lived unsophisticated life and were not fit for administration through the regular judicial and administrative set-up; the regulation and laws passed from time to time in the Legislatures of India were too sophisticated for them. Q. Vict. Act XXXIII, Chap. 2, known as an act to make better provisions for making laws and regulations for certain parts of India and for certain other purposes thereto, authorised to Local Administration to propose to the Governor-General in Council draft of any Regulation, together with the reasons thereof, for the peace and good government of the territories of the Scheduled Districts. Such drafts, when approved of by the Governor-General in Council and after it had received the assent of the Governor-General, were to be notified in the Local Gazette and the *Gazette of India* when it would have the force of law in the Scheduled Districts, or parts of the Scheduled Districts as proposed.[72] Special rules for the administration of justice, both civil and criminal, had already been provided for under provisions of this Act in the Garo, Khasi, Jaintia and Naga Hills; these were reissued under the provisions of the Scheduled District Act.[73] Now these were supposed to be extended to the fringes of the Darrang, Lakhimpur, Sibsagar and Nowgong districts on whose borders lived the hill tribes of the frontiers.

The problem of tribal administration had caught the attention of the Government of India after the rising of the Hos of Singbhum in 1831, the Khonds in 1846 and the Santhals in 1885. Measures to provide for a simpler form of administration for the tribal territories by regulations in which the tribal customs and conventions could be accommodated for settling the disputes had begun to be considered by the Government of India.[74] The results of application of special rules for the administration of justice in the Hill Districts of Assam under Q. Vict. Act XXXIII, Chap. 2 had been found satisfactory. Therefore, to give the Local Administration more powers to deal with the problem of tribal administration, a new Act known as the Scheduled Districts Act was passed by the Government of India in 1874.[75] This Act empowered the Chief Commissioner of Assam to extend to the frontier tracts, for peace and good government, with the previous sanction of the Governor-General in Council, any Act or part thereof passed by the Legislature of any provincial or of the Central Government, by notification in the Local Gazette. Under Section 2 of the said Act, the Chief Commissioner had the power to propose to the Governor-General in Council the draft of any Regulation for the peace and good government of the frontier tracts, which when approved by the Governor-General in Council had the force of law after notification in the Local Gazette. The same

Act authorised the Chief Commissioner, under Section 6, Clause C, to define by what authority and jurisdiction, powers and duties incidental to the operation of any enactment for the time being in force in the frontiers would be exercised and performed.[76]

Meanwhile the Inner Line Regulation was passed in 1873 and the Deputy Commissioners were asked by the Chief Commissioner to propose the Inner Line of their respective districts. The Deputy Commissioner of Lakhimpur, Col. Clarke, while submitting his proposal in respect of his district, stated that the frontier of his district was inhabited by tribesmen, whom it would be inadvisable to administer as people in other parts of the district, which were inhabited by more advanced plains people. The Chief Commissioner wrote to the Government of India that he would prepare the draft of a set of rules for the administration of justice in the frontier tracts which, if approved by the Governor-General in Council, would provide the basis of administration of justice in the frontier. He was advised to consult the rules in force in the Hill Districts of Assam for formulating his proposal.[77] Col. Clarke had drawn up the proposal, but, as he was subsequently transferred from Dibrugarh, Col. Graham, who succeeded him, submitted the proposal in 1876 to the Chief Commissioner.[78] The rules were further modified by the Chief Commissioner and then submitted to the Governor-General in Council for their approval.

The object of the rules was to provide an outline pattern of rules applicable ordinarily to all tracts of the frontier districts allowing exemption to semi-barbarous or barbarous people over whom British control had been exended, from the operation of regular system of procedure prescribed by the Civil and Criminal Procedure Codes, to which they would become subject on the inclusion of their country within the British limits. The end in view was to be attained by issuing a notification under Section 2 of the Scheduled Districts Act of 1874 declaring that the Civil and Criminal Procedure Codes were not to be in force in those tracts, and then under Section 6 (a) and 6 (b) of the said Act declaring by what authority the administration of the tracts was to be conducted and under what rules of procedure, as soon as any tract had been brought within its scope.[79]

But it was necessary to detract the areas of the existing regulation districts which were inhabited by tribal people who were to be exempted from the operation of Regulations and Acts, and define the boundary of the tracts separating them from the adjoining districts and repeal the Acts and Regulations operating in them, and again provide for their proper administration. The proposal had already been made by the Chief Commissioner to the Governor-General while proposing the Inner Line of his province.[80] After the specification of the Inner Line, it now became imperative to detract the tribal areas and provide for their administration. Therefore, the Chief Commissioner now submitted to the Governor-General in Council the draft of the Regulation which would authorise him to remove certain frontier tracts "inhabited or frequented by the barbarous or semi-civilised tribes" and repeal the operation of the enactments existing therein and provide for their proper administration. This draft was approved by the Governor-General in Council and assented to by the Governor-General and notified in the Gazette of India on 24 January 1880 and in the Assam Gazette on 31 January 1880.[81]

The Regulation, known as the Assam Frontier Tract Regulation or Regulation II of 1880, authorised the Chief Commissioner, under Section I, to specify the boundaries of the tracts by which they were to be separated from the regulation districts and define the authorities which would administer them under which Rules or Acts. Section II of the Regulation empowered him to remove or introduce Acts or Regulations for their proper administration.[82] The Chief Commissioner, by notification on 27 August 1884, withdrew the following Acts from the frontier tracts : the Court Fees Act, 1874; the Registration Act, 1877; the Indian Stamp Act, 1899; the Transfer of Properties Acts; the Criminal Procedure Code; and the Civil Procedure Code.[83] On the same date on which the boundary of the Lakhimpur Frontier Tract was defined, that is to say, on 22 August 1884, rules for the administration of justice in the Lakhimpur Frontier Tract were passed by the Chief Commissioner.[84]

But by defining boundary of the frontier tract, the existing responsibilities in regard to extending British control over tribes hitherto not interfered with were in no way increased. The rules for the administration of justice in the Dibrugarh

Frontier Tracts were formulated in such a way that the main principal of the system of administration was to leave the primary responsibility for reporting and preventing crimes on the village authorities, if any such authority existed, or any such authorities created where they did not exist, and to invest those authorities with power of disposing of petty cases among themselves, leaving the remainder to the discretion of the Political Officers.[85]

The Rules for the Administration of Justice, 1884, empowered the Deputy Commissioners of the frontier districts to nominate local authorities, subject to confirmation of the Chief Commissioner, and assign them their functions and define the limits within which they should perform their duties. The Regulation had provision to vest ordinary duties of police and justice, both criminal and civil, in the local authorities who would deal with petty cases according to the existing local customs and conventions. The more serious criminal cases and civil suits involving bigger amounts were to be dealt with by Deputy Commissioner or his Assistants in their political capacity, as also the cases involving the European British subjects or plains people. No legal formalities were to be observed by the tribal local authorities nor would legal advice from professional lawyers be allowed in their courts. The High Court of Judicature in Calcutta which had jurisdiction over the Assam Valley districts was denied jurisdiction over the frontier tracts, the Chief Commissioner being the highest court of appeal in the territory.[86]

ACTS EXTENDED AND ENACTMENTS

The following Acts were extended to the new charges and used for due administration of the frontier tracts : the Indian Penal Code, 1860 (XLV of 1860); the Indian Police Act, 1861 (XI of 1861); the Indian Arms Act, 1878 (XI of 1878); the Assam Land and Revenue Regulation, 1886 (I of 1886) with the exception of Sections 3-5; the Assam Forest Regulation, 1891 (VII of 1891); the Whipping Act, 1909 (IV of 1909); the Eastern Bengal and Assam Military Police Act, 1912 (III of 1912). The Chief Commisssioner explained to the Governor-General the reason for the extension of the above Acts. He wrote that the Assam

Land and Revenue Regulation was necessary in the frontier tracts for repealing any Regulation that might exist there: the Police Act was necessary for enforcing due discipline among the Police in the frontier tracts; Forest and Elephant Preservation Acts were necessary to protect the forests and elephants in the region; and finally, the Penal Code, the Arms Act and the Whipping Act were necessary for proper administration of the new charges.[87]

There were two sets of enactments in force in the frontier tracts—all Acts of the Governor-General in Council which extended *proprio-vigore* to the whole of British India and the operation of which had not been barred under section 2 of Assam Frontier Tract Regulation of 1880 or declared not to be in force under Section 3 of the Scheduled District Act of 1874, and secondly Acts and Regulations either passed specifically for a certain locality or definitely declared in force or extended with or without modification under sections 3 and 5 of Act XIV of 1874. In case of amending Acts, again there were three different classes. In case of all Acts applying *proprio-vigore* to the whole of British India at the time of passing of the Scheduled District Act of 1874, and not barred under the provisions of the Assam Frontier Tract Regulation of 1880 or the Scheduled District Act of 1874, were automatically in force in the Scheduled Districts, unless definitely barred either by the amending Act itself or by action under the Assam Frontier Tract Regulation or the Scheduled District Act. In case of Acts not extending to the whole of British India at that time and not declared to apply under section 3 of the Scheduled District Act amending Acts or separate measures which were extended under section 5 of that Act were only operative. Thirdly, in the case of Acts which though originally applicable to the whole of British India had been barred under Regulation II of 1880, or the Scheduled District Act, amending Acts would not come in force unless and until they were specially extended.[88]

Though the Assam Frontier Tract Regulation and Rules for the administration of justice were passed, no agency was provided for the administration of the new region. But in the late seventies and early eighties, the need for an officer who would serve in the frontier tract for a longer period was felt.

The simple and rude frontier tribes better knew the man whom they dealt with; the Deputy Commissioners, to whom was committed the charge of frontier administration and political relations with the hills tribes, did not stay in the district for a long period. The good relation that developed between a particular district officer and the tribes lapsed after the district officer was transferred. The new-comer lacked experience of frontier tribes and there was no continuity in frontier policy. The officers came on loan to Assam from the Bengal Government and looked for the day when they would go back from Assam. Therefore frontier administration lacked in continuity and understanding of the problems.

ASSISTANT POLITICAL OFFICER APPOINTED

In view of the above-mentioned facts, Sir Charles Elliot, while reviewing the results of the advance of outpost on Nizamghat on the left bank of the Dibang river in the Abor hills, proposed to appoint an Assistant to the Deputy Commissioner of Dibrugarh on the border of whose district lay the extensive Dibrugarh Frontier Tract and the frontier hills of the Abors whom the British regarded at that time as most stubborn and troublesome. He pointed out that an officer, if intelligent in his instinct, quick in his sympathies and a good linguist, might in due course of two or three years attain influence on the frontier and might from that vantage position use any opportunity that might occur of opening friendly communication with the tribes and impress upon them the advantage of regular commerce between the plains and their country. His suggestion was to put a man from police service in charge of frontier relations who would serve for a longer time than any Deputy Commissioner and thus would bring the personal factor in frontier politics.[89]

The first duty of the Assistant Political Officer, Sir Charles Elliot proposed, would be to make himself thoroughly acquainted with the history of relations between the Government and the hill tribes and gain all information that he might acquire from other local authorities; he would become personally acquainted with the leading members of the tribes, their chiefs and Kotokis, and by frequent tour in their territories establish as far as possible friendly and cordial relations with them; he would learn the local languages so as to enable him to speak with the tribesmen without the aid of interpreters and become a past master in border politics which would be his special sphere; and he would acquire as much knowledge as possible to arrive at right judgement and provide sound opinions on questions in relations to borders.[90] But Elliot did not propose to put the Assistant directly under him; he proposed to keep him under the Deputy Commissioner of Lakhimpur, as his subordinate and special adviser on frontier affairs.

In 1882, Jacks Francis Needham of the Bengal Police was appointed as Assistant Political Officer at Sadiya on the suggestion of Elliot. The Agency establisment, consisting of a clerk, an interpreter and the Harkaras of Sadiya, was now put under him. Though apparently the Assistant was appointed to cultivate good relations with the Abors in particular and all other tribes in general by touring the hills inhabited by them, he was saddled with much administrative business. The administration of the Frontier Tracts was now his headache and he was responsible for the arrangement of frontier outposts, their location and supplies and patrolling of the borders of the administrative districts. Moreover, he was assigned criminal work in and around Sadiya, maintain law and order in that territory and look after the collection of revenue in the settled villages within the frontier tracts.[91]

Needham served for 23 years as Assistant Political Officer and was succeeded by Noel Williamson in 1905.[92] During his long tenure of service in the Sadiya Frontier Tract (named after the headquater of the Dibrugarh Frontier Tract) he had succeeded in establishing an image of the government before the tribes and tried vigorously to achieve the objective of the government. The government policy was that of minimum of interference in the tribal life; it aimed at impressing upon the tribesmen the uselessness of raids on the British territory and at making them look upon the British as their master. By his extensive tours and punitive expeditions, Needham had bred in the hill tribes of the frontier a sense of looking towards the British as their master. In 1910, when the Chinese contigent appeared across Rima, the Mishmis reported to the British not only the advent of the Chinese but rejected the orders of the

Chinese, assuming themselves to be under the British paramountcy.[93]

During the term of Needham, the utilisation of the village authorities in the administration of the frontier tracts was not attempted. The administration was busy with preventing the tribesmen from violating the law within the British territory; they were asked not to take the law into their own hands in case of any offence being committed against them or anybody running away from their territory after doing wrong to seek asylum. To prevent the tribesmen's raids in the villages within easy march of the tribes beyond the Inner Line, a tract of territory, 10 miles in width from the Inner Line on both sides, was kept as no-man's land where no settlement was usually allowed.[94] The people who ran away from the tribal territory beyond the Inner Line were kept in detention for sometime for verifying the innocence of the person migrating into British territory; and in case of run-away slaves a ransom was usually paid to the owner of the slave who was allowed to purchase his freedom by earning money.[95] If any tribesman or tribe violated the British law for settlement of dispute, the man or the tribes' leaders were taken into custody and tried according to the Rules for the Administration of Justice in the Frontier Tracts.[96]

Noel Williamson wanted to bring the frontier tracts and the hills beyond the Inner Line under the immediate and direct control of the Government as has already been noted.[97] He envisaged the gradual extension of a system of taxation in the hill areas in recognition of the British authority over the tribes. Further, he wanted to utilise the indigenous tribal institutions for the administration of the frontier hills.[98] The investment with authority of the village headman under the Rules for the Administration of Justice was initiated, and[99] by his tours and display of force Williamson wanted to impress upon the tribes British paramountcy over them. He wanted first to bring under control and authority the Abors who held a position of pre-eminance among the hill tribes, for if the Abors were brought under subservience, the other tribes would be easily brought to terms.[100]

DIVISION OF FRONTIER IN THREE TRACTS

The Chief Commissioner of Assam proposed to the Government of India the division of the frontier tracts which after the Simla Conference was supposed to extend up to the international border, i.e., the McMahon Line into three sections as recommended by General Bower. The three new charges would be known respectively as : (i) Central and Eastern Sections, North-East Frontier Tract; (ii) Western Section, North-East Frontier Tract; and (iii) Lakhimpur Frontier Tract. The Inner boundary suggested for the Central and Eastern Sections ran along the existing Dibrugarh Frontier Tract, but it was stretched a little further south of the existing boundary to accommodate a strip of country south of the existing Dibrugarh Frontier Tract to include lands inhabited entirely by the Miris, as also Saikhowa which was the Bazar for the frontier tribes, though it included five small villages inhabited by the Assamese people. The boundary of the Western Section of the North-East Frontier Tract would run from the river Subansiri which was the boundary between the Central and Eastern Sections and the Western Section. The Inner boundary of this section was also stretched a little within the district boundary to include some lands inhabited by hillmen and to bring them within the jurisdiction of the Political Officers. The Lakhimpur Frontier Tract was so defined as to leave within the regular jurisdiction of the Deputy Commissioner of Lakhimpur the areas in which exploration of coal and oil were being worked and through which the tea railway line of Assam Railways and Trading Company ran, giving him at the same time jurisdiction, under the Assam Frontier Tract Regulation of 1880, over the less civilised area over which the Assam Oil Company prospected for oil.[101]

Draft Notification extending to these territories, the Assam Frontier Tract Regulation of 1880 by the the Governor-General of India in Council, and repealing all enactments in force except the Assam Frontier Tract Regulation of 1880, together with the Scheduled District Act of 1870, were placed before the Government of India. These were accepted. The Governments of India and Assam notified these changes, and now emerged new charges in the Frontier Administration of India in 1914 with provisions for peace and good government in them.[102]

The effect of these notifications was to extend the British authority over the frontier hills beyond the previous Lakhimpur Frontier Tracts and it was now necessary to provide personnel for its proper management. For this purpose, W.C.M. Dundas of Bengal Police, who was on Special Duty on the North-East Frontier with three Assistants, was appointed as Political Officer of the Central and Eastern Sections of the North-East Frontier. Dundas had accompanied the Dibang valley promenade as Political Officer in 1912 and made recommendations for management of the new territory.[103] G.A. Nevill of Bengal Police, on Special Duty in the North-East Frontier, who also had taken part in the exploratory promenade as Political Officer in 1912, was also enlisted for appointment as Political Officer of the new charge of the Western Section.[104] The third Section, of course, was left in charge of the Deputy Commissioner of Lakhimpur, who had jurisdiction over the district of Lakhimpur on whose border this Section stood.[105]

The management of the frontier hills meant, of course, exercise of 'loose political control' over areas to be gradually brought under administrative control. Though the Assam Frontier Tract Regulation of 1880 was extended to the hills following the precedent of 1898 when under Regulation II of that year the Lushai Hills were placed under the jurisdiction of the Chief Commissioner of Assam, the Administration did not at a time bring the hills under immediate authority. It planned to advance gradually into the interior hills, step by step.[106] In exercise of the powers conferred by Section I of the Assam Frontier Tract Regulation of 1880, the Governor-General in Council extended to the new charges Rules for Administration of Justice as they were in force in the Frontier Tracts.[107]

Administrative Structure of Tracts

The Political Officers were provided with establishment for administrative control over the frontier tribes step by step from hill to hill and from hills to the borders. The Central and Eastern Sections were supposed to have three sub-divisions and Dundas was provided with two Assistant Superintendents of Police, T.E. Forze and T.P.M.O. Callaghan, and one Extra-Assistant Commissioner, W.T.H. Ballantine, as Assistant Political Officers to be appointed in Abor Hills, Mishmi Hills and

Sadiya respectively to assist him in controlling and administering the territory. But Nevill was not given any Assistant, as it was expected that the control area in the north-western hills of his charge would not be established in near future, as the First Great War had ensued and border affairs had temporarily lost their importance in the sight of the government.[108]

The duties of the respective office-bearers of the Frontier Service may be noted for understanding the administration of the frontier. The duty of the Political Officer in the former Frontier Tract was to administer justice as per Rules for the Administration of Justice in the Frontier Tracts, maintain law and order, collect revenue and poll-tax from the tribal villages which were gradually brought under assessment, supervise the local authorities which were now invested with powers under the Frontier Tract Regulation, and arrange posting of the Assam Rifles men and patrols.[109]

The Political Officer had the power to expel anybody from his jurisdiction if he considered the presence of such a person prejudicial for the peace and security of his charge. A system of poll-tax began to be levied gradually on the hill tribes, who were exempted so long from taxation. The Political Officer was responsible for its collection.[110] In the event of fighting occurring or being imminent, the officer commanding the escort would take charge of the operation and would be responsible to take measures necessary to ensure the success and safety of the force.[111] The Political Officers were to hold an annual Durbar where they would present *posa* to the tribes, hear their grievances and explain to them the policy of the government.[112]

But to ensure the achievement of the above objective in tracts like the frontier hills it was impossible for the Political Officer with one or two Assistants to carry on the administration. It was wellnigh impossible for the officer to go round the entire area even once in the whole year. Therefore, the services of the Political Jamadars, Harkaras and Kotokis were very important. The Kotokis, now under the Political Officer, were on regular duty and toured the area under him and brought to his notice any breach of rule of peace, and in many cases they attended the meetings of the tribal council which settled disputes. The Political Jamadar did the same job where there was no Kotoki on regular employ. In the Lakhimpur Frontier Tract, the Political Officer disposed of petty cases, both civil and criminal, bringing to the Deputy Commissioner only the serious ones for trial in regular process[113] and he was responsible for collection of poll-tax through the village heads.[114] The Political Jamadar of Margherita held the post almost hereditarily and the tribal people having disputes to settle came to him in the first instance, as if he was the man to satisfy them.[115] The Harkaras served a very useful purpose where there was regular civil police to help the administration in summoning the offenders and bringing them for trial. The Harkaras carried the order of the officers from place to place and served as a check on bad characters.[116]

EXPERIMENTS IN ADMINISTRATION

The Agencies which served to bring the tribes under government influence were administrative posts, trading posts and Military or Armed Police posts which were set up in different parts of the frontier hills. An administrative post was set up with a suitable unit of Military Police or detachment of army and a medical dispensary. While the Political Officer was the symbol of government authority, the Military Police served as a deterrent to any rising or revolt. But the medical dispensaries in the administrative posts served the tribesmen besides treating the administrative and military personnel. These centres relieved the suffering of the tribal people unaccustomed to any sort of medical treatment and thereby won their hearts, preparing them to eagerly welcome the government.[117] Nevill, the Political Officer of the Western Section, repeatedly recommended the extension of administration posts with armed guards and medical dispensaries in the area under his charge.[118] Besides, such an administrative post was expected to have some schools and chapels for community worship which had civilising influence over the tribesmen. The shops in the administrative posts facilitated the marketing of the tribal people and that also endeared the government posts to them.

As a matter of fact, facilities of commerce had a greater effect on the tribes to bring them under the government. The tour diary of the Chief Commissioner of Assam shows that he was very eager to advance trading posts through the Abor hills into the interior with schooling facilities to impress the people and bring them under the influence and control of the government. A trading post consisted of some private shops which would exchange goods with the tribesmen or sell these to them at government-fixed price.[119] The tribes of the interior so long were barred by those on the borders to come for trade into the plains. But when the trading facilities were extended gradually into the interior, people realised their usefulness and welcomed the government. The Chief Commissioner wrote in his tour diary that for opening up the country and advancing trading posts within it was necessary to construct roads linking the interior. For the purpose, a corps of Sappers and Miners were employed to serve under the Political Officers permanently and a plan of advancing gradually into the interior was also chalked out.[120]

He wrote, "as the road is made, I would move the Balek post further and further west until a position is found which would meet all the political considerations in the control area between Pasighat and the Subansiri, and remove the blocks to trade which now exist ...Trade is but one aspect of the case. It is equally important to get near the people over whom we are to exercise loose political control". Later he wrote to the Government of India, "No sort of control can be exercised over the tribes unless the country is gradually opened out. The Chief Commissioner. . . solicits permission only to the gradual extension of the bridle path and the gradual move forward of the trading post in the direction of Riga as well as to move the Balek outpost to Mishing."[121] Agricultural demonstrations in trading outposts educated the tribesmen. Medical benefits and educational facilities attached to the trading posts brought the people under government influence.[122]

An Armed Police or Military post in the frontier not only demonstrated the government authority in the area of its location but the enterprise of the personnel of the force had much educative effect on the people. The forces were employed in building roads and cultivating rice in the terraces or in plain-lands in wet-rice cultivation. The examples of the force were followed by the tribal people which benefited them ; friendship also developed between the forces and the tribesmen. Besides, in big posts there were medical facilities which were made available to the tribal people. With the extension of political control over the Mishmis an armed police post was established at Walong. The members of the force were supposed to produce rice for their consumption and thus demonstrate to the people improved methods of cultivation.[123]

The British Government had, prior to the Simla Conference, scrupulously avoided all responsibility of administration in the frontier hills which were kept beyond the Inner Line. But after that it ushered in an era of activity to endear British authority to the tribal people. Agricultural demonstration, medical benefits and schooling facilities began to be gradually extended in the frontier territory. The Administration tried to provide primary schools and dispensaries with the administrative and trading posts. Agricultural demonstrators were employed to educate the tribal people in the improved methods of cultivation; improved varieties of seeds were supplied in some areas to impress upon the simple tribal folk. But the measures were belated; as the World Wars intervened between their withdrawal from India and the Simla Conference and the freedom movement in India gained momentum during the intervening period, the resources made available for welfare purposes were too meagre to have any significant impact.

Notwithstanding the above factors, the British administrators appreciating the immensity of the problems of the frontier administration carried on experiments till practically the end of their period in the frontier territory. The names of the Western and Central and Eastern Sections of the frontier administration were changed in 1919 and they were henceforth known as Balipara and Sadiya Frontier Tracts respectively.[124] The Frontier Tracts were kept under the charge of the government when reforms were introduced in 1920 in the new Governor's province of Assam.

The authors of the Mont-Ford Reforms emphasised the necessity to protect the backward tribes in the Frontier Tracts and recommended to keep them outside the purview of the reforms.[125] The Government of India Act, 1919, accommodated the recommendation to safeguard the interest of the backward tribes.[126] Therefore, the Governor of Assam continued to administer the frontier tracts with the Political Officers and their Assistants, as the Chief Commissioners had done when the new province of Assam had come into force.

The Indian Statutory or Simon Commission also emphasised the need to keep the frontier hills outside the jurisdiction of the provincial government and, as demanded by the Government of Assam, it also recommended to keep the frontier territories as "Excluded Areas" where Indian Ministers would have no say or control.[127] The Government of India Act, 1935, provided in sections 91-92 for a different sort of administration for the frontier tracts. It provided for creation of "Excluded Areas" by the Secretary of State under section 91 (2), and alter or define the boundary of such Areas. The administration of the said tracts under section 91 (3) was vested in the Governor of the province at his "discretion" as a delegate of the Governor General. Under Section 92 (1), the Indian Legislature had no power to legislate for these areas unless requested by the Governor, and Section 92 (2) provided for special regulations to be framed by the Governor for the peace and good government of the Areas; it also empowered him to extend to the Areas any Act of the Indian or any provincial legislature with or without modifications.[128] By an order of 3 March 1936, the frontier tracts were declared to be "Excluded Areas".[129] In 1937, the frontier tracts were put under the Governor's Secretariat and a new department termed as "Tribal Affairs Department" was created under a separate Secretary and the Chief Secretary was relieved of the frontier affairs. No provision was made to return or nominate representatives from the Areas to sit either in the Provincial or the Central Legislature to take care of their interests. The frontier tracts continued to be administered under the provisions of the Assam Frontier Tracts Regulation, 1880, and the Scheduled District Act, 1874, as they were administered before the introduction of the Reforms in 1920 and 1937.

During the Second Great War, when the Japanese made an attempt to penetrate into India through Manipur and the Naga hills and China was cut off from the world through the sea, the British felt an urge to speed up the direct administrative control over the tribal hills on the frontier. For that purpose, an Adviser to the Governor of Assam was appointed in 1943.

The rank of the Adviser was that of a Senior Secretary to the Government and he was supposed to carry on the administration and development of the hill areas of the North-East Frontier under the nominal authority of the Governor who had many preoccupations and had very little time to devote to the tribal affairs.[130] J.P. Mills, who had much experience of tribal administration, was given charge of the Adviser's portfolio.[131]

Meanwhile the importance of the low-lying hills leading to Burma across the Patkai through the Pangsu pass increased as a result of opening a metalled road to connect China through Burma. For giving more attention to the area, portions of the Sadiya Frontier Tract and the Lakhimpur Frontier Tract were combined to be put under a separate Political Officer in 1943.[132] The charge was named as Tirap Frontier Tract. Towards the close of the Great War, the British once again felt the necessity to advance towards Tawang up to the McMahon Line and, therefore, the Balipara Frontier Tract was bifurcated in 1946 into the Sela Sub-Agency and Subansiri Area.[133]

Thus, it appears from a study of the growth of the administration of the North-East Frontier that the East India Company's Government cared very little to provide a system of administration for the frontier territory, for their concern was to provide for a system of security for the province of Bengal. With that purpose in view, they came to Assam and ultimately annexed it to the Bengal Presidency.

The transfer of authority to the Crown did not immediately bring in a change in the mode of administration of the frontier. But gradually, in the interest of the security of the Indian Empire, the frontier territory had to be demarcated and a system of administration of the hitherto neglected territory began to be devised. As the diverse tribes lived savage and semi-barbarous life, a rough and ready system of administration was created by special provisions like the Assam Frontier Tract Regulation, 1880, Scheduled Districts Act, 1874, and later by providing safeguards in Government of India Acts, 1919 and 1935. The British realised the necessity of developing the area, and small charges under Political Officers began to be created. During the Second Great War, an Adviser to the Governor for fast development of the region was appointed as the Governor and the General Administration were too busy to pay much attention to tribal territories. Before the fruition of the belated measures, the British had to withdraw from India, leaving the burden of developing the system of administration to its logical culmination to the free Indian Government.

REFERENCES

1. Political and Secret Consulations, 2 July 1824, No. 16.
2. *Ibid*, 5 April 1825, No. 24.
3. A.J.M. Mills' Report, p. lxxxiv.
4. *Ibid.*
5. Assam Administration Report, 1920-21, para 75.
6. Letters of the District Officers appended to Mills' Report (1854), show it.
7. Foreign Proceedings (India), July 1838, Nos. 84-85.
8. Political Proceedings (Assam), December 1911, No. 1.
9. *Ibid.*
10. Mills' Report, p. lxxxiv.
11. *Ibid*, p. lxxxvi.
12. Political Proceedings (Bengal), July 1866, No. 70.
13. Mills' Report, p. lxxxiv.
14. Political Proceedings (Bengal), 8 March 1843, No. 147.
15. John Butler, *Travels and Adventures in the Province of Assam*, p. 5.
16. H. Barua, *op. cit.*, p. 36.
17. Judicial Proceedings (Bengal), December 1861, No. 195.
18. Foreign Proceedings (Assam), August 1884, No. 6.
19. Political Proceedings (Assam), April 1905, No. 76.
20. Foreign Proceedings (Assam). August 1884, No. 6.
21. Judicial Proceedings (Bengal), December 1862, No. 195.
22. Political Proceedings (Assam), April 1905, No. 70.
23. Lakhimpur Deputy Commissioner's Collection, No. XII, F. 7, 1904-08.
24. Political Proceedings (Assam), April 1905, No. 59.
25. *Ibid*, No. 64.
26. *Ibid*, No. 71.
27. Foreign Proceedings (Assam), August 1884, No. 5.
28. *Ibid*, March 1874, No. 20.
29. Assam Administration Report, 1920-21, para 75.
30. Assam Administration Report, 1874-76, Part IIA, para 112 & 114.
31. Eastern Bengal and Assam Administration Report, 1905-06, Part IIA, para 120.
32. Mills' Report, p. lxxxiv.
33. Foreign Proceedings (Assam), April 1905, Nos. 59-93.
34. *Ibid*, March 1885, No. 24.
35. *Ibid*, January 1880, No. 1.
36. *Ibid*, March 1885, No. 24.

37. Police Proceedings (Bengal), December 1861, No. 180.
38. Foreign Proceedings (Assam), November 1874, No. 1. The post at Behali consisted of 10 soldiers, Singlijan 20, Ghera 12, Gohpur 12, Katori 12, Barpathar 20, Ooahat 15, Sellonibari 15 and Joyhing 19.
39. *Ibid*, January 1880, No. 1.
40. L.W. Shakespeare, *History of the Assam Rifles*, p. 6.
41. *Ibid*, p. 7.
42. *Ibid*, p. 8.
43. Police Proceedings (Bengal), July 1861, No. 252.
44. Police Proceedings (Bengal), October 1870, No. 137.
45. *Ibid.*
46. *Ibid*, December 1861, No. 179.
47. *Ibid*, September 1861, No. 340.
48. *Ibid.*
49. Home Public Proceedings (India), March 1876, Nos. 33-37.
50. *Imperial Gazatteer*, Vol. IV, p. 101.
51. Sir Charles Alfred Elliot, son of Rev. H.V. Elliot of Brighton was born in December 1835. He was educated at Harrow and Trinity College, Cambridge. He secured Indian Civil Service by open competition and arrived in India in November, 1886. He served in North-West Frontier Province between 1870-77, in Mysore as Famine Commissioner in 1877 and became CSI in 1878. He was Secretary to the Famine Commission of 1878 and Census Commissioner of 1878. In 1881 Sir Elliot was appointed as the Chief Commissioner of Assam and served in the Frontier Province for five years. Subsequently he held the post of President of the Committee for the retrenchment of public expenditure, 1886. He was a member of the Supreme Council between 1887-90 and in 1890 he became the Lt. Governor of Bengal; he served the province for five years. Sir Elliot laboured with ability and energy in all charges and became an expert in Settlement, Famine, Finance and Education. *See* Buckland, *op. cit.*, p. 136.
52. Home Public Proceedings (India), August 1883, No. 86.
53. Judicial Proceedings (Assam), 1917, Nos. 53-54.
54. L.E. Rose, *North-East Frontier Agency of India*, p. 58.
55. Home Public Proceedings (India), December 1884, No. 11.
56. Lakhimpur Deputy Commissioner's Collection, No. XII, F. 58, 1904-06.
57. Judicial Proceedings (Assam), 1917, Nos. 53-54.
58. *Ibid* (Bengal), December 1857, Nos. 182-84.
59. L.E. Rose, *op. cit.*, p. 62.
60. Shakespeare, *op. cit.*, p. VI.
61. See, p. 69, 134.
62. Foreign Secret Proceedings (India), 1871, Nos. 37-39.
63. *Ibid.*
64. *Ibid.*
65. *Ibid.*
66. W.J. Kaye, *The Administration of the East India Company*, p. 433.

67. Home Public Proceedings (India), October 1873, No. 517.
68. *Ibid*, February 1874, No. 165. Also *Gazette of India*, 1874, No. 6.
69. *Imperial Gazetteer*, vol. IV, p. 32.
70. Report on the Constitutional Reforms (1919), para 42. Also Ilbert, *The Government of India*, pp. 92-94.
71. Assam Administration Report, 1874-75, part IIA, para 144.
72. *Ibid*, para 143.
73. *Ibid*, 1882-83, para 103.
74. (Col.) P.N. Luthra, *Constitutional and Administrative Growth of NEFA*, p. 18.
75. *Ibid.*
76. *Ibid*, p. 48-49.
77. Foreign Political Proceedings (India), October 1884, Nos. 366-375.
78. Foreign Proceedings (Assam), April 1884, No. 5.
79. *Ibid.*
80. Foreign Political Proceedings (India), October 1884, Nos. 366-75.
81. Foreign Proceedings (Assam), April 1884, No. 1.
82. *Ibid.*
83. *Ibid*, July 1879, No. 4.
84. Judicial Department (Assam), File No. 134J of 1884.
85. Foreign Proceedings (Assam), April 1884, No. 5.
86. Judicial Department (Assam), File No. 134J, Sl. 21, 1884.
87. Political Proceedings (Assam), December 1914, Nos. 14-50.
88. Lakhimpur Deputy Commissioner's Collection, No. XIV, F. 40, 1910-12.
89. Deputy Commissioner's Collection, No. XII, F. 6 of 1906.
90. *Ibid.*
91. R. Reid, *op. cit.*, p. 184.
92. Lakhimpur Deputy Commissioner's Collection, No. XIV, of 1910-11, F. 3.
93. *Ibid.*
94. Foreign Proceedings (Assam), March 1874, No. 16.
95. *Ibid*, No. XVII, F. 17 of 1916-17; Also Collection XII, F. 6 of 1904-08.
96. See p. 101.
97. Deputy Commissioner's Collection, No. XIV, F. 32 of 1909-10.
98. *Ibid*, Collection No. XII, F. 26 of 1904-08.
99. *Ibid*, Collection No. XIV, F. 18 of 1909.
100. *Ibid*, Collection No. XII, F. 26 of 1904-08.
101. Political Proceedings (Assam), April 1914, No. 2.
102. Political Proceedings (Assam), January 1914, No. 25.
103. Political Proceedings (Assam), May 1913, Nos. 1-15.
104. *Ibid.*
105. Poiltical Proceedings, April 1914, No. 2.
106. Political Proceedings, January 1914, No. 25. Also Administration Report, 1937-39.
107. Deputy Commissioner's Collection, No. XVII of 1916-17, F. 11.
108. Political Proceedings (Assam), May 1913, Nos. 1-15. Hitherto there

were three political establishments at Dibrugarh, North Lakhimpur and Sadiya; there were two Interpreters, 4 Political Jamadars, 1 Hill Kotoki and five Harkaras under the Deputy Commissioner at Dibrugarh, 1 Political Jamadar and 2 Harkaras at North Lakhimpur under the Sub-divisional Officer 1, and 1 Mishmi Interpreter, 1 Harkara and two Chaprasis at Sadiya under the Political Officer at Sadiya. But now the Frontier Tract was divided into three charges and the Deputy Commissioner of Lakhimpur had only to deal with some Singpho and Naga tribes of the newly created Lakhimpur Frontier Tract. He retained one Political Jamadar at Margherita and two Interpreters at Margherita and Joypur respectively and three Harkaras, two for Margherita and one for Joypur, and two Harkaras at his Dibrugarh office. See Political Proceedings, May, 1913, No. 8.

By far the largest charge was supposed to be the Central and Eastern Sections. Four clerks were appointed for the Office of the Political Officer and one Record Keeper was now appointed for his office. Two clerks were provided for two Assistant Political Officers' offices; two Political Jamadars for the Singphos and the Galong Abors respectively were provided for. Besides, there were two Tibetan Interpreters and two Interpreters for Mijus, 2 for Taraons, 2 for Chulikata Mishmis, 5 for Abors and one each for Khamptis and Singphos. As many as 10 Harkaras and 7 Chaprasis were provided for different offices. In the area under the Political Officer there were three big river crossings. Therefore 10 boatmen were employed: 6 for Sadiya, 2 for the Lohit valley and 2 for Pasighat or the Dibang. See Political Proceedings, May 1913, No. 19.

For establishment of Political Officer of the Western Section, one clerk, two Interpreters for Bhutia and Tibetan respectively, 1 Kotoki (for the Akas) and three Chaprasis and two Harkaras to serve in North Lakhimpur were sanctioned. But the Political Officer proposed to have three clerks, 2 Interpreters, 1 Kotoki for the whole year and 4 Kotokis for six months a year, 5 Chaprasis and one Chowkidar for his establishment. As the area under him was full of inaccessible forests having no regular track, he also wanted to have under him one elephant, two Mahuts and two grass-cutters for the elephant. Because of the war exigency, the clerks were not provided for the extra Harkaras and Chaprasis, but the elephant and Mahuts were provided for his service. See Political Proceedings, May 1913, Nos. 62-68.

109. R. Reid, *op. cit.*, p. 183.

110. Political Proceedings, January 1914, No. 25.

111. Political Proceedings, December 1911, No. 1.

112. Political Proceedings, (East Bengal and Assam), February 1911, No. 77.

113. Lakhimpur Deputy Commissioner's Collection, No. IX of 1937, Sl. 1-7.

114. Political Proceedings (Assam), December 1914, Nos. 1-3. Also Collection XII of 1904-05, F. 1.

115. Administrative Jurisictions, p. 1.
116. Lakhimpur Deputy Commissioner's Collection, No. XII, F. 10, 1904-08.
117. Annual Administration Report, Western Section, 1927-28.
118. *Ibid.*
119. Political Proceedings (Assam), July 1913, No. 56.
120. *Ibid.*
121. *Ibid*, January 1915, No. 75.
122. *Ibid*, July 1913, No. 56.
123. *Ibid*, July 1914, No. 27.
124. Administrative Jurisdictions, p. 1.
125. Report on Indian Constitutional Reforms., p. 129.
126. Basu's *Constitutional Documents*, vol. I. p. 91.
127. Report of the Indian Statutory Commission, vol. II, pp. 108-110.
128. Basu's Constitutional Documents, vol. I., pp. 192-93.
129. *Assam Government Hand Book*, p. 1.
130. P.N. Luthra, *op. cit.*, p. 14.
131. *Ibid.*
132. Administrative Jurisdictions, p. 1.
133. *Ibid*, p. 2.

5

British Policy in the North-East Frontier

Sir Alexander Mackenzie writes in his *Memorandum on the North-East Frontiers of Bengal* that "there has been always a decided policy towards those tribes (North-East Frontier tribes) must be evident".[1] That there had been a policy is undisputed, but it is not easy to trace its development. After the First Anglo-Burmese War, the British established themselves in the valley of the Brahmaputra expelling the Burmese from the country. As a result, they now faced a new problem, the problem of the hill tribes of the Assam Burma frontiers. A policy began to be formulated. It was not a static one. It had to be geared up to meet the exigencies in the frontiers. The essence of the policy was to control the tribal areas through the exercise of limited administrative authority.

The political aspect of the policy at its initial stage was to use the tribes on the eastern fringes, as a screen between the newly acquired territories and the Kingdom of Burma, was initiated.[2] With a view to using the Singpho tracts as a screen against the Burmese, treaties were concluded with the Singpho chiefs and the Khampti chiefs. The Moamaria tracts were also kept separate from the Upper Assam principality of Purandar Singh who was enthroned in 1832 and allowed to rule till 1838, with a view to securing ready supply of provisions for British troops passing through the region. But at Sadiya and Joypur, contingents of British Army were deployed to discharge watch and ward functions on the frontiers.

Meanwhile the study of the Ahom relations with the tribes to the west of Sadiya was undertaken and Bhutanese claims upon the Assam Duars were examined. It was found that the territories on the foothills were extremely rich; they contained valuable forests producing timber, rubber and ivory, and the fertile land in the area would produce surplus revenue if farmers could be helped to take up their cultivation.[3] Coal (1825) and petroleum (1825) were discovered in Upper Assam and tea bushes were found in the jungles nearby (in 1823). Tea was an important item of import of Great Britain from China and a very good amount of gold and silver bullions had to be exported from Great Britain to pay for the Chinese tea. The success of its cultivation in Assam in the later half of the century had a decisive effect on the Company's policy in the North-East Frontier. Moreover, the prospects of coal, mined since 1828, and petroleum, drilled from 1866, enhanced the value of Assam to the Company.

A study of the tribes revealed that, except towards the west, outside the eastern boundary of Bhutan there was no organised kingdom and the tribes there were not capable of resisting the British arms. But the attitude of the powers beyond the Chinese and Tibetan Governments had to be ascertained.[4] Therefore, to begin with, the tribes were called upon to forego their rights over the foothills and the adjacent plains as the lands were necessary for settlement of new ryots and tea plantations in lieu of payment by the British Government. Beginning with the Bhutias of Bhutan, a series of engagements were entered into with the tribes by which they undertook to surrender their rights in these territories in consideration of regular payment of compensation by the Company's Government.[5] The Government, however, did not intend to interfere in the affairs of the tribes who were to be left alone up in their hills.

PAYMENT OF 'POSA'

The payment of compensation in the form of *posa* or assignment of a part of revenue was a pre-British system. The Ahoms had introduced the system to reconcile the hill tribes living on the frontier of their kingdom[6]. "The *posa*", writes Mackenzie, "which under the Assam Government was paid to most of the hill tribes bordering on the plains was not, as has been sometimes imagined, an uncertain, ill-defined exaction depending entirely upon the capacity of the different hordes who might descend to lay it; it was really a fixed, well-ascertained revenue payment on account of which a corresponding remission was made in the rent of the ryot satisfying it."[7] The Company's Government made a substantial change in the system which had existed under the Ahom rulers. It stopped the direct collection of the dues by the tribes themselves from the ryots, for it led sometimes to quarrels; instead, it began to pay them some cash, later called 'blackmail' collecting at the same time full dues from the ryots who were exempted from payment of dues to the tribesmen. This arrangement cut off direct contact between the ryots and the tribes.

Posa was payment in lieu of dues which the tribes were entitled to claim on the basis of customs recognised by the Ahom rulers. It was basically different from 'blackmail' which initially meant payment to prevent raids and implied that raiders had no recognised right of admission. 'Blackmail' had originated in Bengal in a different context under British rule.[8] The system of payment of 'blackmail' was a British policy which originated in a different context. The aborigines of the Rajmahal Hills in the Presidency of Bengal had become a terror to the surrounding country and military expeditions had failed to subdue them. Thereupon the Government of Bengal had introduced the system of cash payment to the tribal chiefts of the region on condition of good behaviour and thereafter the tribes remained quiet and peaceful. The amount paid to the Rajmahal chiefs was larger than that paid to the tribes in the North-East Frontier which was meagre. Nevertheless, the principle was the same, *viz.*, protection of the plains against the ravages of tribal raiders, and it was expected to be as efficacious in the North-East Frontier as in the case of Bengal, for it was expected to impress upon the tribes in an indirect manner the consequences of the risk of their raid in the plains.[9]

SHOW OF FORCE AGAINST VIOLATIONS

The consequences of non-compliance with the terms of engagements that different tribes had entered into with the British Government amounted, in some cases, to a 'blockade', that is, the closure of the markets of the plains to the offending tribe. A prohibitive order was issued to the effect that they would not be allowed to come down to the plains to purchase their necessaries; police patrol on the border of their hills was strengthened and watch was kept over their movement. In case of serious offences like murder or kidnapping of British subjects, a demand of surrender of the culprits to the British authority through the native political agent was served for the trial of the offenders under the government. If the demand was not complied with, an expedition to punish the offending tribes was despatched to the hills under a Political Officer with suitable armed forces. The expedition tried first through peaceful means and negotiation to arrest the offenders and realise a fine for non-compliance with the orders of the government and, in case of kidnapping, to secure the release of the persons kidnapped together with those connected with their capture. Sometimes, collective fines were imposed on the village of the offenders or on the tribe in case the culprits could not be arrested. In case the tribesmen resisted in any way the measures of the Administration to punish the guilty or adopted a hostile attitude, the whole village suffered. Fire was set to the houses of the village and all were burnt indiscriminately. The idea behind was to impress upon the whole tribe the dire consequences of the acts of a few guilty persons and to put the wrath of the whole community on the guilty, thus preventing in future the wild acts of its members.

This policy also has been traced back to the days of Ahom rule. The Ahom king Rudra Singh is said to have sent an expedition to the Dafla hills for the violence the Daflas had perpetrated on the plains and the officer in charge of the expedition is said to have brought a number of Daflas to the plains to serve under the government as a punishment.[10] S.K. Bhuyan has equated the Ahom policy to that of the British. He holds that it was a policy of "conciliation backed by a display of force."[11] But our study of the British relations with the frontier tribes shows that the British policy was different. The British law did not permit the molestation or destruction of property of an absconding criminal or his relations, but in the frontier for the supposed crime of a few sometimes the village and even the whole community suffered. It is uncertain as to how far the British Government followed the Ahom practice.

To begin with, the attitude of the tribes towards the British Government did not seem to have been hostile. The Khamptis and the Singphos had accepted the British overtures of friendship and Scott had succeeded in concluding the engagements he had in view. The attitude of the Abors (Adis) was friendly till the middle of the century. Capt. Neufville wrote in 1830 that the Abors were best disposed of all the tribes. The Daflas and the Akas (Hrussos) agreed to accept the money payment in lieu of their right to collect their *posa* in the Duars. The so-called extra-Bhutan Bhutias (Mompas and Sherdukpens) agreed to the British proposal of annual payment by the British Government for surrendering their right of direct collection in their Duars and thereafter never troubled the government or the people of the plains. But after the consolidation of British rule in Assam, the tribes became alive to the inherent dangers of the new system and became restive. The Khamptis were the first to revolt and were assisted by the Singphos. The might of the British arms suppressed the Khamptis attempt to regain their independence. The Khamptis were divided and dispersed over four tracts and brought under the direct control of the government.

The Abors' attempt to assert their supremacy over their fellow-tribes, the Miris, and over their land inhabited by the Assamese gold-washers, resulted in several raids and subsequent punitive British expeditions into their hills.[12] They had to acknowledge the supremacy of the British over the territories up to the foot-hills in an engagement in which the government promised to pay them regular annual subsidy for surrendering their claims over the lands up to the hills.[13] But the Abor discontent continued to mount; any attempt to interfere in their affairs was resented and opposed even after the government took upon itself the administration of the hills directly.[14]

The Akas and Daflas were giving trouble to the government till practically the end of British rule; their submission and the maintenance of peace depended upon the Admintstration's capacity to resist them. In the west, the Mompas and the Sherdukpens did not give the government practically any trouble till the end of their period in India. Perhaps they were not interfered with in any way by the British Government and they had an organised system of government of their own which enforced law and order in their hills where they had extensive territories. The Bhutias followed Buddhism which also instilled in them some sort of obedience, humility and regard for engagement.[15]

In the extreme east the Singphos and the Khamptis settled down to peaceful pursuits because they had learnt that the British were more ferocious and unscrupulous than themselves in avenging their raids. The Naga tribes of the Tirap district continued to commit petty thefts and loot for quite a long time as they began to be pushed up the hills with the extension of the tea plantations and the opening up coal mines.

The gradual increase of the tribal raids may be explained by the sense of their feeling that life inside the hills was hard, and due to poverty and frustration they began raiding the plains below their hills. The government had gradually begun to substitute cash payment in lieu of articles and the money payment which was fixed in the then market price remained fixed althrough the British period.[16] Rather it was reduced in subsequent years. Representation for raising the *posa* met with scant attention and was in no case complied with. The refusal to raise the *posa* resulted in increase of raids which created a problem for the government as well as the people of the plains, for the government felt an obligation to provide protection to the ryots and the tea planters of the plains who had settled on the foot-hills and the businessmen and industrialists who carried on trade with the hill tribes.[17]

OUTPOSTS TO CHECK TRIBAL INROADS

The government began to set up outposts along routes of the tribal movements to check the inroads of the tribes. But the nature of the terrain made such measures inadequate, for the tribes succeeded in attacking their prey by manoeuvring around the border posts. It may be noted that the Ahom king Kamaleswar Singh had created a number of such border forts to check the inroads of the Dafla tribes.[18] But how far the British were guided in their actions by Ahom precedents in setting up border posts cannot be ascertained. Col. Hopkinson, Commissioner of Assam, wrote as far back as 1862, "A military outpost in Assam is a protection against the hill tribes as an umbrella is against rain, but no more".[19]

RESTRICTION ON PLAINS PEOPLE'S ENTRY INTO HILLS

Meanwhile the Inner Line Regulation was passed in 1873. It restricted the entry of the plains people into the tribal hills and thus minimised the contact between the hills and the plains as also the possibility of government action for the settlement of disputes between the plains and the hills people. By passing the Inner Line Regulation and subsequent specification of the Inner Line along the foothills, the government undertook to protect the life and property of the Britsih subjects up to the Inner Line, leaving the tribes beyond to themselves. But except in case of the Akas and the so-called Bhutias of the present Kameng district no restriction was put on the movement of the tribes either inside or outside the Inner Line.[20]

The British administrators were conscious of the fact that the wall they had created by promulgating the Inner Line between the hills and the plains would suffocate the tribes unless some holes were provided for the breathing of the inhabitants of the hills. Therefore, the government took initiative to bring the tribes to the annual fairs which were regularly held along the foothills. But it should be remembered that the term 'fair' as applied to the gatherings of these tribal people in the plains is practically a misnomer. The gathering lasted for over months. The government realised its importance and gave all sorts of encouragement. Government fund was spent to provide shelter, medical care, and proper police guard was provided for security purpose.[21]

FAIRS AND POPULARISING EUROPEAN GOODS

The 'fairs' played a vital role in the economic life of the tribal people. At the onset of the British period in Assam, we find that the tribal people used to collect Assamese goods and sell their own in the plains market. At Udalguri, the Tibetan caravan sold their merchandise and purchased Assamese products. Some tribes, like the Akas and Daflas used to collect their dues from the plains in kind, that is, in Assamese products like cotton piece-goods, handkerchiefs, Mekhala-chaddar, cotton-thread, dao, etc.[22] Even when the Company's Government began to pay them *posa* in cash, the tribal people used to purchase Assamese goods with the money which they now received from the government during the fair.

The British Government began from the very beginning to pursue a policy of popularising the British manufactures. When the government stopped the tribal rights to collect dues from the plains and began to pay them in cash, they used to present the tribal chiefs articles of British produce like wine, cigarette, broad-cloth, handkerchiefs made of cotton and silk, blankets, tobacoo-pipes, knives, etc.[23] The people accustomed to use these things now purchased like goods from the fairs as well. If we look at the itms that the tribal people purchased from the fairs, these findings are corroborated. The report on the trade between Assam and the adjoining areas of 1890 shows that the tendency in trade indicated a steady increase in the demands for European cotton-piece goods, European cotton-twist and yarn, brass and copper, opium, salt and silk manufactures.[24]

In popularising the European goods and promoting their sale the fairs had vital importance. Tribal products, mainly raw materials, came down in the market and European goods poured into the tribal territories. A look into the list of articles brought down by the tribal people show that mainly they brought down raw materials, besides little bit of gold and silver, e.g., wool, yak-tail, musk, chillies, spices, wax madder, ivory, rubber, Mishmi-Teeta, mustard, etc.[25] Their purchases show that they bought mainly manufactured goods, from later part of the last century, mainly European. The tribal people purchased from the fairs salt, mill-made cotton piece-goods, cotton yarn, opium, glass beads, metal and metal wares all imported from abroad.

DESTRUCTION OF TRIBAL CRAFT AND INDUSTRY

The British trade policy led to the destruction of tribal cottage industries and crafts. Salt manufacture and weaving were quite familiar with the tribesmen and salt was an important item of tribal export even at the beginning of British penetration into Assam. Hamilton's account bear testimony to it as also the report on trade in 1890.[26] Pemberton writes that salt was produced at Sadiya and Borhat in good quantity.[27] But the imported salt, sold at cheap rate destroyed its production in the Hills. Weaving and spinning were respectful occupations in the tribal hills of the Frontiers.[28] But the influx of mill-made goods and yarn now discouraged spinning and weaving. Making of dyes from indigenous stuff was a common practice among many tribes. British imports replaced indigenous colours and at the close of the last century it was given up practically.[29] Iron smelting and forging were known and the tribal people forged their own implements and weapons. But now a tendency developed to purchase manufactured tools from the plains. Craftmanship in metals and ivory of high standard were reported from the Khampti villages.[30] At the beginning of the twentieth century, they became things of history.

EXCHANGE OF GOODS

Besides these fairs, trade between the plains and hills continued on a limited scale throughout the year. The tribesmen came down to the shops that were set up by the businessmen at some advance posts on the frontiers and the tribal people came to sell their goods and buy their necessaries from them. But such trade was considered hazardous by both the parties, for sometimes the tribal folk thought that they had been cheated and sometimes they looted the shops and murdered the traders. The government did not encourage trading in any and every place, for in case of trouble they were called upon to provide security and punish the offenders. For controlling the tribes, it was necessary that they should trade through particular marts where they could be subjected to control.[31] Sometimes the Government tried to set up stores for supplying the necessities of the tribes and E.T. Dalton had proposed, as early as 1852, to set up a *Gola* below the Abor hills to purchase their products. But such measures were never practically adopted.

Though the government attempt to open stores to provide the necessaries to the tribes did not materialise, some provisions were made by the Administration for the exchange of goods of the hills and plains. The government presentd to the tribes at the time of payment of *posa* in cash on the occasion of the fairs some necessary items like broad cloth, handkerchief, cigarettes, wine, salt, etc., and received in turn tribal products like ginger, madder, Mishmi-Teeta, Dao, etc. A list of articles for the year 1864 shows that the Deputy Commissioner of Lakhimpur presented to the Khampti, Singpho, Abor, Mishmi, Naga and Doania tribes articles worth Rs. 851-12-0 and received in return goods worth Rs. 364-9-0. Over and above this the Commissioner of Assam presented to the same chiefs goods worth Rs. 2,177-2-0 and received from them articles worth Rs. 551-8-0.[32] It may be mentioned here that the original Abor treaty provided for payment in kind and only in 1878 money payment began to be made. The Daflas were provided with some salt and wine in addition to the *posa* in cash.[33]

From the sixties of the nineteenth century, the officers of the Assam Commission became increasingly concerned at the increase of the tribal raids into the plains of Assam and the need of an officer of higher rank on the spot to give quick orders on issues involved was felt. To meet this requirement, Assam was separated from the Presidency of Bengal in 1874. The policy to be pursued in relation to the hill tribes was also examined. The Government of India asked the Bengal Government to prepare a report on the problem like that of J.A.M. Mills' Report of 1854 on Assam in general. The Memorandum on the North-East Frontier of Bengal written by Alexander Mackenzie, Secretary to the Government of Bengal, came out as a result of the advice in 1869.

CONSOLIDATION AND NO EXTENSION

While discussing the Cachar and Manipur frontier problems, the Deputy Commissioner of Cachar, J.W. Edgar, suggested that for the sake of concerted action, all the Frontier Officers should be brought under one officer who should function under the orders of the Government of Bengal. The Officer in charge of the Frontiers should move from place to place in the region and, receiving reports from the subordinates, dispose of cases as and when required. But the cardinal feature of the policy should be "to acknowledge no territory as ours, unless we are prepared to exercise jurisdiction over the inhabitants and to protect them if attacked.[34]

The leading points in the policy, which he advocated, may be sumed up as follows : (i) the determination not to acknowledge as British territory any area to which British jurisdiction did not extend; (ii) an equally settled determination not to attempt to obtain any control or nominal jurisdiction over tribes settled beyond the boundary so fixed; (iii) endeavours to induce the nearest tribes to settle in the uninhabited jungle between their villages and the administrative districts where cultivation ended ; (iv) the tribes so settled to be treated as independent of British administration and not as protected by the government, but provision to be made for supply of fire arms and cash money on condition of their aiding the administration in stopping the inroads of the interior tribes ; (v) if, inspite of the above measures, outrages were committed, armed forces to punish the offenders should be despatched without loss of time ; and (vi) though the frontier officers should not attempt to bring the tribes under subjection, they should do all in their power to extend their influence over them and encourage them to trade with the plains, impressing upon them the strength of the government and the advantage of good behaviour and peaceful intercourse with the plains. All these depended upon the construction of a good system of roads to facilitate communication between the hills and the plains.[35]

The Government of India was generally in agreement with such a view. While approving the general lines of policy chalked out by the Government of Bengal, it emphasised the point that the object of the government should be not to extend the frontier but to consolidate the portion of the territory already under the possession of the government and to secure its good administration. It further pointed out that it must never be forgotten that while the Government of India acquiesced in the use of all such means of maintaining security on the border, these could be effective only if they were combined with the arrangements calculated at once to overawe and restrain the tribes from attacking the British subjects. "The better prepared we are in this respect, the further will our specific policy be moved from the chance of being misunderstood."[36]

But towards the close of the century, particularly, from the eighties, the need of a local officer functioning among the tribes was felt. The inadequacy of the native agency through which the Deputy Commissioners of Darrang and Lakhimpur conducted their relations with the hill tribes from a distance was realised. Sir Charles Elliot, the then Chief Commissioner of Assam, represented the need for the appointment of a separate officer at Sadiya to conduct the relations with hill tribes of the frontiers while reviewing the effects of the establishment of the Guards posts at Nizamghat on the Abor hills.[37] The issues raised by the proposal of the Chief Commissioner resulted in the appointment of an Assistant Political Officer at Sadiya in 1882.

This appointment, however, did not mean a departure from the traditional policy of the government. In fact, the Government of India under the British Crown did not pursue a policy essentially different from that of the East India Company. It tried to give a trial to the traditional policy by strengthening the administration and reorganising the border post forces as proposed by Col. Hopkinson.

HOPKINSON'S PROPOSAL

As a matter of fact, Col. Henry Hopkinson, the then Commissioner of Assam, had written to the Government of Bengal in 1862 that "in restraining the savage tribes, which infest our frontier, reliance cannot be placed on one course of policy, but there must be a ready adaptation of expedients to suit ever-varying circumstances : some times we must employ coercion pure and simple; sometime blockades; very often a judicious system of subsidising will keep the tribes quiet for a long while; but still the surest foundation on which to build our control over them will be their fear of us." "It is not coercion that has often failed us, but the failure to coerce."[38] "Gold has never yet prevailed in the long run, where there was not iron in reserve to support it," he observed elsewhere.[39]

Col. Hopkinson was the first British officer who had the farsight to see that by the annexation of Assam the British had accepted the obligation to undertake the administration of the tribes of the frontier and he criticised the government for creating a wall of separation between the hills and plains of the province. There would be no rest for the British, he held, in Assam till arrangements for administration of the hills were provided for.[40] In this, he had anticipated the recommendations of Younghusband in his report submitted after the Tibetan expedition of 1904.[41] Col. Hopkinson wrote in his report to the Government of Bengal : "In taking possession of the country (Assam), we incurred a very distinct and positive obligation to administer it to the best of our ability, and at any expense to secure the most absolute protection to life and property by every means available to a civilised government; and it seems inconsistent with this view of our duty that we should have separated the people of the plains from the people of the hills and have made the former our subjects while we renounced the latter, and left them to prey upon those whom we had professed to take under our protection." "Shut out by us from all civilising or elevating influences but our own, we must be responsible for their condition; their murderous raids, their inhuman sacrifices, lie at our door, and we are as much answerable for their continuance in their present state as it used to be held that the States of North America were answerable for the continuance of slavery in the South."[42]

Col. Hopkinson recommended the construction of roads, which, he held, would "afford facilities for intercourse between the world external" and the world of the tribes. He urged the government to help and aid the missionaries in their work among the tribes.[43]

In reply, an Under Secretary to the Government of India wrote to Col. Hopkinson as follows : "I have seen the necessity of patience and forebearance, which I have studiously exercised towards them (hill tribes); these savages are utterly incapable of reasoning, and I fear they attribute our bearing towards them to timidity and either cannot, or will not understand our real motive." He went on to advise that "what is of utmost importance in dealing with the uncivilised tribes is patience. No one supposes that their civilisation is to be effected in a few years, and no one expects that in endeavouring to conciliate them the government will not meet with occasional disappointment;

but the policy is none the less on this account sound and intelligible."[44]

The recommendations of Col. Hopkinson for the reorganisation of the police forces of Assam and the withdrawal of the military and para-military forces from the borders was accepted by the government because it did not mean break with the past policy. He pointed out the inadequacies of the traditional arrangements for the defence of the frontiers of the regularly administered districts by employing the army in the Frontier Service. He observed that the actual frontier duty was performed by the Civil Police who pursued the marauding tribes even into the hills. "Our army administration, our military organisation, the quality of our troops, the conditions of their enlistment, their drill, their discipline, are all, I venture to think inappropriate to the exigencies of hill warfare on our Assam Frontier."[45] He recommended raising of a local force under the orders of the chief civil authority for the defence of the Assam frontier because the management of the frontier tribes was a responsibility of that authority.[46] This view seems to have been accepted by the Government of Bengal which requested the Supreme Government's sanction of the proposal to raise a force like that of the Punjab.[47]

The Army did not share the view of Col. Hopkinson. Lt. Col. W. Agnew did not approve the idea of withdrawal of the troops and leave the defence of the province to the proposed Military Police.[48] But Col. Hopkinson held fast to his view. He pointed out that the tribal raids required prompt and quick action. But employment of the army required the sanction of the Government of India and orders through the army channel which meant delay and loss of time.[49] The Government of India was convinced of the necessity of the reorganisation as suggested by Col. Hopkinson. Accordingly, two battalions of Military Police were recruited; detachments of these were posted along the Inner Line and heavy concentrations were made at the district headquarters for march in emergency immediately.[50]

DIRECT ADMINISTRATION

Thus, so far the administration did not embark upon a new policy. The appointment of the Assistant Political Officer was required by the separation of Frontier Tracts from the regularly administered districts and notification of the Inner Line de-regulationised some parts of the province which now required an officer on the spot to administer those areas. Of course, he was appointed mainly to cultivate friendly relations with the tribal people and help the Deputy Commissioner in frontier politics. But his main duty was to manage the Frontier Tracts which were separated from the regularly administered districts for which purpose the Assam Frontier Tracts Regulation of 1880 had been passed. The reorganisation of the Police Forces or the creation of the Military Police was effected to activise the four planks of the frontier policy, namely, the system of payment of *posa*, the fairs or the safety-valve, the blockade, and the border posts to guard the inroads of the frontier tribes. The traditional policy initiated from the very beginning was given a chance to prove its efficacy.

The appointment of the Assistant Political Officer at Sadiya brought home the necessity of direct administration of the Frontier Tracts. So long the conduct of relations with the tribes was left with the Kotokis on whom the British officers put little reliance and to whom they paid scanty attention. Now the British officer toured the tribal tracts and prepared reports which were read with care and attention and measures suggested by him were considered carefully. At the close of the century again the frontier policy was reopended for consideration by the Lt. Governor of Eastern Bengal and Assam on the recommendations of Noel Williamson, the successor of F.J. Needham.[51]

Noel Williamson who joined as Assistant Political Officer at Sadiya in 1905 acted with indefatigable energy, courage, tact and enthusiasm in putting the frontier service on a new basis till his murder in the Abor hills in 1911. He carried on extensive tours, sometimes unaccompanied by the usual contingents of guards and pomp and splendour, and made good friends with the tribesmen. He had envisaged a course of gradual penetration of frontier hills which ultimately prevailed though the circumstances which burnt the pillars of the frontier policy were different. It was the flame of the fire of the breath of the Chinese Dragon which burnt the pillars of the frontier policy.

Like the realist Williamson the Lt. Governor of the new province of Eastern Bengal and Assam, Sir Lancelot Hare, was also a practical man. He lent his support for the Foward policy of his Assistant Political Officer in the Frontiers. In 1907, he wrote to the Government of India that the "policy of aloofness was foredoomed to failure", and advocated the adoption of the policy of direct and immediate administration of the British territories. Of course, he did not recommend the policy of advancing the administrative centres inside the hills as recommended by Williamson.[52] But the Government of India turned down his proposal in its entirety, and though they accepted the necessity of protecting the British territory, forbade expeditions to be sent beyond the Outer Line.

But the Chinese movement across the boundary (1908-1911) became a matter of concern for the Government of Eastern Bengal and Assam. Reports of Chinese advance into the Aka hills, almost near the administrative boundary of the Assam district of Darrang, Abor hills and Mishmi hills forced the Government of India to propose to the Secretary of State for India to secure as soon as possible a sound strategic boundary between the two countries (India and Tibet) pending the question of demarcation till the explorations were over, as proposed by the Government of Eastern Bengal and Assam. The Government of Eastern Bengal and Assam, however, suggested the erection of a number of boundary pillars along the boundary between the two countries on the common trade routes following the traditional boundary of the two countries. The object of this measure was to be explained to the tribes.[53]

The proposal of the Local Government did not, however, suggest a third line beyond the so-called Outer Line; it meant the fixing up of the traditional boundary between India and Tibet, beyond the Outer Line, and not the shifting of the Outer Line from the foothills to the international boundary. In the second place, they proposed that in future the policy of the government should be one of loose political control, "having as its object the minimum of interference compatible with the necessity of protecting the tribesmen from unprovoked aggression,. the responsibility of whose protection would have to be assumed by the government and at the same time preventing them from the violating either the administrative border or the

Chinese territory". The tribes should be left to themselves as much as possible, but care should be taken to avoid any action or inaction as the case might be which might lead to inculcate in their mind any undue sense of independence as it had happened in the North-West Frontier. They suggested that before the finalisation of measures to be adopted with regard to them, it would be necessary to take effective steps to prevent the violation of the new external boundary as they had proposed.[54]

The Government of India accepted the recommendation but did not permit the extension of the administrative boundary beyond the existing line. They also sanctioned exploratory and survey expeditions to be sent to the Mishmi, Miri and Dafla Hills. They addressed a despatch to the Secretary of State for India on the frontier issues recommending the lines of action proposed by the Government of Eastern Bengal and Assam, C.A. Bell and the General Staff of the Army. The Secretary of State, however, preferred not to push the posts within the tracts. The Government of India protested, for they contemplated to exercise loose political control over the tribes which could not be done from beyond the Inner Line boundary. The Secretary of State for India now concurred with the proposal and the hill tracts were subsequently divided into three sections as proposed in 1914.[55]

It is interesting to note that the Simla Conference, which the British Officers like Charles Bell and Henry McMahon utilised to finalise the Indo-Tibetan boundary, did not engage the attention of the Government of India insofar as they suggested creation of an administrative apparatus for the frontier region. In the Memorandum appended to the proceedings of the Simla Conference, Charles Bell had suggested the creation of new administration consisting of Bhutan, Sikkim, Tibet, Tawang and the North-Eastern Frontier Tracts. He held that though the frontier tribes were ethnologically different from the Tibetans, they had close relation with the Tibetans and it was imperative to pursue a common policy towards the frontiers. Besides one agency for the entire belt would result in economy and service in a large agency would be more popular than in smaller ones in different regions. He urged that in any case the frontier administration should be placed under the

Foreign Department of the Government of India than under the Local Administration of Assam and he recommended for the appointment of a separate discreet and tactful British Officer for Tawang.[56]

Sir Henry McMahon did not give much importance to what Charles Bell had suggested. He agreed that military aid should be given to the Tibetan authorities as Charles Bell had also suggested and recommended for the appointment of a separate British Officer for Tawang too. Next he thought of clearing the Chinese out of the Tibetan territories and set-up a strong British post at Gyantse.

But practically no arrangement was made for the proper and direct administration of the tribal tracts. The Government of India did not even forward the proceedings of the Simla Conference to the Local Administration and did not recommend any special measure for implementation of the recommendations of Henry McMahon or Charles Bell.[57] The Political Officers who continued to be under the Local Administration were instructed to exercise loose political control over the tribes. The wall of separation, the Inner Line, was also not removed. The Government of India was influenced by the "buffer" concept of Sir Henry McMahon. They seem to have believed that it was not the boundary line which mattered in a tract like the North-Eastern Frontier; what was important was a "buffer" which meant a belt of neutral territory between the two countries. Moreover, Sir Henry McMahon had cautioned the Government of India not to offend the Tibetan vested interests in the tribal tracts south of the McMahon Line. McMahon's recommendation to send a British officer to proceed to the Tawang area and arrange for its administration, therefore, received no attention from the British Indian Government.[58]

Proposal for simple administration

Capt. Nevill who was in charge of the Balipara Frontier Tract, as the western section of the Frontier Tracts was known from 1919, paid a visit to Mompa territory and reported that in order to bring about a state of prosperity in this region and to promote the growth of trade it was necessary to establish some sort of simple administration within the Frontier Tracts by establishing outposts attached with dispensaries well connected by roads. Nevill tried to buttress his arguments to bring the hills under close control by evaluating the political developments in China and Tibet. He pointed out, "as soon as China settles down, this Tibetan frontier will become of great importance. China has still its eyes on Tibet and on Lhasa; the pro-Chinese party is growing in influence and should China gain control of Tibet, the Tawang country is particularly adapted for a secret and easy entrance into India. Russia is also trying to establish her influence in Tibet and, if successful, could safely and secretly send her emissaries into India by this route."[59] But then the Government of India did not take interest in the affairs of the frontier tribes and they shelved the issue of frontier problem by sending a despatch to the Secretary of State.

After the first World War, a siprit of humanism spread far and wide in the world. People began to talk of human rights and protest against exploitation. The concept of 'Mandate' was developed for protecting the interest of the underdeveloped peoples under the supervision of the League of Nations. As a part of this worldwide change of outlook, the protection of tribal rights now caught the attention of the philanthropic people. In India, British administrators like J.P. Mill and J.H. Hutton who served in the hills in the north-east were struck by the exploitation of the simple tribal people by adventurers and businessmen which, if not actively patronised, was at least tolerated by the government. Essays appeared in journals to enlist popular support for stopping such practices towards the tribal people.[60] The government now adopted a more or less benevolent attitude towards the tribal people. But in an atmosphere of political tension between the rulers and the politically conscious sections of the Indian nation, the government solicitude for tribal welfare was utilised more for segregation of the tribal folk from the rest of the Indian community than for actual amelioration of their condition.

ISOLATING TRIBAL AREAS FROM REGULAR ADMINISTRATION

The policy of segregation was given shape for the first time in the Reforms of 1919 although its beginnings may be traced in the late 19th century. It has already been observed that the

Scheduled Districts Act was passed in 1874 to provide for the administration of the tribal areas in a rough and ready manner and the Inner Line Regulation of 1873 began to be applied to segregate tribal areas of the North-East Frontier from 1875 onwards. When Edwin Montagu, in concert with Lord Chelmsford, under the directions of the House of Commons, prepared their report on constitutional reforms in India, they recommended measures to be taken for reconstruction of the Indian Government, but the tribal issue was not given any new complexion. While recommending the increasing association of Indians in every branch of administration and "the gradual development of self-governing institutions with a view to progressive realisation of responsible government in India as an integral part of the British Empire", they did not deem it proper to either encourage the tribal people to participate in their own administration or to associate the Indian ministers and legislators with the administration of the tribal hills of the frontiers.[61]

The Mont-Ford scheme, which involved the division of functions of the Provincial Government between elected Indian Ministers and appointed Executive Councillors, proposed to keep the tribal areas separate from the regularly administered territory, on the ground that in those areas "there was no material on which to found political institutions."[62] It was held that the tracts mentioned in the schedules and appendices to the Scheduled Districts Act, 1874, with "certain exceptions and possibly certain additions, should be reserved for further consideration." But the "typically backward tracts (frontiers) should be excluded from the jurisdiction of the reformed provincial governments and administered by the head of the province."[63] In these areas, therefore, the old system was to continue, and the tribes were to be kept apart—ostensibly for their own welfare—from the people of the plains.

The reaction of the Government of India to the recommendations of the Joint Report was embodied in the Ninth Despatch on the Constitutional Reforms. The Government of India was anxious to limit exclusion as much as possible both in its local extent and in its degree. With this end in view, it estimated the degree of backwardness of each of the tracts and recommended varying degrees of exclusion to conform with such estimates. The recommendation that the backward tracts should be directly administered by the Governors was not finally carried out, except in the Shan States of Burma.[64] For Assam, the reserved half of the government was given full discretion to administer the tracts as per enactments under the Government of India Act, 1919.

The Government of India Act, 1915, as amended by the Government of India Act, 1919, which carried into effect the recommendations of the Mont-Ford Report provided, *inter alia*, that "the Governor-General in Council may declare any territory in British India to be a 'Backward Tract' and may, by notification, with such sanction as aforesaid, direct that this Act shall apply to that territory subject to such exceptions and modifications as may be prescribed in the modifications."[65] When the Reforms were introduced in Assam in 1920, the frontiers affairs were placed under the reserved half of the government and the elected half of the government did not have any jurisdiction over them. This was a modified policy of segregation, for the reserved half of the government was not under the administrative or financial control of the Legislature.

Increasing British influence

Meanwhile the government has pursued a policy of bringing the frontier territory under its political influence. The tour reports of the Political Officers showed the popularity of the government in the tribal hills. A little good humour by the government officers endeared the government to the tribal folk. While the government officials in the plains dreaded the Indian Nationalists, they felt quite comfortable in the tribal territory. Rather in Christian areas, like the Lushai hills and the Naga hills, they felt secure and firm. Step by step they developed the theory of exploitation of the tribal people by the Indians and they claimed to stand against such exploitation as friends of the tribal people.

By the time of the coming of the Statutory Commission, the officers serving in the frontiers and adjacent tribal hills, like the Lushai and Naga hills, had arrived at the conclusion that the British would withdraw some day from India and Burma, but if they could create a separate tribal belt along the North-East Frontiers they might continue to possess a foothold on Indian territory. The result of the policy of keeping the frontier tribes in isolation would be, they hoped, the perpetuation of their control in a part of this country. The conversion of the tribal people in the Lushai and Naga hills into Christianity had accustomed them to look upon the British as their co-religionists and upon the Indian people as heathens and exploiters. The Nagas put before the Simon Commission a demand to keep their areas excluded from the authority of the Indian Government, and anti-Congress ryots broke out in Shillong, the capital of Assam, which was located in the Khasi area.[66] In Burma, the British officers, by manipulating affairs in the Shan States and in the unadministered areas in the northern triangle of Burma on the Indian border, succeeded in developing in the local population a separatist outlook. The Burma Government wrote, "These.... areas are all unfit to participate in a constitution on representative lines suitable for Burma proper. Their peoples are educationally backward, and have evinced no desire to be linked with the Burmans, who in turn betray little interest in these hill tracts."[67] The calculating British officers of the Assam Government now thought on the same lines and wanted to exclude the North-East Frontier hills from India.

Asked for opinions on the reforms and further changes in the mode of government, the officers of the frontiers as well as hill areas of Assam advocated exclusion of the hill tribes of the frontiers and the Hill Districts of Assam from the jurisdiction of the Indian ministers who, it was understood, would assume—on the abolition of the system of Dyarchy—control of entire provincial government. J.H. Hutton, Deputy Commissioner of Naga Hills District, wrote an exhaustive letter to the Government of Assam giving the history of the the hill areas; basing his arguments on the social, economic, religious and cultural grounds of the region, he propagated the idea of a separate state for the hill tribes.[68] On the Burmese side, a similar proposal was made to unite the northern triangle of Burma and the Shan States with the hill areas on the north-eastern corner of India and create a separate state.[69] But the Government of Assam, as suggested by its Political Officers, urged retention of the frontier tracts under direct control and authority of the Governor-General in Council who would be responsible only to the British Parliament.

Development and Education of Tribals

In view of this trend of opinion in official circles the Simon Commission, which was appointed to report on further progress on constitutional reforms in India, did not find it possible to recommend the incorporation of the hill tracts of the North-East Frontier for administrative purposes in the province of Assam. It wrote that the "backward tracts of Assam are of great importance and extent, and nowhere in India is the contrast between the life and outlook of these wild hill-men and the totally distinct civilisation of the plains more manifest...." The report went on, "To the economic self-sufficiency of the indigenous hill races—the Nagas, Kukis, Mishmis, and the rest the tea-planters and the immigrant Bengali alike—constitute a real danger."[70] The Commission recommended that the British Parliament should avow its special obligation for the tribal folk, educate them to stand on their own feet, give them protection against exploitation, and prevent their raids on the plains. The hills were, or course, not to be branded as backward tracts but termed as 'excluded areas'. For the administration of the tribal areas, excluded from the regularly administered districts of the province, the Governor-General in Council should use the agency of the Governor.[71]

The Commission expected that for developing the tribal areas and for educating the tribal people, huge money would be required. The money would not be forthcoming from the revenue of a poor State like Assam. Further the Commission apprehended that the representatives of the provincial legislature would not vote for the appropriation of money for development purposes in the hill tracts since that would not immediately benefit the constituencies of the members who would vote.[72] Perhaps the Commission applied a British analogy to an Indian perspective; in any case it overlooked the fact that the Federal Government could provide the money for development purposes and yet put the charge of the tribal affairs under the Provincial Government. The Government of Assam, controlled by the elected representatives, who came from the vicinity of the tribal tracts and who understood the tribal problems and possibilities much better, could undertake the development work more meaningfully and satisfactorily. In the prevailing atmosphere of distrust and political animosity, the British statesmen and administrators alike wanted to sympathise with the tribal folk and alienate them from the Indian people though the tribal people were a part and parcel of the myriad Indian population.

But inspite of the recommendations of the Simon Commission, the British Prime Minister disavowed any intention of the British Parliament to control any territory of British India; the hopes of the British officers in the tribal areas were thus dashed to the ground.[73] The Government of India now asked for reconsideration of the issues of Frontier administration by the Government of Assam since the previous scheme of retention of tribal territory under the British Parliament could not be worked upon after declaration of the British Prime Minister.[74] The Government of Assam, nevertheless, proposed the perpetuation of the separation of the tribal tracts of the frontiers from the regularly administered areas in the province of Assam. It wrote, "Its (tribal tracts) progressive absorption into the province of Assam in the past was forced upon the government by the unavoidable necessity of securing from the marauding and revengeful raids of its denizens, the safety of the plain districts for which the government had made itself responsible. . . what was needed for the future is a policy of development and unification on lines suited to the genius of the hill people, an object in itself of formidable magnitude."[75]

The formulation of such a policy could no longer be divorced from political factors. The Government of Assam pointed out that there had already developed in the hills an anti-Indian feeling, probably due to a fear of economic exploitation. It was even apprehensive that a change in policy with regard to the frontiers might provoke rebellion. Therefore, it recommended that in developing a scheme of administration for the hill tribes "the essence of the system in the administration of the definitely excluded areas would the personal rule of the Governor exercised through selected officers."[76] In course of time, it suggested, an indigenous staff of officers of all ranks might be provided for the Hill Districts and frontiers.

The Government of India Act, 1935, which was passed after taking into consideration the Simon Commission's recommendations as well as the points of view of the provincial governments concerned with tribal areas, provided in sections 91 and 92 that His Majesty by an order in Council might declare some territory in India as "Excluded Area" or "Partially Excluded Area" and empower the Governor of a province to administer that area under the authority of the Governor-General. The Governor was given discretion to extend Acts or parts thereof passed by any provincial legislature or the federal legislature to the excluded areas which otherwise would not apply there. Moreover, the Governor was given the power to prepare and approve drafts of Regulations for the peace and good government of the excluded areas with the previous sanction of the Governor-General in Council.[77]

GAINING INFLUENCE IN TIBET

Now the problem of the delineation of the Frontier Tracts cropped up when the question of notification of the boundary of the excluded areas and the definition of the Indo-Burmese boundary came up before the King in Council. In the meantime, an English botanist W.F. Kingdon-Ward, who toured the Dafla Hill areas, was arrested by the Tibetan authorities for crossing the Indian boundary. The British Government secured his release and said Kingdon-Ward, in an article, posed once again the problem of the McMahon Line.[78] The Government of India, which had almost forgotten the issue of McMahon Line and had not even informed the Local Government of Assam about the delineation of the boundary at the Simla Conference, was now at a loss. It was now found that the Russians had once again began—in view of the increasing Russo-Mongolian collaboration and the conclusion of the Russo-Mongolian Protocol of Mutual Assistance (1936) it now became imperative to pursue the Indo-Tibetan boundary as agreed to in 1914 in the Simla Conference—to gain influence in Tibet. As early as 1927, a Russo-Mongolian delegation visited Lhasa and another Military Officer remained in Lhasa in 1928.[79]

In view of these, the Governor of Assam Sir Robert Reid proposed that a tactful and discreet officer with knowledge of frontier diplomacy should be posted, at least for the summer months, at Tawang with instructions: (*i*) to collect a light tax, leaving to the people management of their own affairs, (*ii*) to offer an assurance to owners of private estates that their proprietory rights would be respected; and (*iii*) to give an nnder taking to the Tawang monastery that the Tibetan Government would be consulted whenever a new Head Lama was appointed.[80]

Capt. Lightfoot, who held the post of Political Officer in Balipara Frontier Tract, was authorised to lead an expedition to Tawang in 1938 and on his return he submitted a report which contained almost the same recommendations as were proposed by Capt. Nevill 24 years before. Capt. Lightfoot proposed that the Tibetan Government should be asked to withdraw their officials and assistants from south of the McMahon Line which would terminate automatically the exactions and forced labour and at the same time establish British title over the area. He advised to make the Tawang monastery a purely Mompa affair in default of which the Tibetan intrigues would continue and also to abolish the system of payment in kind which entailed forced labour. He suggested to abolish the monopoly in salt and rice enjoyed by Tibetan officials. Further, he recommended establishment of a control area at Tawang and Dirangzong where Political Agents ought to be appointed who would manage tribal affairs through the Panchayats consisting of the representatives of the village headmen and monastic council and imposition of a house tax of Rs. 5 per annum in assertion of the British jurisdiction over the tribes of the area. The duty of the Agent would be to collect the house tax and hear appeals from the Panchayats. The Senior Agents were to visit the areas of the Junior Agents and reports were to be sent to the Political Officer whose subordinates the Agents would be. The Political Officer might hear appeals from the Political Agents.[81]

The acting Governor of Assam, Hogg, forwarded the recommendations of Capt. Lightfoot and observed that the existing situation in Tawang area was intolerable and should be teminated as early as possible. He also advocated the creation of control area within the Mompa hills under Political Agents as recommended by the Political Officer and imposition of a house tax of Rs. 5 in substitution of theexisting tax in kind. He recommended the proposal to reconstitute the Tawang Monastery excluding the Tibetan officials and abolition of salt and rice monopoly at Dirangzong. Further, he requested the Government of Indiato approve an expedition to Tawang even if the measures proposed were not approved for implementation.[82]

But the world was heading towards the Second Great War. Sir Henry Tuynam, acting Governor of Assam, in a letter to the Governor-General emphasised the risk of antagonising Tibet-China and financial involvement for the measure. The Government of India decided to implement the policy as proposed after one year and the proposed tour was not authorised since that might result in permanent occupation of the Mompa Tracts and, thus, entail an obligation to provide for its administration. When the World War broke out and the British were involved in it as a belligerent, they began to muster all their resources to win the war in Europe and for a time the affairs in the North-East Frontier were subordinated to war considerations. A Conference of Political Officers held in 1940 at Shillong decided not to pursue the occupation of Tawang area and offend the Tibetan sentiment over the issue.[83]

If the Government of India's attitude towards the Western Hills of the North-East Frontier was a little hesitating and procrastinating, its support for implementing the new policy in the Abor and Mishmi hills was not lacking. The British Government tried to build up a chain of outposts along the border of Abor and Mishmi hills and a number of control areas to exercise British jurisdiction.[84] Trading posts which benefited the people at large and reconciled them to the new government were opened in the interior as brigade tracks were constructed to connect the border from whitin the country. The Governor's proposal to extend control area as proposed by the Political Officer of Abor hills was approved by the Government of India in 1914, with the proviso that no extra cost should be incurred as it was then engaged in the Great War. The proposal of the Local Government to resist the Tibetan tax collectors from within the McMahon Line, of course, did not get approval of the Indian Government as it still followed the policy of good humouring China.[85]

The veil of the Frontier drama, however, was again lifted when the Japanese overran the whole of South-East Asia, and entered into India through Manipur and Nagaland in 1943. The rapid advance of the Japanese through the tribal territories surprised the British authorities and the difficulty of military movement through these hills made them aware of the backwardness of the region. Increasing Chinese activity in

Tibet once again made the government uneasy over the situation in Tawang and as suggested by Chief of Staff Sir Reid, Governor of Assam recommended the occupation of Tawang to forestall Chinese advance in the region. J.P. Mill went up the hills and opened an advanced post in Dirang Dzong area.[86] The development of the area was undertaken immediately and to help and advise the Governer of Assam for development of the tribal region an advisor of the rank of Secretary to the Government was placed at his disposal, but the gradual recession of the Japanese invasion again removed priority on tribal development.

PRESERVING INFLUENCE POCKETS BEFORE DEPARTURE

Meanwhile, when talks of transferring power to the Indians began, British politicians, scholars and administrators began to moot projects which would enable the British Crown to maintain a foothold in a part of the Indian territory in the name of protecting the tribal people and strengthening the defence of India. The union of the North-East Frontier, together with the Naga, Lushai and North Cachar Hills of India, with the northern triangle and Shan States of Burma seemed to them to provide a strategic platform wherefrom watch could be kept over Communist China, Burma, India and East Pakistan (now Bangladesh). Reginald Coupland, who had accompanied Sir Stafford Cripps, while delivering a talk at Oxford in 1945, developed on the British obligation to the tribal people of India as also of the British obligation for the defence of India.[87] The learned professor was still troubled by the thought of the white-man's burden in the East. He suggested the creation of a Crown Colony in the North-East of India, including the Shan State and the northern tringle of Burma. He further advocated the encouragement of the Christian missions to undertake humanitarian and welfare measures in the area. In India and Burma, people scented a design by the British to keep under their domination portions of Indian and Burmese territory to serve as bases of British imperialism.[88] All suspicions, however, were laid at rest when the Labour Government that came to power in Britain after the World War, left the entire territory of India to the independent Indian Government on whom then devolved the great task of harmonising tribal needs and aspirations with the larger interests and security of the country.

CONCLUSION

Thus reviewing the British policy in the North-East Frontier Agency Area, it can be concluded that, to begin with, the British policy was to wait and watch the existing conditions and then gradually they began to enter into a system of engagement with the hill tribes of the region. The engagements provided them an opportunity to sense the reaction of the cross-country Powers on British relations with the tribes and at the same time provided a basis of intercourse with the tribes. It may be mentioned in this context that the Mughals from whom the British gradually assumed sovereignty of India had similarly dealt with the indigenous potentates of India.[89] The petty chiefs of Hindustan were gradually brought under the complete control of the Mughal Emperors when the former began to assume obligations to the latter. The British Government in Assam introduced Mouzardi system for the collection of revenue in the Brahmaputra valley and thus created a class of people who were regarded by the local people as their representatives but were bound to the Government by the factor of their position.[90] In the frontier hills, they similarly entered into engagements with the different tribes and thus brought them under some obligations and later on, as and when necessary, the British imposed their control over them.

Again, a dividing line in British policy may be found in the year 1910. Till that year the British policy in relation to the North-East Frontier was to keep the frontier tribes in good humour by providing them some "blackmail" on condition of their good behaviour. They were hedged in by promulgating the Inner Line which was guarded by Frontier posts. But to provide for the economic requirements of the tribes, 'fairs' were held along their foothills. In case of any tribal raid on the plains villages on this side of the Inner Line, punitive expeditions were sent to chastise the attacking tribe. No interference was made in the purely tribal affairs. No agency operated for administration within the hills. But from 1910 this policy was substituted by the policy of direct control of the tribes from within the hills and the Indo-Tibetan border, which had remained undefined, was settled. The control of the Government was pushed to the border which was, of course, a strategic line drawn following the natural line of the Himalayas.

If the policy with regard to the tribal people in the North-East was that of non-interference in tribal affairs and non-exercise of jurisdiction, either political or administrative, beyond the Outer Line before 1914, after that year political jurisdiction was extended up to the international border which was now known and consequently, British jurisdiction now ran up to a definite area. Political and administrative agencies which did not operate before beyond the Outer Line, were now functioning beyond that line. Communication within the hills were neglected till now, but henceforth they began to be opened up and developed and this facilitated defence requirements but benefited the people of the region. Medical establishments with police posts were established in some places which won over the hearts of the people by their services. While the police succeeded in stopping Tibetan exploitation and inter-tribal blood feuds, the medicalmen became friends of the people by attending on the sufferers. The government, which disregarded the tribal rights and privileges, now posed as friends to protect the tribals from external aggression and internal enemies and diseases.

Major Sitaram Johri has rightly observed, "During and before the 19th century, the United States and of the United Kingdom's policy towards the aborigines of North America and Australia was to disregard their rights."[91] Pages of history are full of accounts of exploitation by the European colonists in United States of the Red Indians who were even hunted down and dispersed from the lands as the Frontiers men advanced towards the Pacific. The instances of British exploitation of tribal rights in India, particularly in Assam, are abundant. In fact, such things did not prick the conscience of the adventurers who ventured out of their home for riches. The commercial attitude, a legacy of the East India Company, was handed down to the British merchants in India whose interest the Supreme and Provincial Governments were bound to protect, even after the transfer of India to the Crown. No wonder, the appeal of T.H. Lewin in 1869, "let us not govern these hills for ourselves, but administer the country for the well-being and happiness of the people dwelling there", fell on deaf ears.[92]

REFERENCES

1. A. Mackenzie, *Memorandum*, p. 71.
2. *Ibid*, p. 114.
3. Foreign Political Proceedings (India), 12 September 1838.
4. Bengal Papers in Assam State Archives, 1873-77, F. 22.
5. Judicial Proceedings (Bengal), June 1865, No. 71.
6. *Ibid.*
7. Mackenzie, *History*, p. 5.
8. Judicial Proceedings (Bengal), June 1865, No. 73.
9. *Ibid.*
10. L. Devi, *op. cit.*, p. 179.
11. S.K. Bhuyan, *Anglo-Assamese Relations*, p. 33.
12. *Ibid*, pp. 91-95.
13. *Ibid*, p. 96.
14. *Ibid*, pp. 101-102.
15. Elwin, *The Art*, p. 16.
16. Foreign Proceedings (Assam), March 1885, No. 34.
17. Lakhimpur Deputy Commissioner's Collection, No. xii, F. 59, 1904-08.
18. G.C. Barua, *Ahom Buranji*, p. 61.
19. Foreign Political Proceedings (India), June 1866, Nos. 37-39.
20. Lakhimpur Deputy Commissioner's Collection, No. xiv, F. 36, 1910-12.
21. Report on the trade between Assam and the adjoining Foreign Countries, 1890.
22. Revenue Proceedings (Bengal), No. 5 of 11 August 1834.
23. Political Proceedings (Bengal), May, 1864.
24. Report on the Trade between Assam and adjoining Foreign Countries, 1890.
25. *Ibid.*
26. S.K. Bhuyan, (ed), *An Account of Assam*, p. 28.
27. Pemberton, (Capt.) R.B., *Report on the Eastern Frontier of British India*, p. 84.
28. H.F. Sinman, *A Monograph on Cotton.*
29. W.A.M. Duncan, *A Monograph on Dying.*
30. E.T. Dalton, *op. cit.*, p. 7.
31. Lakhimpur Deputy Commissioner's Collection, No. xii, F. 2, 1904-08.

32. Political Proceedings (Bengal), May 1864, 'B' Nos. 24-26.
33. Lakhimpur Deputy Commissioner's Collection, No. xii, F. 7, 1886.
34. Judicial Proceedings (Bengal), January 1870, No. 80.
35. *Ibid.*
36. Foreign Political Proceedings (India), June 1865, No. 82.
37. Lakhimpur Deputy Commissioner's Collection, No. xii, F. 59, 1904-08.
38. Political Proceedings (Bengal), June 1866, Nos. 37-39.
39. Foreign Political Proceedings (India), 1865, Nos. 80-82.
40. Political Proceedings (Bengal), June 1866, Nos. 37-39.
41. F. Younghusband, *India and Tibet*, p. 428.
42. Political Proceedings (Bengal), June 1866, Nos. 37-39.
43. *Ibid.*
44. *Ibid.*
45. *Ibid.*
46. *Ibid.*
47. *Ibid.*
48. Judicial Proceedings (Bengal), May 1870, No. 202.
49. Political Proceedings (Bengal). June, 1866, Nos. 37-39.
50. L.W. Shakespeare, *op. cit.*, p. 8.
51. Lakhimpur Deputy Commissione's Collection, No. xii, F. 6, 1904-08.
52. *Ibid*, F. 59.
53. *Ibid*, No. 204.
54. *Ibid.*
55. *Ibid.*
56. Foreign Political (Secret) Proceedings (India), May 1915, Nos. 36-50.
57. P. Mehra, *The McMahon Line and After*, p. 425.
58. Proceedings of the Governor's Secretariat, December 1937, Nos. 1-19.
59. Annual Administration Report, Western Section, Noth-East Frontier, 1927-28.
60. *Journal of Royal Asiatic Society of Bengal*, vol. lxix, p. LIII: Census Report of India, 1931, p. IV.
61. Report on Indian Constitutional Reforms, 1918, p. 1.
62. *Ibid*, p. 129.
63. *Ibid.*
64. Report of the Indian Statutory Commission, vol. I, p 159.
65. D. Basu, *Constitutional Documents*, vol. I, p. 91.
66. *Tribal Awakening*, p. 101.
67. Report of the Indian Statutory Commission, voll. II, p. 82.
68. Report on Constitutional Reforms, 1930, vol. XIV, pp. 111-117.
69. D. Woodman, *The Making of Burma*, p. 520.
70. Report of the Indian Statutory Commission, vol. I, pp. 75-76.
71. *Ibid*, vol. II, pp. 109-10,
72. *Ibid.*
73. Political Proceedings (Assam), September 1931, Nos. 130-134.
74. *Ibid.*
75. *Ibid.*

76. *Ibid.*
77. D. Basu, *op. cit.*, p. 93.
78. P. Mehra, *op. cit.*, p. 420.
79. *Ibid*, p. 423.
80. Proceedings of the Government Secretariat, June 1940, Nos. 535-636.
81. *Ibid.*
82. *Ibid.*
83. K. Gupta, *The Hidden History of the Sino-Indian Frontier*, p. 86.
84. Political Proceedings (Assam), December, 1914, Nos. 19-54.
85. R. Reid, *op. cit.*, p. 264.
86. K. Gupta, *op. cit.*, p. 90.
87. R. Coupland, *The Future of India : Report on the Constitutional Problems in India*, pp. 164-65.
88. *Ibid.*
89. W.H. Moreland, "*The Revenue System of the Mughal Empire*," *The Cambridge, History of India*, p. 455.
90. M. Bora, *Assam in 1857*, p. 46.
91. S. Johri, *op. cit.*, p. 62.
92. V. Elwin, *North-East Frontier*, p. xix.

APPENDIX A

THE INNER LINE REGULATION, 1873[1]

Regulation under Act XXXIII Vic. Chap. 3. Sec. I.

A Regulation for the Peace and Government of certain districts on the Eastern Frontier of Bengal.

Whereas the Secretary of State for India in Council as by resolution in Council declared the provisions of the Q Vict. Act XXXIII, Chap. 3, Section 1, to be applicable to the districts of Kamrup, Darrang, Nowgong, Sibsagar, Lakhimpur, Garo hills, Khasi and Jaintia hills, Naga hills, Cachar and Chittagong hills;

And whereas the Lieutenant Governor of Bengal has proposed to Governor-General in Council a draft of the following Regulation, together with the reasons for proposing the same, for the peace and good government of the said districts ;

And whereas the Governor-General in Council has taken such draft and reasons into consideration and has approved of such draft and the same has received the Governor-General's assent :

The following Regulation is now published in *Gazette of India* and will be published in the Calcutta Gazette, and thereupon will have the force of law under thirty third of Victoria, Chapter III ;

1. This Regulation shall extend to the districts named in the preamble, and shall come into force on the 1st of November 1873.
2. It shall be lawful for the Local Government of Bengal, with the previous sanction of the Governor-General in Council, from time to time alter by notification in the *Calcutta Gazette*, a line to be called "The Inner Line" in each or any of the above named districts. The Local Government may, by notification in the *Calcutta*

1. Bengal Papers in Assam Archives, F. No. 521 of 1873.

Gazette, prohibit all British subjects, or any class of British subjects, or any persons residing in, or passing through such districts, from going beyond such line without a pass under the hand and seal of the executive officer as be may authorised to grant such pass; and the Local Government may from time to time cancel or vary such prohibit.

3. Any British subject or other person so prohibited who goes beyond the 'Inner Line' fixed in accordance with Section 2 of the Regulation, after its notification, in the *Calcutta Gazette*, without a pass, shall be liable on conviction before a Magistrate to a fine not exceeding Rs. 100 for the first offence and to a fine of not exceeding Rs. 500 or to simple or rigorous imprisonment for a term not exceeding three months, or to both for each subsequent offence.
4. The Local Government may, from time to time prescribe, by notification in the *Calcutta Gazette*, a form of pass for each district and may in such form of pass fix such restrictions or conditions the Local Government may deem fit and may require the payment of such dues and fees for such passes as the Local Government may deem proper. Any holder of such pass shall on breach of any such restriction or conditions be liable on conviction to a fine not exceeding Rs. 100 for a first offence and to a fine not exceeding Rs. 500 or to simple or rigorous imprisonment which may extend to three months or to both for each subsequent offence.
5. Any rubber, wax, ivory or other jungle product found in possession of any person convicted of an offence under this Regulation may be confiscated to the Government by an order to be passed at the time of conviction by the Magistrate.
6. The Chief Executive Officer of any district comprised in any notification as aforesaid may, subject to the approval of the Local Government, authorise, by a written instrument under his hand, any public servant to arrest and bring before him with the least practicable delay :

Firstly—Any person prohibited from crossing the Inner Line prescribed for such district if such person shall be found beyond the line and when asked to produce his pass shall refuse or be unable to do.

Secondly—Any person to whom a pass may have been granted, and who has committed any infraction of its conditions.

7. It shall not be lawful for any British subject, or other persons not being a native of the district comprised in the preamble of this Regulation to acquire any interest in the land or the product of land beyond the said Inner Line without the sanction of the Local Government officer as the Local Government shall appoint in this behalf. Any interest so acquired may be dealt with as the Local Government or its said officer shall direct. The Local Government may also by notification in the Local Gazette extend the prohibition contained in this section to any class of persons natives of the said districts and may from time to time in like manner cancel or vary such extension.

8. Wherever, without the written permission of the officers authorised by the Local Government to grant such permission kills or captures or attempts to kill or capture, or abets the killing or capturing of a wild elephant in any of the districts to which this Regulation extends, shall be liable to a fine not exceeding Rs. 200 for each elephant so killed or captured and any elephant so killed or captured shall be confiscated to Government provided that no person who kills or abets the killing of an elephant in protection of himself, his house or his crops, shall be liable to punishment; and provided also that every person who in the like case captures, or abets the capture of an elephant shall not be liable to fine, but shall be bound to surrender such captured elephant to the government or to pay such royalty thereon as the Local Government may from time to time direct.

9. It shall be competent for the Local Government to make rules for the issue of licence to kill or capture elephant and for all purposes connected with the capture of elephant.

10. The prosecution for every offence punishable under section 8 of the Regulation shall be commenced within 6 months after the offence is committed.

11. Offences against this Regulation may be tried by Magistrate of the first or second class and shall be bailable.

APPENDIX B

INDIA-TIBET FRONTIER, 1914; EXCHANGE OF NOTES BETWEEN THE BRITISH AND TIBETAN PLENIPOTENTIARIES[1]

To

Lonchen Shatra, Tibetan Plenipotentiary.

In February last, you accepted the India-Tibet frontier from the Isu Razi Pass to the Bhutan frontier, as given in the map (two sheets), of which two copies are herewith attached, subject to the confirmation of your Government and the following conditions :

(*a*) The Tibetan ownership in private estates on the British side of the frontier will not be disturbed.

(*b*) If the sacred places of Tso Karpo and Tsari Sarpa fall within a day's march of the British side of the frontier, they will be included in Tibetan territory and the frontier modified accordingly.

I understand that your Government have now agreed to this frontier subject to the above two conditions. I shall be glad to learn definitely from you that this is the case.

You wished to know whether certain dues now collected by the Tibetan Government at Tsona Jong and in Kongbu and Kham from the Mompas and Lopas for articles sold may still be collected. Mr. Bell has informed you that such details will be settled in a friendly spirit, when you have furnished him the further information which you promised.

The final settlement of this India-Tibet frontier will help to prevent causes of future dispute and thus cannot fail to be of great advantage to both Governments.

A.H. McMahon,
British Plenipotentiary.

Delhi 24th March, 1914.

---

1. Foreign Political (Secret) Proceedings (India), October 1914, Nos. 136-396.

(Translation)

To

Sir Henry McMahon,

British Plenipotentiary to the China-Tibet Conference.

As it was feared that there might be friction in future unless the boundary between India and Tibet is clearly defined, I submitted the map, which you sent to me in February last, to the Tibetan Government at Lhasa for orders. I have now received orders from Lhasa, and accordingly agree to the boundary as marked in red in the two copies of the maps signed by you subject to the condition mentioned in your letter, dated 24th March, sent to me through Mr. Bell. I have signed and sealed the two copies of the maps. I have kept one copy here and returned herewith the other.

Sent on the 29th day of the 1st month of the Wood-Tiger year (25th March 1914) by Lonchen Shatra, the Tibetan Plenipotentiary.

Seal of Lonchen Shatra

APPENDIX C

SCHEDULED DISTRICTS ACT, 1874[1]

An Act to ascertain the enactments in force in various parts of British India, and for other purposes.

Whereas various parts of British India have never been brought within, or have from time to time been removed from, the operation of the general Acts and Regulations and the jurisdiction of the ordinary Courts of Judicature;

And whereas doubts have arisen in some cases as to which Acts or Regulations are in force in such parts and in other cases as to what are the boundaries of such parts;

And whereas among such parts are the territories specified in the first schedule hereto annexed, and it is expedient to provide readier means than now exist for ascertaining the enactments in force in such territories and the boundaries thereof, and for administering the law therein;

And whereas it is expedient to declare that certain Acts are in force in a tract of land lying between the Railway Station at Satna and the eastern boundary of the Jabalpur Division;

(It is hereby enacted as follows:)

1. This Act may be called the Scheduled District Act, 1874.

This Act extends in the first instance to the whole of British India other than the territories mentioned in the first schedule hereto annexed, and it shall come into force in each of the Scheduled Districts on the issue of a notification under section 3 relating to such district.

In this Act the term "Scheduled Districts" means the territories mentioned in the first schedule hereto annexed; and from the date fixed in the resolution next hereinafter mentioned, it shall also include any other territory to which the Secretary of State for India, by resolution in Council may

1. Luthra (Col.) P.N., *Constitutional and Administrative Growth of NEFA*, (Shillong. 1972).

declare the provisions of the 33rd of Victoria, chapter 3, section 1, to be applicable.

2. The enactments mentioned in the second schedule hereto annexed shall be repealed.

3. The Local Government **** may from time to time, by notification * * in the local Gazette* *—

(a) declare what enactments are actually in force in any of the Scheduled Districts, or in any part of the any such district,

(b) declare of any enactment that it is not actually in force in any of the districts or in any part of any such district,

(c) correct any mistake of fact in any notification issued under this section :

Provided that a declaration once made under clause (a) or clause (b) of this section shall not be altered by any subsequent declaration other than a declaration under clause (c) of this section.

4. On the issue, under section 3, of the notification declaring what enactments are in force, or not in force in any Scheduled District, the enactments so notified shall be deemed to be in force or not in force, according to the tenor of the notification, in such district, and every such notification shall be binding on all courts of law.

5. The Local Government * * * may, from time to time, by notification * * * in the local Gazette * * * extend to any of the Scheduled Districts or to any part of any such district, any enactment which is in force in any part of British India at the date of such extension.

5A. In declaring an enactment in force in a Scheduled District or part thereof under section 3 of this Act, or in extending an enactment to a Scheduled District or part thereof under Section 5 of this Act, the Local Government * * * * may declare the operation of the enactment to be subject to such restrictions and modifications as that Government thinks fit.

6. The Local Government may from time to time :

(a) appoint officers to administer civil and criminal justice and to superintend the settlement and collection of the public revenue, and all matters relating to rent and otherwise to conduct the administration, within the Scheduled District,

(b) regulate the procedure of the officers so appointed; but not so as to restrict the operation of any enactment for the time being in force in any of the said districts,

(c) direct by what authority any jurisdiction, powers or duties incident to the operation of any enactment for the time being in force in such district shall be exercised or performed.

7. All rules heretofore prescribed by the Governor-General in Council or the Local Government for the guidance of officers appointed within any of the Scheduled Districts for all or any of the purposes mentioned in section 6, and in force at the time of the passing of this Act, shall continue to be in force unless and until the Governor-General in Council or the Local Government, as the case may be, otherwise directs.

All existing officers so appointed previous to the date on which this Act comes into force in such districts shall be deemed to have been appointed hereunder.

8. Whenever any question arises as to the line of boundary between any of the Scheduled Districts and other territory, such officer as the Local Government or (where the said district and the other territory are not subject to the same Local Government) as the Governor-General in Council from time to time appoints, may consider and determine such line of boundary; and the order made thereon by such officer, if confirmed by the Government which appointed him, shall be conclusive in all Courts of Justice.

9. Any person liable to be imprisoned or to be transported beyond sea under any order or sentence passed by any officer appointed under section 6 may (subject to such rules as the Local Government may from time to time prescribe in this behalf) be imprisoned in such jail or transported to such place as the Local Government directs.

10. Acts No. III of 1867, * * * and No. XXV of 1869 are hereby declared to be in force in the tract of land ceded to the British Government in the year 1863 and lying between the Railway Station at Satna and the eastern boundary of the Jabalpur District.

11. Nothing contained in this Act or in any notification issued under the power hereby conferred shall be deemed;

(a) to affect the criminal jurisdiction of any Court over European British subjects, or

(b) to effect any law other than laws contained in Acts or

Regulations or in Rules made in exercise of powers conferred by such Acts or Regulations.

THE FIRST SCHEDULE

See Section I

Part I

Scheduled Districts, 5 Madras

1—In Ganjam

Part X

The Chief Commissionership of Assam

APPENDIX D

ASSAM FRONTIER TRACT REGULATION, 1880[1]

Whereas it is expedient to provide for the removal of certain frontier tracts in Assam inhabited or frequented by barbarous or semicivilized tribes from the operation of enactments in force therein; It is hereby enacted as follows :

1. This regulation may be called the Assam Frontier Tracts Regulation, 1880.

It extends to such frontier tracts within the territories (for time being) administered by the Chief Commissioner of Assam (as he) may, by notification in the (local Gazette) from time to time direct;

and it shall come into force in each of such tracts on such day as (he) in like manners directs in this behalf.

2. When this Regulation has been extended in manner hereinbefore prescribed to any tract, the Chief Commissioner may from time to time * * * * by notification in the local Gazette, direct that any enactment in force in such tract shall cease to be in force therein, but not so as to affect the criminal jurisdiction of any Court over European British subjects.

3. Whenever any question arises as to the line of boundary between any tract to which the provisions of this Regulation have been extended as aforesaid and the adjoining territory in British India, such officer as the Chief Commissioner of Assam from time to time appoints may consider and determine such line of boundary ; and the order made thereon by such officer, if confirmed by the said Chief Commissioner, shall be conclusive.

---

1. Foreign Proceedings (Assam), April 1884, No. 1.

APPENDIX E

RULES FOR THE ADMINISTRATION OF JUSTICE IN THE DIBRUGARH FRONTIER TRACT[1]

No. 7751P.—In exercise of the powers conferred upon him by section 6 of Act XIV of 1874 (the Scheduled Districts Act), the Chief Commissioner is pleased to prescribe the following rules for the administration of justice in the Dibrugarh Frontier Tract. This cancels all previous orders on the subject, but does not affect the rules published with Notification No. 142J., dated the 23rd December 1888:—

Administration of the Dibrugarh Frontier Tract

I.—GENERAL

1. The administration of the Dibrugarh Frontier Tract is vested in the Chief Commissioner of Assam, the Political Officer, Central and Eastern Sections, North-East Frontier, his Assistants, and the native village authorities, or such other officer or officers as the Chief Commissioner may see fit from time to time to appoint in that behalf, subject to the restrictions and rules hereinafter recorded.

2. The Political Officer shall nominate and appoint the village authorities, if any, subject to the confirmation of the Chief Commissioner and shall assign to them their respective functions under these rules, and define, so far as may be necessary, the local limits within which such duties shall be exercised by each, respectively, and may cancel or modify any such order. When no village authorities have been so nominated and appointed, the powers and duties assigned to them by these rules shall be exercised and performed by the Political Officer or by such other officers as he may depute for this purpose.

1. Foreign Proceedings (Assam), April 1884, Nos. 1-38.

II—POLICE

3. The ordinary duties of police in respect of crime will be discharged by the village authorities. They shall arrest all criminals and maintain peace and order within their respective local limits.

4. It shall be the duty of the village authorities to report to the Political Officer or such other officer as may be authorised by him in that behalf, at the earliest practicable moment, all crimes, violent deaths, and serious accidents occurring within their respective local limits, and all occurrences, whether within or beyond such limits, which may come to their knowledge and which are likely to affect the public peace; and to deliver up offenders as soon as may be to the officer authorised to try them.

5. The village authorities shall watch and report, or apprehend and deliver up, all vagrants or bad and suspicious characters found within their respective local limits.

Administration of the Dibrugarh Frontier Tract

6. On the occurrence of any heinous crime* or of offences under the Arms Act or Excise Act within their local limits, the inhabitants of the village shall at once, if possible, apprehend the offender, and in any case shall at once inform the chief village authority, who, if the offender has not been apprehended, shall proceed without delay to the place where the crime occurred, and enquire into the matter. He shall further, as soon as possible, report any such offence to the Political Officer or such other officer as may be duly authorised by him in that behalf, whether the offender has been apprehended or not.

7. The village authorities may pursue an offender fleeing beyond their jurisdiction and arrest him, but shall not ordinarily attempt to arrest an offender beyond their own jurisdiction without the cognisance and co-operation of the village authorities within whose limits the offender has fled. When an offender is traced from one jurisdiction to another, it will be sufficient to

---

* Heinous crimes are—
Arson, Cattle Stealing, Counterfeiting coin or passing it, Dacoity, Wounding to the danger of life or limb, House breaking, Murder, Rape, Rebellion, Robbery, and Riot.

point him out to the village authorities within whose limits he may be found, aiding them, if required, to effect his capture.

8. When the village authorities are unable to arrest an offender, they shall apply to the Political Officer or such other officer as may be duly authorised by him in this behalf for the aid of the regular police.

9. All inhabitants of the tract are bound to aid the village authorities when required to do so for the maintenance of order or apprehending offenders, and are liable to fine for failing to give such assistance; the fine to be adjudged by chief village authority to the extent of his powers in criminal cases, or by the Political Officer or his Assistants. And if it appears that the community is to blame, and that particular offenders cannot be discovered a fine may be imposed upon the community, but by the Political Officer only.

10. Misconduct on the part of the village authorities in police matters shall be punishable by the fine which may extend to Rs. 500, or by simple imprisonment to the extent which would be awardable under the Penal Code or other law for a like offence, or by both. Imprisonment may be awarded in lieu of fine in accordance with the provisions of the Penal Code or any other law in force.

11. An appeal shall lie from all orders of the chief village authority in police matters to an Assistant Political Officer authorised by the Political Officer in that behalf, and from him to the Political Officer, whose orders are final; but the Chief Commissioner may at any time call for the proceedings, and modify or reverse any order of the Political Officer.

III—CRIMINAL PROCEDURE

12. Criminal justice shall be ordinarily administered by the Political Officer and his Assistants and by the chief village authority duly authorised in this behalf.

13. The Political Officer shall be competent to pass sentence of death, transportation, or imprisonment up to the maximum amount provided for the offence, of whipping, and of fine up to any amount: Provided that all sentences of death or transportation or imprisonment for a term of seven years and upwards shall be subject to the confirmation of the Chief Commissioner.

The Chief Commissioner or Political Officer may call for the proceedings of any officer subordinate to him and reduce, enhance or cancel any sentence passed or remand the case for retrial; but no offence shall be punished by a sentence exceeding that awardable under the Indian Penal Code. The Assistant Political Officers shall exercise such powers not exceeding these of a Magistrate of the first class as defined in the Criminal Procedure Code, as they may be invested with by the Chief Commissioner.

Administration of the Dibrugarh Frontier Tract

14. The chief village authorities may themselves dispose of the cases of persons residing within their jurisdiction charged with the following offences :—

Theft.
Injury to property of whatever kind.
Injury to person not endangering life or limb.
House-trespass.
Affronts of whatever kind.

15. The chief village authorities may impose a fine for any offence which they are competent to try up to a limit of Rs. 50 and may award restitution or compensation to the extent of the injury sustained. Fines may be enforced by distraint of the property of the offender.

16. The chief village authorities may not decide in cases:—

(*a*) where their father, mother, son, daughter, their wife, or the children, husbands, or wives of any of these are concerned; or

(*b*) where the defendant does not reside within their jurisdiction;

(*c*) where the offence is one against the State or of causing death or danger to life or limb, or of robbery of any sort with violence or of arson or of making or passing counterfeit coins or of making fraudulent documents, or offences under the Arms Act or Excise Act, and generally any offences of a heinous nature.

17. The chief village authorities shall decide all cases in open Darbar in the presence of at least three witnesses and of

the complainant and accused whose attendance they are empowered to compel.

18. The chief village authority may carry out his decision as soon as pronounced, unless the accused person appeals. If the sentence is fine, and the accused person does not pay, he shall be sent to the Political Officer or any Assistant authorised by him in that behalf to be dealt with while the fine is being realised.

19. Either party may appeal from the decision of the chief village authority at the time the decision is pronounced. The case shall then be tried de novo.

20. An appeal shall lie from the decision of an Assistant Political Officer to the Political Officer if preferred within thirty days.

21. No appeal shall lie as a matter of right from any sentence passed by the Political Officer involving less than three years' imprisonment. An appeal shall lie to the Chief Commissioner against sentences of three years' imprisonment and upwards, and from all sentences of death or transportation. Appeals must be presented within thirty days of the date of the order appealed against excluding the time required for procuring copy of the order; Provided that an appeal from a sentence of death shall be preferred within seven days from the date of the sentence.

22. The Political Officer and the Assistant Political Officers shall be guided in regard to procedure by the principles of the Code of Criminal Procedure so far as they are applicable to the circumstances of the district and consistent with these rules. The chief exception are :—

Administration of the Dibrugarh Frontier Tract

(*a*) Verbal orders or notice only shall be requisite in any case except when the regular police are employed, or when the person concerned is not a resident of or in the tract at the time; but orders or summonses shall in every case be for a fixed day, and the order shall be made known to the person concerned or to some adult member of his family, and failing this shall be openly proclaimed at the place where he is, or was last known to be, in sufficient time to allow him, if he sees fit, to appear.

(*b*) The proceedings of the chief village authorities need not be recorded in writing, nor shall it be necessary that examinations before the Political Officer and the Assistant Political Officers be signed by the parties examined; but the Political Officer may require the chief village authorities to report their proceedings in any way which appears to him suitable.

(*c*) There shall be no preliminary enquiries by regular or village police unless the Political Officer or Assistant Political Officers see fit to directions.

(*d*) Recognisance to appear shall not be taken unless it appears necessary to the Political Officer or Assistant Political Officer.

(*e*) Examinations and proceedings generally shall be recorded in English only.

(*f*) Oaths shall be administered to parties and witnesses in cases where the accused is charged with murder, but not in other cases unless the Court or either party so require. It is, however, at all times optional with the Court to put witnesses on oath; but witnesses, whether on oath or not, shall be punishable for giving false evidence. In all cases where oaths are administered, all persons shall be sworn in the mode most binding on their conscience.

IV—CIVIL PROCEDURE

23. The administration of civil justice in the Dibrugarh Frontier Tract shall be conducted by the Political Officer, the Assistant Political Officers and the chief village authorities.

24. The chief village authorities may try cases in which plaintiff and defendant are living in their jurisdiction without limit as to amount, but with the following reservations.

25. The chief village authorities may not try suits in which their fathers, mothers, sons or daughters, uncles or aunts, sisters or brothers, the children of any of the foregoing, their wives, or persons in the above relationship to a wife, or any near relative, are concerned.

26. All suits shall be decided in open Darbar in the presence of the parties, and at least three respectable witnesses.

27. The chief village authorities shall have power to compel attendance of parties to any suit and witnesses, and to fine up to a limit of Rs. 50 to persons failing to attend when ordered to do so. They have power to award all costs, also

compensation to defendants for unfounded or vexatious suits brought against them.

28. All proceedings shall be viva voce, but the Political Officer may require the chief village authorities to report their proceedings in any way which appears to him suitable. After hearing both parties and their witnesses, if any, they shall, with or without the opinion of assessors, as they may see fit, forthwith pronounce a decision.

Administration of the Dibrugarh Frontier Tract

29. The chief village authorities may carry out their decisions at once, if necessary, by destraint of any property belonging to the person found liable, to pay (unless appeal is made, or security given to the chief village authorities' satisfaction); but if an appeal is made at the time of decision, the chief village authority shall send up the parties and their witnesses to the Political Officer or any other officer authorised by him in that behalf forthwith, as soon as may be. He shall either accompany them himself or send at least one respectable person who has been present at the trial with them.

30. The Political Officer and the Assistant Political Officers shall not ordinarily hear any suits triable by the chief village authorities; but suits which under these rules the chief village authority cannot try shall be tried by the Political Officer or an Assistant Political Officer.

31. The Political Officer and the Assistant Political Officers shall in all cases coming before them, in which the parties are indigenous inhabitants of the frontier tract, endeavour to induce them to submit their case to a Panchayat. In that event, each party shall name an equal number of arbitrators, and the Court shall either choose, or leave the arbitrators to choose, an umpire. The name and residence of the arbitrators and umpire and the matter in dispute shall be recorded before their proceedings commence, and the Court shall direct the chief village authority, or some other person, to assemble the Panchayat and witnesses within such reasonable period as the Court may fix. When the case has been decided, the umpire shall appear with the parties before the Court, which shall proceed to record the decision and enforce it as its own. From such decision there shall be no appeal.

32. On appeals to the Political Officer from a decision of

the chief village authority, a record shall be made of the matter in dispute, and of the decision of the chief village authority; if necessary, the Court shall examine the parties, and, if the decision appears to be just, it shall be affirmed and enforced by the Court as its own. If, on the other hand, the Court sees grounds to doubt the justice of the decision, it shall try the case *de novo*, or refer it to a Panchayat, as provided above.

33. Decrees against persons resident beyond the jurisdiction of the Court in the Dibrugarh Frontier Tract, if satisfaction cannot be obtained within the Dibrugarh Frontier Tract, shall be transferred for execution to the Court having jurisdiction.

34. Houses, needful clothing, or cooking utensils, or implements whereby the owner or his family subsists, shall not be attached, soil, or transferred in execution of a decree, unless the house or other thing above exempted is the actual subject-matter of the suit. Land may be sold or temporarily transferred where custom admits of individual right in it being recognised.

35. There shall be no imprisonment for debt, excepting when the Political Officer is satisfied that fraudulent disposition or concealment of property has taken place. In such case the debtor may be detained for a period not exceeding six months.

Administration of the Dibrugarh Frontier Tract

36. The Chief Commissioner or a Political Officer may, on application or otherwise, call for the Proceedings of any case decided by any officer subordinate to him and pass such orders as he may deem fit.

37. An appeal shall lie to the Political Officer against any decision of an Assistant Political Officer, and to the Chief Commissioner against an original decision of the Political Officer, if the value of the suit be rupees five hundred or over, or if the suit involve a question of tribal rights or customs, or of right to, or possession of, immoveable property : Provided that the petition of apeal accompanied by a copy of the order appealed against and by a clear statement of the grounds of appeal be filed within thirty days from the date of decision, excluding the time required for obtaining a copy of the decision. An appeal which lies to the Chief Commissioner may be presented to the Political Officer, who shall, if it be in order

and presented in due time, endorse upon it the date of receipt and transmit it with the records of the case to the Chief Commissioner.

The decree of the Appellate Court shall be transferred to the Court passing the original order for execution as a decree of its own.

37. The Courts of the Chief Commissioner, Political Officer and Assistant Political Officers, shall be guided by the spirit, but not be bound by the letters of the Code of Civil Procedure.

38. No professional pleader or mukhtar shall be allowed to appear in any case except with the sanction of the Court. Near relatives may appear for persons incapacitated by age, sex, or sickness.

39. Oaths shall not be administered to parties or witnesses in suits unless the Court or either party to a suit so require. In all cases where oaths are administered, all persons shall be sworn in the manner most binding on their consciences. It is at all times optional with the Court to put witnesses on oath; but witnesses whether on oath or not, shall be punishable for giving false evidence.

40. The Political Officer is empowered to try suits up to any amount. The Assistant Political Officers shall hear and decide original civil suits up to a value of Rs. 1,000 and shall hear and decide appeals from the decision of the chief village authorities up to a value of Rs. 300.

Bibliography

PRIMARY SOURCES

1. UNPUBLISHED RECORDS :

(*i*) *Proceedings of the Government of Bengal*:

(a) Political Department, 1824-1873;

(b) Judicial Department, 1824-1873;

(c) Police Department, 1824-1873.

(*ii*) *Proceedings of the Government of Eastern Bengal and Assam, Political Department, 1905-1912.*

(*iii*) *Proceedings of the Government of Assam*:

(a) Foreign Proceedings of the Chief Commissioner of Assam, 1874-1905.

(b) Political Proceedings of the Chief Commissioner of Assam, 1912-1920.

(c) Political Proceedings of the Government of Assam, 1921-1937.

(d) Proceedings of the Tribal Affairs Department, Governor's Secretariat, 1937-1947.

(*iv*) *Foreign Political Proceedings af the Government of India, 1824-1915.*

(*v*) *Lakhimpur Deputy Commissioner's Collection, 1874-1947.*

2. PUBLISHED RECORDS, REPORTS AND GAZETTEERS :

(*i*) *Aitchison, C.U., A Collection af Treaties, Engagements and Sanads Relating to India and Neighbouring Countries, (Calcutta 1862).*

(*ii*) *Survey of India Records, 1874-75.*

(iii) *Selection from the Records of the Bengal Government, XXIII, 1855.*

(iv) *White Papers of the Government of India* (*on India-China Border Issues*), *vols. I-XIV.*

(v) *A.J.M. Mills' Report on Assam, 1854.*

(vi) *Census of India Reports, 1881-1941.*

(vii) *Annual Political Reports on the Frontier Tracts, 1874-1945.*

(viii) *Assam Administration Reports, 1874-1946.*

(ix) *Report on Indian Constitutional Reforms, 1918.*

(x) *Report of the Indian Statutory Commission, Vol. I & II, 1930.*

(xi) *Report of the Officials of the Government of India and the People's Republic of China on the Boundary Question.*

(xii) *Assam Government Hand Book,* (*Shillong, 1938*).

(xiii) *Assam District Gazetteers,* (*Shillong, 1906*).

(xiv) *Imperial Gazetteer, vol. IV, 1905.*

3. MAPS :

(i) *Atlas of the Northern Frontier of India, Ministry of External Affairs, New Delhi, 1960.*

(ii) *Augusto Gansser's Geology of the Himalayas Maps.*

(iii) *Evolution of the Administrative Jurisdictions of the North-East Frontier Agency, Shillong, 1965.*

SECONDARY WORKS

Aidye, (General) Sir J., Indian Frontier Policy (London, 1897)

Amanatulla (Khan Choudhury), Ahmed, A History of Cooch Behar, (Cooch Behar, 1936).

Bailey, F.M., No Passport to Tibet, (London, 1957).

———, China, Tibet and Assam (London, 1945).

Banerjee, A.C., Eastern Frontier of British India, (Calcutta, 1943, 3rd edition 1954).

———, Annexation of Burma (Calcutta, 1944).

Barooah, N., David Scott in North-East India 1802-1831, A Study in British Paternalism (New Delhi, 1970).

Baruah, G., Ahom Buranji (Gauhati, 1930).

Barua, H., Asom Buranji (Gauhati, 1930).
Baruah, T., The Idu Mishmis, (Shillong, 1961).
Basu, D., Constitutional Documents, vol. I, (Calcutta, 1969).
Baveja, J.D., Across the Golden Heights of Assam and NEEA.
Bell, C., Tibet—Past and Present (London, 1924-1948).
Beresford, G.W., Notes on the North-East Frontier of Assam, (Shillong, 1881, reprinted 1906).
Bhuyan, S.K., Anglo-Assamese Relations, 1771-1826 (Gauhati, 1947).
Buckland, C.E., Dictionary of Indian Biography, (London, 1906).
Butler, John, Travels and Adventures in the Province of Assam, (London, 1855).
Chakravarti, P.C., Evolution of India's Northern Borders (New Delhi, 1971).
Chakravorty, B.C., British Relations with the Hill Tribes of Assam since 1858 (Calcutta, 1964).
———, India-China Relations, (Calcutta, 1965).
Chakravorty, L.N., Glimpses of the History of Arunachal Pradesh, (Shillong, 1973)
Chowdhury, J.N., A Comparative Study of the Adi Religion (1971).
———, The Hill Miris (Shillong, 1970).
———, Arunachal Panorama (Shillong, 1973).
Dalton, E.T., Descriptive Ethnology of Bengal, (Calcutta, 1872, 1960).
Dalvi,(Brigadier) J.P., The Himalayan Blunder, (Bombay, 1969).
Devi, L., Ahom-Tribal Relations, (Gauhati, 1968).
Duff-Sutherland-Dunbar, G., Abors and Galongs (Memoirs of Asiatic Society of Bengal, Vol. V, 1913-17).
Dun, G. W., Preliminary Notes on Daphlas (Simla, 1896).
———, Preliminary Notes on Miris (Simla, 1896).
Dutta, P., The Tangsas of the Namchik and Tirap Valleys, (Shillong, 1959).
Elwin, V., A Philosophy for NEFA (Shillong, 1957, 1959)
———, Democracy in NEFA (Shillong, 1965).
———,India's North-East Frontier in the Nineteenth Century (Oxford, 1959, 1962).
———,Myths of the North-East Frontier of India (Shillong, 1958).

———, The Art of the North-East Frontier of India (Shillong, 1959)

———,'The North-East Frontier Agency of India', (Geographical Magazine, vol. XXIX, 1956, pp. 405-16).

———, The Tribal World of Verrier Elwin (Oxford, 1964).

Furer-Haimendorf, C. Von., 'Agriculture and Land Tenure Among the Apa Tanis' (Man in India, vol. XXVI, 1946, pp. 20-49).

———, Ethnographic Notes on the Tribes of the Subansiri Region (Shillong, 1947).

Gait, E., A History of Assam, (Calcutta, 1926).

Gansser, A., Geology of the Himalayas, (New York, 1964).

Gogoi, L., The Tai Khamtis, (Namsoon, NEFA, 1971).

Grierson, G., Linguistic Survey of India, vols. I-IV (Calcutta, 1905).

Gupta, K., The Hidden History of the Sino-Indian Frontier, (Calcutta, 1974).

Hamilton, F., An Account of Assam, compiled between 1907-14; edited by S.K. Bhuyan (Gauhati, 1940).

Hannay, S.F., Sketch of the Singphos, or the Kakhyens of Burma; the Position of the Tribes as regards Bauno and the Inland Trade of the Irrawaddy with Yunnan, followed by an Account of the Shans (Calcutta, 1847).

Hesselmeyer, C.H., 'The Hill Tribes of the Northern Frontier of Assam' (J.A.S.B., vol. XXXVII, 1968, pp. 192-208).

Hunter, W.W., A Statistical Account of Assam (London, 1879).

Hutton, J.H., A Primitive Philosophy of Life (Oxford, 1938).

———, 'Head Hunters of the North-East Frontier' (Journal of Royal Society of Arts, vol. LXXXII, 1936, pp. 134-44).

Ilbert, (Sir) Courtenay, The Government of India (London, 1915).

James, O.E., The Beginning of Religion (New York, 1958).

Johri, (Major) S., Where India, China and Burma Meet, (Calcutta, 1962).

Kennedy, R.S., Ethnological Report on the Akas, Khoas, and Mijis and the Membas of Tawang (Shillong, 1914).

Lahiri, R.N., Annexation of Assam (Calcutta, 1954).

Lamb, Alastair, India-China Border : The Origins of the Disputed Boundaries (London, 1964).

———, The McMahon Line: A Study of Relations between India, China and Tibet 1904-1914, (London, 1966).

Mackenzie, A., Memorandum on the North-East Frontier of Bengal, (Calcutta, 1869).

———, History of the Relations of the Government with the Hill Tribes of the North-East Frontier of Bengal (Calcutta, 1884).

Maxwell, N., India's China War, (Bombay, 1970).

Mehra, P., The Younghusband Expedition, (Bombay, 1968).

———, The McMahon Line and After, (Madras, 1974).

Mehta, K.L., 'The North-East Frontier Agency Today' (March of India, vol. VIII, 1956, pp. 8-12).

Mills, J.P., The Mishmi Hills of the Lohit Valley (Reprint, Shillong, 1962).

Mishra, S.D., Rivers of India, NBT, (New Delhi, 1970).

Pemberton, R.B., Report on the Eastern Frontier of British India, (Calcutta, 1835).

Rahul, Ram, The Himalaya Borderland, (Delhi, 1970).

Rao, K. Krishna, The Sino-Indian Boundary Question and International Law (New Delhi, 1963).

Reid, R., History of the Frontier Areas bordering on Assam from 1883-1941, (Shillong, 1942).

———, Years of Change in Bengal and Assam, (London, 1966).

Richardson, H.E., Tibet and Its History, (Oxford, 1962).

Robinson, W., A Descriptive Account of Asam (London, 1841).

Rustomji, N., Tribal Administration in the North-East Frontier Agency, (Delhi, 1955).

Rose, L.E., and Fisher, M.W., North-East Frontier Agency of India, (California, 1967).

Shakespeare, L.W., History of the Assam Rifles, (London, 1929).

Sharma, S.P., The India-China Border Dispute: An Indian Perspective, (New Delhi, 1967).

Sing, (Buragohain) P., Asom Buranji, Transcript No. 109 (Director of Historical & Antiquarian Studies, Gauhati).

Sing, R.L., (ed), India—A Regional Geography, (Varanasi, 1971).

Thomas, M.M. and Taylor, R.W., (ed), Tribal Awakening: A Group Study, (Bangalore, 1965).

Younghusband, F., India and Tibet, (London, 1910, Reprinted, 1971).

Index